W9-CHP-653

Focus on GRAMMAR 5A

FOURTH EDITION

Focus on GRAMMAR 5A

FOURTH EDITION

Jay Maurer

ALWAYS LEARNING

PEARSON

Focus on Grammar 5A: An Integrated Skills Approach, Fourth Edition

Pearson Education, 10 Bank Street, White Plains, NY 10606

Staff credits: The people who made up the *Focus on Grammar 5A, Fourth Edition*
team, representing editorial, production, design, and manufacturing, are John Barnes, Andrea
Bryant, Elizabeth Carlson, Tracey Cataldo, Aerin Csigay, Dave Dickey, Christine Edmonds,
Nancy Flaggman, Ann France, Shelley Gazes, Lise Minovitz, Barbara Perez, Robert Ruvo, and
Debbie Sistino.

Cover image: Shutterstock.com
Text composition: ElectraGraphics, Inc.
Text font: New Aster

PEARSON LONGMAN ON THE **WEB**

Pearsonlongman.com offers online
resources for teachers and students. Access
our Companion Websites, our online catalog,
and our local offices around the world.

Visit us at **pearsonlongman.com**.

Printed in the United States of America

ISBN 10: 0-13-216981-9
ISBN 13: 978-0-13-216981-3

1 2 3 4 5 6 7 8 9 10—V082—16 15 14 13 12 11

ISBN 10: 0-13-216982-7 (with MyLab)
ISBN 13: 978-0-13-216982-0 (with MyLab)

1 2 3 4 5 6 7 8 9 10—V082—16 15 14 13 12 11

CONTENTS

WELCOME TO *FOCUS ON GRAMMAR*

Now in a new edition, the popular five-level *Focus on Grammar* course continues to provide an integrated-skills approach to help students understand and practice English grammar. Centered on thematic instruction, *Focus on Grammar* combines controlled and communicative practice with critical thinking skills and ongoing assessment. Students gain the confidence they need to speak and write English accurately and fluently.

NEW for the FOURTH EDITION

VOCABULARY

Key vocabulary is highlighted, practiced, and recycled throughout the unit.

PRONUNCIATION

Now, in every unit, pronunciation points and activities help students improve spoken accuracy and fluency.

LISTENING

Expanded listening tasks allow students to develop a range of listening skills.

UPDATED CHARTS and NOTES

Target structures are presented in a clear, easy-to-read format.

NEW READINGS

High-interest readings, updated or completely new, in a variety of genres integrate grammar and vocabulary in natural contexts.

NEW UNIT REVIEWS

Students can check their understanding and monitor their progress after completing each unit.

MyFocusOnGrammarLab

An easy-to-use online learning and assessment program offers online homework and individualized instruction anywhere, anytime.

Teacher's Resource Pack   One compact resource includes:

THE TEACHER'S MANUAL: General Teaching Notes, Unit Teaching Notes, the Student Book Audioscript, and the Student Book Answer Key.

TEACHER'S RESOURCE DISC: Bound into the Resource Pack, this CD-ROM contains reproducible Placement, Part, and Unit Tests, as well as customizable Test-Generating Software. It also includes reproducible Internet Activities and PowerPoint® Grammar Presentations.

THE *FOCUS ON GRAMMAR* APPROACH

The new edition follows the same successful four-step approach of previous editions. The books provide an abundance of both controlled and communicative exercises so that students can bridge the gap between identifying grammatical structures and using them. The many communicative activities in each Student Book provide opportunities for critical thinking while enabling students to personalize what they have learned.

- **STEP 1: GRAMMAR IN CONTEXT** highlights the target structures in realistic contexts, such as conversations, magazine articles, and blog posts.
- **STEP 2: GRAMMAR PRESENTATION** presents the structures in clear and accessible grammar charts and notes with multiple examples of form and usage.
- **STEP 3: FOCUSED PRACTICE** provides numerous and varied controlled exercises for both the form and meaning of the new structures.
- **STEP 4: COMMUNICATION PRACTICE** includes listening and pronunciation and allows students to use the new structures freely and creatively in motivating, open-ended speaking and writing activities.

Recycling

Underpinning the scope and sequence of the *Focus on Grammar* series is the belief that students need to use target structures and vocabulary many times, in different contexts. New grammar and vocabulary are recycled throughout the book. Students have maximum exposure and become confident using the language in speech and in writing.

Assessment

Extensive testing informs instruction and allows teachers and students to measure progress.

- **Unit Reviews** at the end of every Student Book unit assess students' understanding of the grammar and allow students to monitor their own progress.
- Easy to administer and score, **Part and Unit Tests** provide teachers with a valid and reliable means to determine how well students know the material they are about to study and to assess students' mastery after they complete the material. These tests can be found on MyFocusOnGrammarLab, where they include immediate feedback and remediation, and as reproducible tests on the Teacher's Resource Disc.
- **Test-Generating Software** on the Teacher's Resource Disc includes a bank of *additional* test items teachers can use to create customized tests.
- A reproducible **Placement Test** on the Teacher's Resource Disc is designed to help teachers place students into one of the five levels of the *Focus on Grammar* course.

COMPONENTS

In addition to the Student Books, Teacher's Resource Packs, and MyLabs, the complete *Focus on Grammar* course includes:

Workbooks   Contain additional contextualized exercises appropriate for self-study.

Audio Program   Includes all of the listening and pronunciation exercises and opening passages from the Student Book. Some Student Books are packaged with the complete audio program (mp3 files). Alternatively, the audio program is available on a classroom set of CDs and on the MyLab.

THE *FOCUS ON GRAMMAR* UNIT

Focus on Grammar introduces grammar structures in the context of unified themes. All units follow a **four-step approach**, taking learners from grammar in context to communicative practice.

STEP 1 GRAMMAR IN CONTEXT

This section presents the target structure(s) in a natural context. As students read the **high-interest texts**, they encounter the form, meaning, and use of the grammar. **Before You Read** activities create interest and elicit students' knowledge about the topic. **After You Read** activities build students' reading vocabulary and comprehension.

Vocabulary exercises improve students' command of English. Vocabulary is **recycled** throughout the unit.

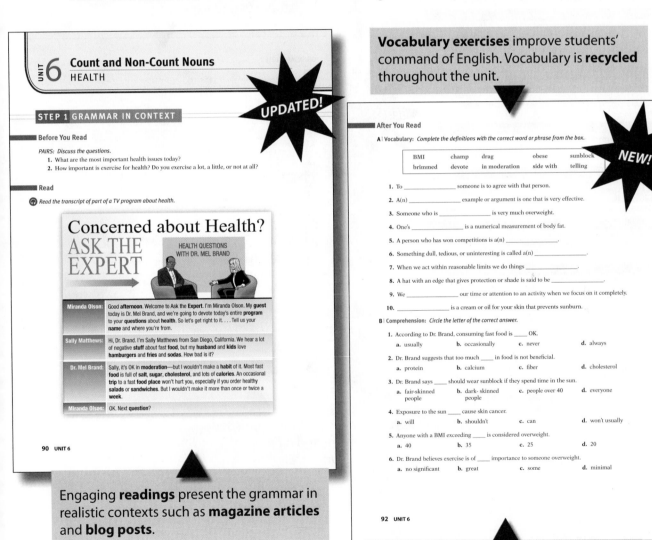

UPDATED!

NEW!

Engaging **readings** present the grammar in realistic contexts such as **magazine articles** and **blog posts**.

Reading comprehension tasks focus on the meaning of the text and draw students' attention to the target structure.

This section gives students a comprehensive and explicit overview of the grammar with detailed **Grammar Charts** and **Grammar Notes** that present the form, meaning, and use of the structure(s).

Grammar Charts present the structure in a clear, easy-to-read format.

Grammar Notes give concise, simple **explanations** and **examples** to ensure students' understanding.

Additional **Notes** provide information about spelling, common errors, and differences between spoken and written English.

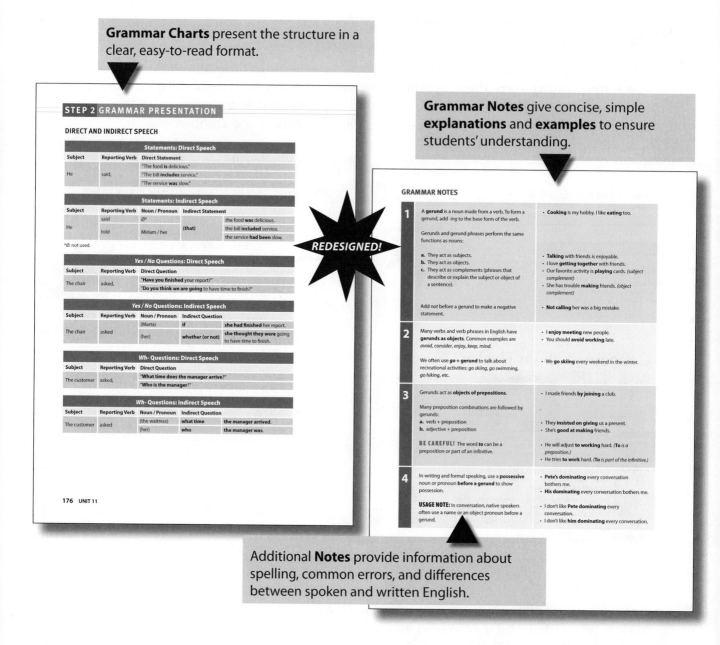

Controlled practice activities in this section lead students to master form, meaning, and use of the target grammar.

STEP 3 FOCUSED PRACTICE

EXERCISE 1: Discover the Grammar

A | *Read the sentences. Underline each noun clause and identify it as* **S** *(used as a subject),* **O** *(used as an object), or* **C** *(used as a complement).*

_____ 1. Moe was sure that the mansion would be her favorite gift.

_____ 2. What wasn't so admirable was their rivalry.

_____ 3. All I know is that the chicken you gave me was delicious.

_____ 4. Their mother said there was nothing she needed.

B | *Look at the sentences. Underline the embedded question in each. For each embedded question, write the direct question it was derived from.*

1. Each brother constantly tried to figure out <u>how he could outdo the other two.</u>

   How can I outdo the other two?

2. Curly was wondering what he could do to top his brothers.

3. At first he wondered if he could afford it.

4. I don't know if you believed me.

5. I don't know what you mean.

EXERCISE 2: Embedded Questions   *(Grammar Notes 4–7)*

Based on the exchanges in the chart, complete the story with embedded **yes** / **no** *and* **wh-***questions. Put the verbs in the simple past or the past perfect.*

1. **A:** Excuse me. How far is the nearest town?   **B:** I don't know.
2. **A:** Well, what's the name of the nearest town?   **B:** I'm not sure.
3. **A:** Can I borrow your cell phone?   **B:** What's a cell phone?

Discover the Grammar activities develop students' recognition and understanding of the target structure before they are asked to produce it.

A **variety of exercise types** engage students and guide them from recognition and understanding to accurate production of the grammar structures.

An **Editing** exercise ends every Focused Practice section and teaches students to find and correct typical mistakes.

EXERCISE 5: Editing

Read the letter. It has eight mistakes in the use of direct and indirect speech. The first mistake is already corrected. Find and correct seven more.

November 20

Dear Emily,

I just wanted to fill you in on Tim's school adventures. About two months ago
Melanie said she ~~feels~~ *felt* we should switch Tim to the public school. He'd been in a
private school for several months, as you know. I asked her why did she think
that, and she said, "He's miserable where he is, and the quality of education is
poor. He says he doesn't really have any friends." I couldn't help but agree. She
said she thought we can move him to the local high school, which has a good
academic reputation. I told that I agreed but that we should ask Tim. The next
morning we asked Tim if he wanted to stay at the private school. I was surprised
at how strong his response was. He said me that he hated the school and didn't
want to go there any longer. So we changed him. He's been at the new school for
a month now, and he's doing well. Whenever I ask him does he have his homework
done, he says, "Dad, I've already finished it." He's made several new friends.
Every now and then he asks us why didn't we let him change sooner. He says
people are treating him as an individual now. I'm just glad we moved him when
we did.

Not much else is new. Oh, yes—I do need to ask are you coming for the
holidays. Write soon and let us know. Or call.

Love,

Charles

This section provides practice with the structure in **listening** and **pronunciation** exercises as well as in communicative, open-ended **speaking** and **writing** activities that move students toward fluency.

Listening activities allow students to hear the grammar in natural contexts and to practice a range of listening skills.

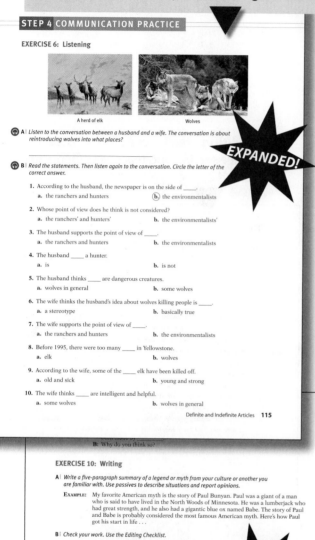

STEP 4 COMMUNICATION PRACTICE

EXERCISE 6: Listening

A herd of elk   Wolves

🎧 **A |** *Listen to the conversation between a husband and a wife. The conversation is about reintroducing wolves into what places?*

_____

🎧 **B |** *Read the statements. Then listen again to the conversation. Circle the letter of the correct answer.*

1. According to the husband, the newspaper is on the side of _____.
   a. the ranchers and hunters   (b.) the environmentalists

2. Whose point of view does he think is not considered?
   a. the ranchers' and hunters'   b. the environmentalists'

3. The husband supports the point of view of _____.
   a. the ranchers and hunters   b. the environmentalists

4. The husband _____ a hunter.
   a. is   b. is not

5. The husband thinks _____ are dangerous creatures.
   a. wolves in general   b. some wolves

6. The wife thinks the husband's idea about wolves killing people is _____.
   a. a stereotype   b. basically true

7. The wife supports the point of view of _____.
   a. the ranchers and hunters   b. the environmentalists

8. Before 1995, there were too many _____ in Yellowstone.
   a. elk   b. wolves

9. According to the wife, some of the _____ elk have been killed off.
   a. old and sick   b. young and strong

10. The wife thinks _____ are intelligent and helpful.
    a. some wolves   b. wolves in general

Definite and Indefinite Articles   **115**

EXPANDED!

Pronunciation Notes and **exercises** improve students' spoken fluency and accuracy.

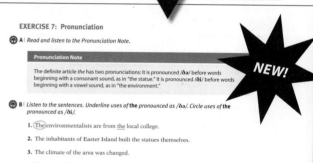

EXERCISE 7: Pronunciation

🎧 **A |** *Read and listen to the Pronunciation Note.*

Pronunciation Note

The definite article *the* has two pronunciations: It is pronounced /ðə/ before words beginning with a consonant sound, as in "the statue." It is pronounced /ði/ before words beginning with a vowel sound, as in "the environment."

NEW!

🎧 **B |** *Listen to the sentences. Underline uses of* **the** *pronounced as /ðə/. Circle uses of* **the** *pronounced as /ði/.*

1. (The) environmentalists are from the local college.
2. The inhabitants of Easter Island built the statues themselves.
3. The climate of the area was changed.
4. The forests that used to cover the island are gone.
5. The sad truth is that the Earth's resources are limited.
6. Fortunately, that's not the end of the story.
7. The 11 ruling chiefs were responsible for the problem.
8. Are we overfishing the ocean in the mistaken belief that the supply of seafood is unlimited?

C | *PAIRS: Practice the sentences. Take turns.*

EXERCISE 8: Picture Discussion

GROUPS: Form small groups and discuss the picture. Identify some of the items you see. Then discuss the situation. How can we dispose of items we no longer need or want? What solutions are there to this problem?

EXAMPLE: **A:** I see a lot of plastic bags and cardboard boxes.
B: How do you think we should dispose of things like those?
C: We could recycle as much as possible . . .

116   UNIT 7

B: Why do you think so?

EXERCISE 10: Writing

A | *Write a five-paragraph summary of a legend or myth from your culture or another you are familiar with. Use passives to describe situations and report opinions.*

EXAMPLE: My favorite American myth is the story of Paul Bunyan. Paul was a giant of a man who is said to have lived in the North Woods of Minnesota. He was a lumberjack who had great strength, and he also had a gigantic blue ox named Babe. The story of Paul and Babe is probably considered the most famous American myth. Here's how Paul got his start in life . . .

B | *Check your work. Use the Editing Checklist.*

Editing Checklist

Did you use . . . ?
☐ passives to describe situations correctly
☐ passives with *it* and *that* clauses correctly
☐ passives with *to* phrases correctly

NEW!

Writing activities encourage students to produce meaningful writing that integrates the grammar structure.

An **Editing Checklist** teaches students to correct their mistakes and revise their work.

Speaking activities help students synthesize the grammar through discussions, debates, games, and problem-solving tasks, developing their fluency.

Unit Reviews give students the opportunity to check their understanding of the target structure. **Answers** at the back of the book allow students to monitor their own progress.

NEW!

UNIT 5 Review

Check your answers on page UR-1.
Do you need to review anything?

A | *Circle the correct word or phrase to complete each sentence.*

1. That <u>must / may</u> be the answer to the mystery. All evidence points to it.
2. Ellen <u>might / will</u> be here later, but I don't know for sure.
3. A monk <u>must / might</u> have made the trip, but the evidence isn't conclusive.
4. It <u>couldn't / shouldn't</u> have been Newfoundland, which is too far north.
5. We <u>should / may</u> find out what really happened later today. Louis says he knows.
6. You <u>may not / ought not to</u> have trouble solving the problem—you're good at math.
7. They <u>had to / might</u> have been home—I heard their music.
8. She <u>might be / 's got to be</u> the one who took it. No one else had access to it.
9. They <u>had to be / must have been</u> away last week. Their car was gone.
10. There <u>must / might</u> be a key around here somewhere. Dad said he had one.

B | *In the blank after each sentence, write a modal or modal-like expression of certainty with a meaning similar to the underlined phrase.*

1. <u>It's possible that Jeremy</u> had to work late. _____
2. <u>It's very likely that Mari</u> missed her flight. _____
3. <u>It's impossible that they</u> heard the news. _____
4. <u>It's likely that we'll</u> know the answer soon. _____
5. <u>You had the opportunity to get</u> a scholarship. _____

C | *Circle the letter of the one underlined word or phrase in each sentence that is not correct.*

1. <u>Might</u> she <u>have forgotten</u>, or <u>could she had</u> <u>had to</u> work?   A B C D
      A   B   C   D
2. I <u>think</u> Ed <u>isn't</u> here because he <u>should</u> <u>be</u> sick.   A B C D
        A   B   C D
3. Al <u>can't get</u> here by 7:00, but he <u>shouldn't</u> <u>make</u> it b
       A   B   C D
4. I suppose they <u>couldn't</u> <u>be working</u> late at the office
             A   B
   <u>didn't mention</u> it, and neither <u>did</u> Mary.
      C   D
5. I'm sorry; I <u>could had</u> called to say <u>I'd be</u> late, but I
        A   B   C

84 Unit 5 Review: Modals to Express Degrees of Certainty

Extended writing tasks help students integrate the grammar structure as they follow the steps of the **writing process.**

PART II From Grammar to Writing

TOPIC SENTENCES

An important way to strengthen your writing is to provide a **topic sentence** for each paragraph. A topic sentence is a general sentence that covers the paragraph's content. All the supporting examples and details of the paragraph must fit logically under this sentence, which usually comes first.

EXAMPLE: **For me, a dog is a better pet than a cat.** When I come home from work, for example, my dog comes to meet me at the door. He is always glad to see me. My cat, on the other hand, couldn't care less whether I'm at home or not, as long as I keep filling her food dish. Another good thing about a dog is that you can teach him tricks. Cats, however, can't be bothered to learn anything new. The best thing about a dog, though, is that he's a great companion. I can take my dog on hikes and walks. He goes everywhere with me. As we all know, you can't take a cat for a walk.

The topic sentence for this paragraph tells the reader what to expect in the paragraph: some reasons why the writer considers a dog a superior pet.

1 | *Each of the word groups is a fragment but is also a potential topic sentence. Make necessary additions to each.*

EXAMPLE: Reasons why the legal driving age should be raised. (not an independent clause)
Correction: There are several reasons why the legal driving age should be raised.

1. A city where exciting and mysterious things happen.

   _____

2. Reasons why college isn't for everybody.

   _____

3. Wild animals not making good pets.

   _____

4. Regular exercise and its benefits.

   _____

2 | *Look at the following paragraphs containing supporting details but no topic sentences. For each set of details, write an appropriate topic sentence.*

1. _____
   a. For one thing, there's almost always a traffic jam I get stuck in, and I'm often late to work.
   b. Also, there's not always a parking place when I do get to work.
   c. Worst of all, I'm spending more money on gas and car maintenance than I would if I took public transportation.

(continued on next page)

From Grammar to Writing **85**

The *Focus on Grammar* Unit **xiii**

SCOPE AND SEQUENCE

UNIT	READING	WRITING	LISTENING
1 page 2 **Grammar:** Present Time **Theme:** The Digital World	An article: *Connected!*	Two or three paragraphs about electronic devices in your life	A conversation about identity theft
2 page 15 **Grammar:** Past Time **Theme:** Marriage	An article: *A Marriage Made on the Internet?*	Two or three paragraphs about a situation that turned out unexpectedly	A broadcast about an unusual wedding
3 page 32 **Grammar:** Future Time **Theme:** Travel	An article: *Getting the Most Out of It!*	Two or three paragraphs about a world traveler's opinions or on your dream vacation	A family conversation about what to do on a trip

PART I   From Grammar to Writing, page 45
The Sentence: Avoiding Sentence Fragments: Write a composition about a travel experience.

UNIT	READING	WRITING	LISTENING
4 page 50 **Grammar:** Modals to Express Degrees of Necessity **Theme:** Cultural Differences	An article: *What We Should and Shouldn't Have Done*	Two or three paragraphs about a situation you should have handled differently	A conversation about a gift for a surprise party
5 page 69 **Grammar:** Modals to Express Degrees of Certainty **Theme:** Puzzles	An article: *Who Really Discovered America?*	Three or four paragraphs about a world mystery	A discussion about hearing one's recorded voice

PART II   From Grammar to Writing, page 85
Topic Sentences: Write a composition about a cross-cultural experience.

UNIT	READING	WRITING	LISTENING
6 page 90 **Grammar:** Count and Non-Count Nouns **Theme:** Health	A transcript of a TV program: *Concerned about Health? Ask the Expert*	Three or four paragraphs about health issues	A conversation between a doctor and a patient about health needs

SPEAKING	PRONUNCIATION	VOCABULARY	
Group Discussion: Electronic devices which are important in your life *Class Discussion:* The dangers of texting while driving	Two pronunciations of the letters *ng*	24/7 contemplating digitally do without	profile staying on top of telecommute tends
Information Gap: A married couple who took risks and made changes *Picture Discussion:* A married couple's relationship *Group Discussion:* Changes in one another's lives	Contracting auxiliary verbs in past forms	came up with out of the blue pondered tie the knot	turned in turned out ultimately*
Picture Discussion: What you think will happen in the future *Group Discussion:* Opinions of a world traveler	Contracting auxiliary verbs in future forms	chart your own course excruciatingly hectic landmarks	maximize* mindset out of whack scrapbook

SPEAKING	PRONUNCIATION	VOCABULARY	
Information Gap: Cultural differences and travel problems *Discussion:* Correct behavior in your culture	Reduction of modals and modal-like auxiliaries	chuckle decline* gracious have someone over	perplexed pointer praise rectify
Pair Discussion: Possible solutions to various puzzling events *Group Discussion:* Explanations to the mystery of Atlantis	Reductions of *to* and *have* in modal constructions	artifacts cohorts contenders debris	monasteries monks potential* stems from

SPEAKING	PRONUNCIATION	VOCABULARY	
Discussion: Statements about personal experiences *Personal Inventory:* Responses to a survey about health	Reduction of *of*	BMI brimmed champ devote* drag	in moderation obese side with sunblock telling

* = AWL (Academic Word List) items

SPEAKING	PRONUNCIATION	VOCABULARY	
Picture Discussion: Solutions to the problem of disposing of unwanted items *Game:* Asking *who* and *what* questions	Two pronunciations of *the*	bark desolate drastically hauling	ostrich-like rivalry toppled over trunk
Game: World facts *Personal Inventory:* Your life now compared to your life five years ago	Unstressed vowels	correspondingly* crisp e.g. fiat i.e.	the jury is still out live beyond our means succeeding take plastic
Story Discussion: A famous Arabic story *Picture Discussion:* A famous disaster at sea	Pausing between modifiers in the same category	buff exploit* irony live up to marathon	otherworldly relinquish surge syndrome tedious
Pair Discussion: Airline humor *Class Discussion:* Presenting a joke or amusing story	Intonation in *wh-, yes/no,* and embedded questions	ecstatic exemplary in a dilemma inclination* on call	one-upmanship outdo supplant uniqueness*
Group Reporting: Game about miscommunication *Picture Discussion:* An auto accident	Blending of /t/ or /d/ plus /y/	bottom line chair civility distressed glared	minimize* rancor short-handed spin sugarcoat
Pair Discussion: Dealing with conflict *Class Activity:* Identifying classmates based on descriptions given by others	Pauses in identifying and nonidentifying adjective clauses	charismatic correlation embrace entrepreneurs	gravitate toward insight* spotlight without mincing words

* = AWL (Academic Word List) items

UNIT	READING	WRITING	LISTENING
13 page 211 **Grammar:** Adjective Clauses with Prepositions; Adjective Phrases **Theme:** Movies	Movie reviews: *Five to Revisit*	A movie review of three or more paragraphs	Weekly movie reviews by a TV film reviewer
PART V **From Grammar to Writing,** page 229 **Punctuating Adjective Clauses and Phrases:** Write a composition about a photograph.			
14 page 234 **Grammar:** The Passive: Review and Expansion **Theme:** Unsolved Mysteries	An article: *Did He Get Away with It?*	Five or more paragraphs about an unsolved mystery	A news bulletin about an accident
15 page 250 **Grammar:** The Passive to Describe Situations and to Report Opinions **Theme:** Legends and Myths	An article: *The Strangest of Peoples*	A five-paragraph summary of a legend or myth	A news bulletin about a natural disaster
PART VI **From Grammar to Writing,** page 266 **Parallel Structure: Nouns, Articles, and Voice:** Write a composition about an unsolved mystery or unusual experience.			
16 page 270 **Grammar:** Gerunds **Theme:** Friendship	An article: *Friends*	Five or more paragraphs about a friend who fits a particular category	A telephone conversation about a club
17 page 285 **Grammar:** Infinitives **Theme:** Procrastination	An article: *Seize the Day*	Three or more paragraphs about a time you put off doing something that needed to be done	A news bulletin about a prison escape
PART VII **From Grammar to Writing,** page 303 **Parallel Structure: Gerunds and Infinitives:** Write a composition about a task you have difficulty accomplishing.			
18 page 308 **Grammar:** Adverbs: Sentence, Focus, and Negative **Theme:** Controversial Issues	A transcript of a radio call-in show: *Time to Sound Off*	Five paragraphs on a controversial topic	A radio call-in show about military service

SPEAKING	PRONUNCIATION	VOCABULARY	
Information Gap: Movie review: *A Beautiful Mind* *Group Discussion:* The current movie rating system *Picture Discussion:* The behavior of moviegoers	Vowel sound changes in words with the same spellings but different meanings	compilation* engrossing estranged incumbent on me	polarized spice up transcend vanquishing
Information Gap: Guessing a mystery object based on clues *Survey and Discussion:* Crime and punishment	*Has been* and *is being* in passive constructions	accomplice alias divulged gear get away with	hijacked inadvertently remains rotting
Game: People and places *Picture Discussion:* Famous people	The vowel sounds /ei/ and /ɛ/	bewitch font lacerates potions	repulsive rituals shrine supernatural
Personal Inventory: Life events *Group Discussion:* What you value in friendships	Pronunciation of nouns and verbs with the same spellings	catching up on coincide* context* counterpart	meander naive spare your feelings vulnerable
Personal Inventory: Personal beliefs and experiences *Group Discussion:* Famous sayings	The vowel sounds /æ/, /ɑ/, and /ʌ/	connotation flunk learned longhand	ring a bell scenario* tough nut to crack wretched
Personal Inventory: Personal beliefs and experiences *Pros and Cons:* Brainstorming ideas about controversial topics *Debate:* Debating a controversial topic	Sentence stress and meaning	compulsory controversial* fuzzy shed some light on	spirited stereotype uncensored willingly

* = AWL (Academic Word List) items

UNIT	READING	WRITING	LISTENING
19 page 323 **Grammar:** Adverb Clauses **Theme:** Sports	An editorial: *Are Sports Still Sporting?*	Three or four paragraphs about a sports topic	An interview with a sports star
20 page 340 **Grammar:** Adverb and Adverbial Phrases **Theme:** Compassion	An article: *Compassion*	Three or four paragraphs about a compassionate act you have witnessed	A news broadcast on world events
21 page 358 **Grammar:** Connectors **Theme:** Memory	An article: *Try to Remember*	Three or four paragraphs about a significant memory you have	An excerpt from a memory-training workshop
PART VIII From Grammar to Writing, page 374 **Using Transitions:** Write a composition that expresses a strong opinion.			
22 page 378 **Grammar:** Conditionals; Other Ways to Express Unreality **Theme:** Intuition	A story: *Intuition*	Four or five paragraphs about a time when you ignored your intuition	A conversation about a student's moral quandary
23 page 396 **Grammar:** More Conditions; The Subjunctive **Theme:** Advice	Letters to an advice columnist and responses: *Ask Rosa*	Four or five paragraphs about a time when you took good advice and another when you took bad advice	A conversation advising a friend about her daughter's demands
PART IX From Grammar to Writing, page 414 **Avoiding Run-On Sentences and Comma Splices:** Write a composition about an intuitive experience.			

SPEAKING	PRONUNCIATION	VOCABULARY	
Personal Inventory: Future possibilities *Picture Discussion:* Sports and violence	Placement of dependent adverb clauses and pauses in speaking	also-ran awry inevitable* lurking	partisanship prevalence stamina venues
Personal Inventory: Personal beliefs and expressions *Group Discussion:* Animal emotions	Vowel changes and stress shift in words of the same family	bandanna a blow was struck corneas dawned on decrepit	elude floored oozing petty weighed
Game: Connecting ideas *Picture Discussion:* A famous painting about memory	Pronunciation of clauses connected by conjunctions and those connected by transitions	core* glucose lobes mitigate	peg recollect tap vivid
Conditional Game: People and things *Personal Inventory:* Personal hopes and wishes *Group Discussion:* Story outcome	Contractions of the auxiliaries *would* and *had*	beastly bureau fluttered hailing inkling	mutilated sweltering token weirdo
Personal Inventory: Personal beliefs and experiences *Group Discussion:* Moral and political issues *Picture Discussion:* Advice about visiting another country	Silent consonants that are sometimes pronounced	at the end of my rope doormat intransigent lighten up neatnik	overbearing pigsty right the ship semblance slob

* = AWL (Academic Word List) items

ABOUT THE AUTHOR / ACKNOWLEDGMENTS

Jay Maurer has taught English in binational centers, colleges, and universities in Spain, Portugal, Mexico, the Somali Republic, and the United States; and intensive English at Columbia University's American Language Program. In addition, he has been a teacher of college composition, literature, and speech at Santa Fe Community College and Northern New Mexico Community College. He is the co-author with Penny LaPorte of the three-level *Structure Practice in Context* series; co-author with Irene Schoenberg of the five-level *True Colors* series and the *True Voices* video series; co-author with Irene Schoenberg of *Focus on Grammar 1*; and author of *Focus on Grammar 5*, editions 1 through 4. Currently he lives and writes in Arizona and Washington State. *Focus on Grammar 5: An Integrated Skills Approach*, Fourth Edition, has grown out of the author's experiences as a practicing teacher of both ESL and college writing.

Writing the fourth edition of *Focus on Grammar 5* has been even more interesting and rewarding than doing the first three editions. I'm indebted to many people who helped me in different ways. Specifically, though, I want to express my appreciation and gratitude to:

- My students over the years.
- **Marjorie Fuchs**, **Margaret Bonner**, and **Irene Schoenberg**—the other members of the FOG author team—for their support and encouragement.
- That genius, whoever he or she is, who created the joke about the parrot that has been floating around in cyberspace for a considerable time now. The same to the unknown authors of the bumper stickers.
- **Lise Minovitz** for her many well-taken comments about the manuscript, particularly in the early stages of the revision.
- **Amy Shearon** of Rice University for her careful review of the third edition and her many perceptive suggestions for improvement.
- **Debbie Sistino** for her vision and her excellent direction of the entire project. Thank you very much.

Above all I am grateful to:

- **John Barnes**, my editor, for his patience, his excellent eye for detail, his perceptive understanding of what works well in the classroom, and his overall vision. He has been instrumental in making this a better book.
- My wife **Priscilla** for her love, wonderful support, and assistance with the manuscript.
- My best friend.

REVIEWERS

We are grateful to the following reviewers for their many helpful comments:

Aida Aganagic, Seneca College, Toronto, Canada; **Aftab Ahmed**, American University of Sharjah, Sharjah, United Arab Emirates; **Todd Allen**, English Language Institute, Gainesville, FL; **Anthony Anderson**, University of Texas, Austin, TX; **Anna K. Andrade**, ASA Institute, New York, NY; **Bayda Asbridge**, Worcester State College, Worcester, MA; **Raquel Ashkenasi**, American Language Institute, La Jolla, CA; **James Bakker**, Mt. San Antonio College, Walnut, CA; **Kate Baldrige-Hale**, Harper College, Palatine, IL; **Leticia S. Banks**, ALCI-SDUSM, San Marcos, CA; **Aegina Barnes**, York College CUNY, Forest Hills, NY; **Sarah Barnhardt**, Community College of Baltimore County, Reisterstown, MD; **Kimberly Becker**, Nashville State Community College, Nashville, TN; **Holly Bell**, California State University, San Marcos, CA; **Anne Bliss**, University of Colorado, Boulder, CO; **Diana Booth**, Elgin Community College, Elgin, IL; **Barbara Boyer**, South Plainfield High School, South Plainfield, NJ; **Janna Brink**, Mt. San Antonio College, Walnut, CA; **AJ Brown**, Portland State University, Portland, OR; **Amanda Burgoyne**, Worcester State College, Worcester, MA; **Brenda Burlingame**, Independence High School, Charlotte, NC; **Sandra Byrd**, Shelby County High School and Kentucky State University, Shelbyville, KY; **Edward Carlstedt**, American University of Sharjah, Sharjah, United Arab Emirates; **Sean Cochran**, American Language Institute, Fullerton, CA; **Yanely Cordero**, Miami Dade College, Miami, FL; **Lin Cui**, William Rainey Harper College, Palatine, IL; **Sheila Detweiler**, College Lake County, Libertyville, IL; **Ann Duncan**, University of Texas, Austin, TX; **Debra Edell**, Merrill Middle School, Denver, CO; **Virginia Edwards**, Chandler-Gilbert Community College, Chandler, AZ; **Kenneth Fackler**, University of Tennessee, Martin, TN; **Jennifer Farnell**, American Language Program, Stamford, CT; **Allen P. Feiste**, Suwon University, Hwaseong, South Korea; **Mina Fowler**, Mt. San Antonio Community College, Rancho Cucamonga, CA; **Rosemary Franklin**, University of Cincinnati, Cincinnati, OH; **Christiane Galvani**, Texas Southern University, Sugar Land, TX; **Chester Gates**, Community College of Baltimore County, Baltimore, MD; **Luka Gavrilovic**, Quest Language Studies, Toronto, Canada; **Sally Gearhart**, Santa Rosa Community College, Santa Rosa, CA; **Shannon Gerrity**, James Lick Middle School, San Francisco, CA; **Jeanette Gerrity Gomez**, Prince George's Community College, Largo, MD; **Carlos Gonzalez**, Miami Dade College, Miami, FL; **Therese Gormley Hirmer**, University of Guelph, Guelph, Canada; **Sudeepa Gulati**, Long Beach City College, Long Beach, CA; **Anthony Halderman**, Cuesta College, San Luis Obispo, CA; **Ann A. Hall**, University of Texas, Austin, TX; **Cora Higgins**, Boston Academy of English, Boston, MA; **Michelle Hilton**, South Lane School District, Cottage Grove, OR; **Nicole Hines**, Troy University, Atlanta, GA; **Rosemary Hiruma**, American Language Institute, Long Beach, CA; **Harriet Hoffman**, University of Texas, Austin, TX; **Leah Holck**, Michigan State University, East Lansing, MI; **Christy Hunt**, English for Internationals, Roswell, GA; **Osmany Hurtado**, Miami Dade College, Miami, FL; **Isabel Innocenti**, Miami Dade College, Miami, FL; **Donna Janian**, Oxford Intensive School of English, Medford, MA; **Scott Jenison**, Antelope Valley College, Lancaster, CA; **Grace Kim**, Mt. San Antonio College, Diamond Bar, CA; **Brian King**, ELS Language Center, Chicago, IL; **Pam Kopitzke**, Modesto Junior College, Modesto, CA; **Elena Lattarulo**, American Language Institute, San Diego, CA; **Karen Lavaty**, Mt. San Antonio College, Glendora, CA; **JJ Lee-Gilbert**, Menlo-Atherton High School, Foster City, CA; **Ruth Luman**, Modesto Junior College, Modesto, CA; **Yvette Lyons**, Tarrant County College, Fort Worth, TX; **Janet Magnoni**, Diablo Valley College, Pleasant Hill, CA; **Meg Maher**, YWCA Princeton, Princeton, NJ; **Carmen Marquez-Rivera**, Curie Metropolitan High School, Chicago, IL; **Meredith Massey**, Prince George's Community College, Hyattsville, MD; **Linda Maynard**, Coastline Community College, Westminster, CA; **Eve Mazereeuw**, University of Guelph, Guelph, Canada; **Susanne McLaughlin**, Roosevelt University, Chicago, IL; **Madeline Medeiros**, Cuesta College, San Luis Obispo, CA; **Gioconda Melendez**, Miami Dade College, Miami, FL; **Marcia Menaker**, Passaic County Community College, Morris Plains, NJ; **Seabrook Mendoza**, Cal State San Marcos University, Wildomar, CA; **Anadalia Mendoza**, Felix Varela Senior High School, Miami, FL; **Charmaine Mergulhao**, Quest Language Studies, Toronto, Canada; **Dana Miho**, Mt. San Antonio College, San Jacinto, CA; **Sonia Nelson**, Centennial Middle School, Portland, OR; **Manuel Niebla**, Miami Dade College, Miami, FL; **Alice Nitta**, Leeward Community College, Pearl City, HI; **Gabriela Oliva**, Quest Language Studies, Toronto, Canada; **Sara Packer**, Portland State University, Portland, OR; **Lesley Painter**, New School, New York, NY; **Carlos Paz-Perez**, Miami Dade College, Miami, FL; **Ileana Perez**, Miami Dade College, Miami, FL; **Barbara Pogue**, Essex County College, Newark, NJ; **Phillips Potash**, University of Texas, Austin, TX; **Jada Pothina**, University of Texas, Austin, TX; **Ewa Pratt**, Des Moines Area Community College, Des Moines, IA; **Pedro Prentt**, Hudson County Community College, Jersey City, NJ; **Maida Purdy**, Miami Dade College, Miami, FL; **Dolores Quiles**, SUNY Ulster, Stone Ridge, NY; **Mark Rau**, American River College, Sacramento, CA; **Lynne Raxlen**, Seneca College, Toronto, Canada; **Lauren Rein**, English for Internationals, Sandy Springs, GA; **Diana Rivers**, NOCCCD, Cypress, CA; **Silvia Rodriguez**, Santa Ana College, Mission Viejo, CA; **Rolando Romero**, Miami Dade College, Miami, FL; **Pedro Rosabal**, Miami Dade College, Miami, FL; **Natalie Rublik**, University of Quebec, Chicoutimi, Quebec, Canada; **Matilde Sanchez**, Oxnard College, Oxnard, CA; **Therese Sarkis-Kruse**, Wilson Commencement, Rochester, NY; **Mike Sfiropoulos**, Palm Beach Community College, Boynton Beach, FL; **Amy Shearon**, Rice University, Houston, TX; **Sara Shore**, Modesto Junior College, Modesto, CA; **Patricia Silva**, Richard Daley College, Chicago, IL; **Stephanie Solomon**, Seattle Central Community College, Vashon, WA; **Roberta Steinberg**, Mount Ida College, Newton, MA; **Teresa Szymula**, Curie Metropolitan High School, Chicago, IL; **Hui-Lien Tang**, Jasper High School, Plano, TX; **Christine Tierney**, Houston Community College, Sugar Land, TX; **Ileana Torres**, Miami Dade College, Miami, FL; **Michelle Van Slyke**, Western Washington University, Bellingham, WA; **Melissa Villamil**, Houston Community College, Sugar Land, TX; **Elizabeth Wagenheim**, Prince George's Community College, Lago, MD; **Mark Wagner**, Worcester State College, Worcester, MA; **Angela Waigand**, American University of Sharjah, Sharjah, United Arab Emirates; **Merari Weber**, Metropolitan Skills Center, Los Angeles, CA; **Sonia Wei**, Seneca College, Toronto, Canada; and **Vicki Woodward**, Indiana University, Bloomington, IN.

PART
1

PRESENT, PAST, AND FUTURE

UNIT	GRAMMAR FOCUS	THEME
1	Present Time	The Digital World
2	Past Time	Marriage
3	Future Time	Travel

Present Time
THE DIGITAL WORLD

STEP 1 GRAMMAR IN CONTEXT

Before You Read

PAIRS: Discuss the questions.

1. What electronic devices do you use for communication with others? How often do you use them?
2. Do you think digital advances have changed our world for the better or for the worse?

Read

🎧 *Read the article about staying in close connection with other people.*

CONNECTED!

by James Marx

Most of us hardly **go** anywhere today without a cell phone or iPhone, an iPod, or a laptop —or so it **seems**. We**'re trying** to stay in 24/7 communication with each other. We **want** to be "connected." How **do** we **accomplish** this? We **use** the Internet to contact friends on MySpace or Facebook. We **send** and **receive** emails, **write** and **read** blogs, **call** others and **text** them on our cell phones. We**'re** "available" most of the time. **Is** this constant communication good? I **think** it**'s** positive overall, though there **is** a downside to living digitally.

My daughter, Allison, **is** an excellent example. Consider the social networking sites MySpace and Facebook. MySpace **has been** around since 2003 and Facebook since 2005. When you **join** one of them, you **develop** your own web page where you **present** your personal profile, **post** pictures, and **write** on your friends' "walls." Allison **has** a page on both of them and **spends** a lot of time keeping in touch with her friends. This evening Allison **is sitting** in front of the computer, **reading** posts on her wall, and **writing** responses. At the moment, she**'s laughing**, probably at a picture or amusing comment.

Then there**'s** my 15-year-old son, Nick, who **appears** addicted to his cell phone, which he**'s had** since his birthday four months ago. Right now Nick **is texting** friends—he**'s been doing** that for the last half hour—and **shows** no signs of stopping. I**'ve had** conversations with Nick's teachers, who **say** Nick **isn't doing** well, that they**'ve been having** difficulty getting his attention. Most of them **have outlawed** the use of cell phones in class. They **feel** bad about this but **believe** education **comes** first.

Then there**'s** my wife Elena, who **loves** email. After dinner every night Elena **gets** out her laptop, **logs** on to the Internet, and **reads** and **answers** her messages. That**'s** what Elena **is** doing right now. She **says** she**'s getting** about 100 email messages daily and **is having** trouble staying on top of them.

And then there**'s** yours truly. As a writer for *In Touch Magazine*, I **go** to the office three days a week and **telecommute** the other two. When I**'m working** at home, I **write** a blog. By the way, **do** you **know** the origin of the word "blog"? It**'s** a contraction of "web log," which **is** a type of website. On my blog I **write** and **read** regular entries, **describe** events, and **comment** on what others **say**. There**'s** a blog on the Internet for just about everything. **Do** you **remember** the movie *Julie and Julia*? It**'s** about a young woman who, bored with her day

job, **decides** to cook all of TV chef Julia Child's famous recipes and then **writes** a blog about each day's meal.

The downside I mentioned above **is** simply this: Staying in near-constant communication with others often **leads** to stress. It **takes** our time and **tends** to prevent us from spending quiet time alone, from reading, from contemplating things, from enjoying nature. We **hear** people saying things such as, "I just couldn't do without my BlackBerry." So would I give it all up? Not on your life! Through the Internet I **stay** in touch with friends I seldom **see**. But as with so many other things in our lives, we **need** to put things in balance.

After You Read

A | **Vocabulary:** *Match the blue words and phrases on the left with their meanings on the right.*

_____ 1. We're trying to stay in **24/7** communication with each other.

_____ 2. There is a downside to living **digitally**.

_____ 3. You present your personal **profile** online.

_____ 4. She's having trouble **staying on top of** her email.

_____ 5. I **telecommute** two days a week.

_____ 6. It **tends** to prevent us from spending quiet time alone.

_____ 7. It also prevents us from **contemplating** things.

_____ 8. Some say they couldn't **do without** their cell phone.

a. thinking about with attention

b. short description

c. continue to live minus (something)

d. is likely

e. managing

f. with electronic devices

g. constant

h. work from home

B | **Comprehension:** *Circle T (True) or F (False). Correct the false statements.*

1. According to the author, most people today want to be in frequent
   communication with others.   T   F

2. The author thinks digital living is positive overall.   T   F

3. MySpace and Facebook are computer search engines.   T   F

4. Facebook became available before MySpace.   T   F

(continued on next page)

5. The author says most teachers have outlawed computers in class.	**T**	**F**
6. The word "blog" is a short form of "web log."	**T**	**F**
7. The film *Julie and Julia* is about a woman who writes a blog.	**T**	**F**
8. The author thinks staying in near-constant communication with others is always stressful.	**T**	**F**

STEP 2 GRAMMAR PRESENTATION

PRESENT TIME

Present Time: In General or Now

Simple Present	Present Progressive
	Be + Base Form + *-ing*
Today we **spend** a lot of money on electronic devices.	Jack **is looking** for a new iPod.

Present Time: From a Time in the Past Until Now

Present Perfect	Present Perfect Progressive
Have + Past Participle	*Have been* + Base Form + *-ing*
We **have had** email for 12 years.	He**'s been texting** his friends for the last half hour.

Action and Non-Action Verbs

Action Verbs		Most Non-Action Verbs
Simple Form	Progressive Form	Simple Form
They normally **drive** to work.	Today they**'re taking** the bus.	Teachers **know** he is a good student. They **want** to understand his problem.

Some Non-Action Verbs	
Simple Form (Stative Use)	Progressive Form (Active Use)
I **have** a new iPhone.	I'm **having** problems with it.
They **think** they need a better computer.	Please don't bother me; I'm **thinking**.
Our laptop **is** a great computer.	It**'s being** difficult today, though.

Action Verbs	Some Non-Action Verbs	
+ Adverb	+ Adjective (Stative Use)	+ Adverb (Active Use)
She **works constantly**. He**'s doing badly** in class.	Your car **looks good**. The soup **tastes delicious**. She **feels bad** about what she said.	He **looked thoughtfully** at the text message. You should **taste** that **carefully**—it's hot! The doctor **felt** the bruise **gently**.

GRAMMAR NOTES

1 Use the **simple present** to show actions, events, or states that are true in general or happen habitually.

- We **use** the Internet to stay in touch with friends. *(true in general)*
- After dinner every night, Elena **gets out** her laptop. *(habitual)*

We also use the simple present to narrate events in sequence.

- Elena **logs** on to the Internet, **reads** her email, and **starts** responding.

2 Use the **present progressive** to show actions or events in progress at the moment (not finished).

- Allison **is sitting** in front of the computer.

BE CAREFUL! We generally don't use the progressive with non-action verbs.

- We **need** to put things in balance.
  Not: We're needing to put things in balance.

3 The **present perfect** and the **present perfect progressive** connect the past with the present. Use them to show actions and states that began in the past and continue until now.

- I**'ve had** my iPod for six months.
- He**'s been writing** a blog since 2008.

They are often used with *for* + a length of time and *since* + a starting point.

Use the **present perfect**, not the present perfect progressive, to describe completed actions with a connection to the present.

- I**'ve bought** four cell phones in the last two years.
  Not: I've been buying four cell phones in the last two years.

4 **Action** verbs (also called **active**) describe actions.

- Computers **perform** tasks quickly. *(action)*

Use **simple** verb forms (without *-ing*) to describe all of an action—the action in general.

- I **write** articles for a psychology magazine. *(in general)*

Use **progressive** verb forms (with *-ing*) to describe part of an action—in progress at a specific time.

- Right now I**'m writing** my blog. *(in progress at the moment)*

(continued on next page)

5	Non-action verbs (also called stative) describe states such as appearance (seem), emotions (love), mental states (know), perceptions (hear), possession (own), and wants (need).	• You **seem** stressed. • Elena **loves** email. • We **hear** that all the time. • They **own** four computers. • I **need** a new phone.
	We most often use non-action verbs in the simple form and not in the progressive.	• I **know** my coworker well. NOT: I'm knowing . . .
	Some non-action verbs can be used to describe either states or actions. When they are used to describe actions, they usually have different meanings.	• We **have** a new laptop. *(possess)* • We**'re having** trouble with it. *(experiencing)* • He **is** a nice fellow. *(a state)* • Today he**'s not being** nice. *(behaving)*
6	We normally use **adverbs** with **action verbs**.	• She always **listens carefully**. • She **works hard** at her job.
	We normally use the verbs *look*, *sound*, *feel*, *smell*, and *taste* to show states, in which case they are used with **adjectives**, not adverbs.	• You **sound** really **excited**! NOT: You sound really excitedly! • She **feels bad** about what she said. NOT: She feels badly . . .
	BE CAREFUL! The sense verbs are sometimes used to show actions, in which case they are used with adverbs.	• I don't **hear well** when other people are talking. *(an action—using one's ears)* • The fire alarm **sounded** a warning **loudly**. *(an action—making a noise)*

REFERENCE NOTES

For definitions and examples of **grammar terms**, see Glossary on page G-1.

For a list of **non-action verbs**, see Appendix 2 on page A-2.

For a list of **non-action verbs sometimes used in the progressive**, see Appendix 3 on page A-3.

STEP 3 FOCUSED PRACTICE

EXERCISE 1: Discover the Grammar

A | *Look at the sentences. Do the underlined verbs show habitual action (**HA**) or action in progress (**AP**)?*

____HA____ **1.** Most of us hardly <u>go</u> anywhere today without an electronic device.

_____ **2.** We<u>'re trying</u> to stay connected.

_____ **3.** We <u>use</u> the Internet to contact friends.

_____ **4.** Allison <u>is sitting</u> in front of the computer.

_____ **5.** At the moment, she<u>'s laughing</u>.

_____ **6.** Nick's teachers say he <u>isn't doing</u> well.

_____ **7.** Elena <u>is having</u> trouble staying on top of her email.

_____ **8.** When <u>I'm working</u> at home I write a blog.

_____ **9.** When I'm working at home I <u>write</u> a blog.

_____ **10.** Through the Internet I <u>stay</u> in touch with friends.

B | *Look at the sentences. Decide whether the underlined verbs describe actions (**A**) or states (**S**).*

1. Most people today hardly <u>go</u> anywhere without an electronic device.	Ⓐ	**S**
2. At least it <u>seems</u> that way.	**A**	**S**
3. We <u>want</u> to be connected 24/7.	**A**	**S**
4. We <u>text</u> people on our cell phones.	**A**	**S**
5. Nick <u>appears</u> to be addicted to his cell phone.	**A**	**S**
6. On MySpace and Facebook you <u>develop</u> your own page.	**A**	**S**
7. Teachers <u>feel</u> bad about outlawing cell phones in class.	**A**	**S**
8. Elena <u>loves</u> her email.	**A**	**S**
9. I <u>telecommute</u> two days a week.	**A**	**S**
10. We <u>need</u> to put things in balance.	**A**	**S**

EXERCISE 2: Simple Present / Present Progressive   *(Grammar Notes 1, 2)*

Complete the account of a day in the life of James Marx, magazine writer and Internet blogger. Circle the correct forms of the underlined verbs.

Today is Monday, one of the two days a week that I <u>telecommute</u>/ 'm telecommuting. On these
                                                                    1.
days, I <u>walk</u> / 'm walking about 50 steps to my home office, <u>turn on</u> / am turning on the computer,
          2.   **3.**
and <u>start</u> / am starting writing. For some reason, my computer printer <u>gives</u> / is giving me problems
        4.   **5.**
today, so at the moment I <u>try</u> / 'm trying to fix it. Ah, here we go. It <u>works</u> / 's working again.
                              6.   **7.**

This week I <u>write</u> / 'm writing on my blog about the dangers of text messaging. Currently our state
                8.
legislature <u>considers</u> / is considering a law that would prohibit texting while driving or operating
                9.
machinery. I <u>think</u> / 'm thinking it would be a good idea to pass it.
                10.

It's now 12:30 P.M., time for lunch. On these home days, I <u>make</u> / 'm making my own lunch. On
                                                              11.
the other three days, I <u>have</u> / 'm having lunch in the company cafeteria.
                            12.

It's 3:30 P.M. I finished my blog an hour ago, and now I <u>do</u> / 'm doing some Internet research for
                                                            13.
an article I'm going to write in a few days. I <u>love</u> / 'm loving these quiet days at home.
                                                    14.

EXERCISE 3: Present Perfect / Present Perfect Progressive

(Grammar Note 3)

Complete the sentences with present perfect or present perfect progressive forms of the verbs in parentheses. Use the progressive form if possible.

James and Elena Marx _____*have known*_____ each other
1. (know)
for 20 years and _____ married for 18. They
2. (be)
_____ in their current house for three years.
3. (live)
James _____ a writer for 10 years. He
4. (be)
_____ for *In Touch Magazine* for eight years
5. (work)
and _____ an Internet blog for six. He
6. (write)
_____ four books on popular culture.
7. (also write)
Elena _____ a high school English teacher for the last 12 years. During that time
8. (be)
she _____ at six different schools. She _____ at her current school for
9. (teach)   **10. (teach)**
five years now.

The Marxes are a "wired" family. They _____ at least one home computer for
11. (have)
15 years. Over the years they _____ six computers. James, Elena, Allison, and Nick
12. (own)
_____ with friends and relatives online for almost as long as they can remember.
13. (communicate)

EXERCISE 4: Action / Non-Action Verbs; Adverbs / Adjectives

(Grammar Notes 4–6)

Complete the statements with the correct verb from the box. Use each verb once in the simple present and once in the present progressive. Also choose the correct adverb or adjective.

be	feel	have	look	think

1. Your new iPhone _____*looks*_____ (similar)/ similarly to mine.

2. Our computer crashed, so we _____ frantic / frantically for a new one.

3. If your day is going bad / badly, you _____ a bad day.

4. Cell phone use has grown so rapid / rapidly that more people _____ cell phones today than land lines.

5. A person who _____ bad / badly about saying something should apologize.

6. I was fine yesterday, but today I _____ terrible / terribly.

7. When a person _____ clear / clearly, that person is using his or her brain.

8. Many people today _____ a home computer is <u>essential / essentially</u>.

9. That child _____ <u>normal / normally</u> a well-behaved student.

10. Today, however, she _____ <u>obnoxious / obnoxiously</u>.

EXERCISE 5: Editing

Read the student essay. There are eleven mistakes in the use of present-time verbs, adjectives, and adverbs. The first mistake is already corrected. Find and correct ten more.

No Cell Phone Restrictions!

It seems
~~It's seeming~~ that I constantly hear the same thing: "Cell phones are dangerous. We're needing to restrict them. People are dying because of cell phones." Well, I'm thinking cell phones themselves aren't the problem. I'm completely opposed to restrictions on them, and here's why:

First, people say cell phones are dangerous to health, so they should be limited. Supporters of this idea say there are studies showing that cell phones produce harmful radiation and can even cause cancer. I think this is nonsense. There hasn't been any real proof. It's sounding like just another study that ultimately isn't meaning anything.

Second, teachers say we shouldn't allow cell phones in classes because they're a distraction. I feel pretty angrily about this. Here's an example: Two weeks ago in my history class, a student had her cell phone on because her mother was really sick and might need a ride to the hospital. The student's mother couldn't contact anyone else. Actually, the mother did call, and the student called someone to help her mother. What if the phone hadn't been on? The teacher would feel pretty badly.

Third, people argue that using a cell phone while driving is dangerous. I disagree. It's no more dangerous than turning on the car radio or eating a sandwich. People do those things when they drive. The law says you have to have one hand on the steering wheel at all times. It's possible to use a cell phone correct with one hand. I use my cell phone careful; I always keep one hand on the wheel. Maybe there should be training in ways to use a cell phone good, but we shouldn't prohibit using handheld phones in cars.

This has always been a free country. I hope it stays that way.

EXERCISE 6: Listening

A | *Listen to the conversation. Check (✓) the topic that is <u>not</u> mentioned.*

☐ credit cards ☐ cell phones

☐ identity theft ☐ the Internet

B | *Read the questions. Listen to the conversation. Then listen again and answer the questions in complete sentences.*

1. How are things going for Mary?

   Things aren't going well for her.

2. What kind of problem is Mary having?

   _____

3. What is wrong?

   _____

4. What is this a good example of?

   _____

5. What has the person who got the number been doing?

   _____

6. How much money is involved?

   _____

7. Does Mary have to pay back the money?

   _____

8. When are people supposed to report problems like this?

   _____

9. What does Mary say about the Internet?

   _____

10. According to Jim, what is the downside of the Internet?

    _____

EXERCISE 7: Pronunciation

A | *Read and listen to the Pronunciation Note.*

> **Pronunciation Note**
>
> The letters ***ng*** have two pronunciations: with the /g/ sound, /ŋg/, as in the word *English*, and without it, /ŋ/, as in the word *sing*. Note that the /g/ sound is never pronounced when a word ends in ***ng***.

B | *Listen to the sentences. Circle the letters **ng** when the **g** is pronounced (/ŋg/). Underline the letters **ng** when the **g** is not pronounced (/ŋ/).*

1. Elena has been teaching English for a long time.

2. A lot of new things are happening in the digital world.

3. James has been writing for a magazine and blogging on the Internet for years.

4. The longer he spoke, the angrier we got.

5. Bill is strong, but Bob is stronger.

6. My fingers are sore because I've been working in the yard.

7. He's been single for years, but now he's going to get married.

C | *PAIRS: Practice the sentences.*

EXERCISE 8: Group Discussion

A | *Fill out the chart on page 12 for yourself.*

Electronic Device or System	Have It	Don't Have It	Works Well	Often Use It	Seldom or Never Use It	Comments
Home computer	✓		✓	✓		*Spend several hours a day on it. Use it for writing, research, entertainment. Couldn't do without it.*
Laptop computer						
Email						
Cell phone or iPhone						
iPod or MP3 player						

B | *GROUPS: Discuss your answers. Talk about which electronic devices are important in your life and which are not.*

> EXAMPLE: **A:** I have a home computer and love using it. I couldn't do without it.
> **B:** Why?
> **A:** I use it for a lot of things—for writing, doing research, watching things for entertainment.
> **C:** Do you think you spend too much time on the computer?
> **A:** Well . . .

C | *Report your answers to the class.*

EXERCISE 9: Class Discussion

A | *Read the excerpt from an Internet article on the dangers of texting while driving.*

> According to a poll given Tuesday, August 7, 2007, 91 percent of Americans agree that text messaging while driving is just as dangerous as driving after having a few alcoholic beverages, but 57 percent admit that they do it.
>
> The Harris Interactive survey, given by the cell phone messaging service Pinger Inc., found that 89 percent of respondents believe that messaging while driving should be banned because the act is very dangerous.
>
> Of those polled, 66 percent said they had read text messages and emails while driving, and another 57 percent said they have sent them while driving. In May, Wisconsin was the first state to ban text messaging while driving, and now six other states are considering the same law. The poll included 2,049 people from the United States and took place from June 29 to July 3.
>
> The majority of people that text message while they drive are young people, many of whom have only been driving a few years. Having these inexperienced drivers texting on the road is a very dangerous combination. Text messaging while driving significantly slows your reaction time. . . .

B | *CLASS: Discuss the following questions related to the article:*

1. Do you agree that text messaging while driving should be banned?
2. Do you agree that the majority of people who text message while they drive are young people?
3. What is the best way to solve this problem? Make several suggestions.

EXERCISE 10: Writing

A | *Write two or three paragraphs on the following topic, using present-time verbs.*

Of all the electronic devices mentioned in this unit—home computer, cell phone, iPod, MP3 player, laptop—which is the most beneficial to you? Which would be hard for you to do without? Give several reasons for your opinion.

EXAMPLE: My cell phone is the electronic device that is most beneficial to me. There are several reasons why. The first is convenience: I carry my phone with me wherever I go. I have it whenever I need it. Also, it's light and fits easily into my pocket or book bag . . .

B | *Check your work. Use the Editing Checklist.*

Editing Checklist
Did you use . . . ?   ☐ simple present correctly   ☐ present progressive correctly   ☐ action verbs correctly   ☐ non-action verbs correctly

UNIT 1 Review

Check your answers on page UR-1.

Do you need to review anything?

A | *Complete the letter by circling the correct verb form.*

Dear Amy,

Just a note to tell you how we <u>do / are doing</u>. Tim <u>loves / is loving</u> his job. Our house is on
1.   2.
a bus line, so he <u>takes / is taking</u> the bus to work. I <u>get / 'm getting</u> to know our neighbors, who
3.   4.
<u>seem / are seeming</u> friendly. Nancy <u>attends / is attending</u> kindergarten four days a week, but
5.   6.
today is a holiday, so she <u>plays / is playing</u> outside. We really <u>like / are liking</u> Phoenix.
7.   8.

Love,
Martha

B | *Complete the paragraph with correct forms of the verbs in parentheses. Use the present perfect progressive if possible.*

Tim and Martha Baldwin _____ in Phoenix since
1. (live)
last March. Tim is a film director. He _____ five movies
2. (direct)
in his career and _____ on a sixth since they moved to
3. (work)
Phoenix. They _____ their own house for six months and
4. (own)
_____ it since they bought it. Martha is a language teacher and
5. (remodel)
_____ an online tutoring service for three months.
6. (run)

C | *Circle the letter of the one underlined word or phrase in each sentence that is not correct.*

1. Frank <u>feels</u> <u>badly</u> that he <u>got</u> <u>angry</u> at the staff meeting.　　　**A B C D**
      A   B   C   D

2. Helen <u>sounded</u> <u>tremendously</u> <u>excitedly</u> when she <u>called</u>.　　　**A B C D**
       A   B   C   D

3. The food <u>didn't smell</u> <u>good</u>, but it <u>certainly</u> tasted <u>well</u>.　　　**A B C D**
       A   B   C   D

4. Melanie <u>looked</u> <u>angry</u> at the person who <u>suddenly</u> <u>cut</u> in front of her in line.　　　**A B C D**
       A   B   C   D

5. The teacher <u>feels</u> <u>bad</u> yesterday when her students <u>behaved</u> <u>badly</u> in front　　　**A B C D**
        A   B   C   D
of the school principal.

6. The situations <u>looked</u> <u>similar</u> at first, but they <u>were</u> really <u>differently</u>.　　　**A B C D**
          A   B   C   D

Past Time
MARRIAGE

Before You Read

PAIRS: Discuss the questions.

1. What do you think the term "arranged marriage" means?
2. Would you rather find your own person to marry or have someone else select that person for you?
3. Do you think an arranged marriage is likely to be a happy marriage?

Read

Read the article about an unusual marriage.

LIFESTYLES

A *Marriage* Made on the **Internet?**

$\mathcal{H}$ ow many Americans **have** ever **considered** asking friends or relatives to select their spouse for them? Not many. Yet this is exactly what David Weinlick **did**. He **had** long **been pondering** marriage and **had known** for some time that he **was going to get** married in June of 1998. When the wedding **would take place** and who **would be invited** he already **knew**. He just **didn't know** whom he **would be marrying**. You see, he **hadn't met** his bride yet.

It **started** some years ago. Friends **would ask** Weinlick, an anthropology student at the University of Minnesota, when he **was going to tie** the knot. He **would say** he **didn't know**. Eventually he **got** tired of these questions, so he **picked** a date out of the blue: June 13, 1998. As this date **was getting** closer, Weinlick, who **was** 28 at the time, **knew** he **had** to do something. His friend Steve Fletcher **came up with** the idea of a democratic selection process. Weinlick **liked** the idea, so he **advertised** for a bride on the Internet on a Bridal Nomination Committee website.

He **created** an application form and **asked** friends and relatives to interview the candidates and select the winner. They **did** this at a party before the ceremony on the day of the wedding.

Weinlick's friends and relatives **took** the request seriously. Though Weinlick **wasn't** sure who his bride **would be**, he **did want** to get married. He **said** he thinks commitment is important and that people have to work at relationships to make them successful.

(*continued on next page*)

Internet Marriage

Weinlick's sister **said** she **thought** all of the candidates **were** nice, but she **was looking** for someone really special—a person who **would fit** into family celebrations.

So who **won** the election? It **was** Elizabeth Runze, a pharmacy student at the University of Minnesota. She **hadn't met** Weinlick before she **picked up** a candidate survey on the Monday before the wedding. They **talked** briefly on that day and again on Tuesday when Runze **turned in** the completed survey. However, neither Weinlick nor Runze **knew** who **would** ultimately **be chosen** by Weinlick's friends and family on Saturday, the day of the wedding. After her Saturday selection by the committee, Runze **said** the day **was** the most incredible she **had** ever **experienced**.

Weinlick **was** happy too. After the selection, the groom **said** the plan **had turned out** almost exactly as he **had hoped**. By the time the wedding day **arrived**, Weinlick **had prepared** everything. The two **took** their vows at the Mall of America in Minneapolis while about 2,000 shoppers **looked on**.

Probably few Americans would do what Weinlick and Runze **did**. Their union qualifies as an "arranged marriage," a phenomenon that **has not been** popular in America. Arranged marriages are common in many other parts of the world, though, or at least they **used to be**. Maybe they're not such a bad idea.

After You Read

A | Vocabulary: *Match the blue words and phrases on the left with their meanings on the right.*

_____ 1. Weinlick had **pondered** marriage for quite some time.

_____ 2. Friends would ask Weinlick when he was going to **tie the knot**.

_____ 3. Weinlick picked a date **out of the blue**.

_____ 4. A friend of Weinlick **came up with** the idea of a democratic selection process.

_____ 5. Weinlick and Runze talked briefly when she **turned in** her application.

_____ 6. No one knew who would **ultimately** be chosen.

_____ 7. Weinlick said the plan had **turned out** almost exactly as he'd hoped.

a. at random

b. had a particular result

c. considered

d. in the end

e. wed

f. submitted

g. originated, produced

B | Comprehension: *Circle* **T (True)** *or* **F (False)**. *Correct the false statements.*

1. Weinlick had considered marriage for a long time before his wedding.	T	F
2. Weinlick had met his bride before the planning of his wedding.	T	F
3. He didn't know whom he would marry until shortly before the wedding.	T	F
4. He advertised for a bride in a newspaper.	T	F
5. The selection of Weinlick's bride was a democratic process.	T	F
6. Arranged marriages have traditionally been common in America.	T	F

PAST TIME

Past Time: General or Specific (Definite)

Simple Past
Weinlick **needed** to find a bride.
He **advertised** on the Internet.

Past Progressive
Was / Were + Base Form + *-ing*
He **was looking** for someone special.

Past Time: Not Specific (Indefinite)

Present Perfect
Has / Have + Past Participle
The couple **has** already **sent** the invitations.
They **have chosen** the date for the party.

Past Time: Habitual or Repeated

Used to + Base Form
She **used to be** a pharmacist.

Would + Base Form
Some days she **would work** 12 hours.

Past Time: Before a Time in the Past

Past Perfect
Had + Past Participle
He **had met** her before the wedding.

Past Perfect Progressive
Had been + Base Form + *-ing*
He **had been planning** the wedding for months.

Past Time: After a Time in the Past But Before Now ("Future in the Past")

Was / Were going to + Base Form
He knew he **was going to marry** soon.

Would + Base Form
He knew when the wedding **would be**.

GRAMMAR NOTES

1   Use the **simple past** to express an action, event, or state occurring at a general or specific time in the past.

- Runze **wanted** to get married. *(general)*
- She **filled out** an application form several days before the wedding. *(specific)*

2   Use the **past progressive** to express an action that was in progress (not finished) at a time in the past.

- Runze **was studying** pharmacy at the University when she decided to get married.

3   Use the **present perfect** to express an action, event, or state occurring at an **indefinite** time in the past.

BE CAREFUL! Don't use the present perfect with a past-time expression.

NOTE: The simple past is the definite past. The present perfect is the indefinite past.

Remember that the present perfect also connects the past and the present. (See Unit 1.)

- How many Americans **have** ever **considered** an arranged marriage?

- Weinlick **got married a few years ago**.
  Not: Weinlick ~~has gotten~~ married a few years ago.

- The two **met** on June 8, 1998.
- They **have** already **met**.

- I **have attended** many weddings since then.

4   Use **used to** + base form to show a habitual action, event, or state that was true in the past but is no longer true.

You can also use **would** + base form to express actions or events that occurred regularly during a period in the past.

BE CAREFUL! *Used to* and *would* are similar in meaning when they express past actions. However, only *used to* can show past location, state of being, or possession.

- Kayoko **used to play** tennis a lot.

- When we were children, we **would spend** every summer in Maine.

- I **used to live** in Chicago. *(location)*
- Mia **used to be** a nurse. *(state of being)*
- We **used to have** a summer home. *(possession)*
  Not: I ~~would live~~ in Chicago.
       Mia ~~would be~~ a nurse.
       We ~~would have~~ a summer home.

5   Use the **past perfect** to show an action, event, or state of being that happened **before** a certain time in the past.

Use the past perfect with the simple past to show which of two past actions, events, or states happened first.

The past perfect is usually used when we talk about the first event second.

The past perfect is not often used in sentences with *before* or *after*. The simple past is generally used to describe both events.

- By June 13, the family **had interviewed** dozens of candidates.

- Weinlick and Runze **had known** each other for five days **when** they got married.

- By the time the wedding day arrived, Weinlick **had prepared** everything.

- Weinlick **started** advertising for a bride after he **graduated** from college.

6	Use the **past perfect progressive** to express an action that was in progress **before** another past event.	• She **had been working** when she got married.
7	Use *was / were going to / would* + base form to describe an action, event, or state that was planned or expected in the past (before now). Sentences with *was / were going to / would* are sometimes called **future in the past**.	• Weinlick knew that he **was going to get** married on June 13, 1998. • He knew where the wedding **would be**.

REFERENCE NOTE

For a list of **verbs with irregular past forms and past participles**, see Appendix 1 on page A-1.

STEP 3 FOCUSED PRACTICE

EXERCISE 1: Discover the Grammar

A | *Look at these sentences based on the reading. Write the earlier-occurring action or state on the left and the later-occurring action or state on the right.*

1. Weinlick had known for a long time that he was going to get married on June 13, 1998.

   Weinlick had known for a long time / he was going to get married on June 13, 1998.

2. He just didn't know who he would be marrying.

   _____

3. Friends would repeatedly ask Weinlick when he was going to tie the knot.

   _____

4. Runze hadn't met Weinlick when she picked up her candidate survey.

   _____

5. By the time the wedding day arrived, Weinlick had prepared everything.

   _____

B | *Look at these sentences containing* **would**. *Is* **would** *used for future in the past* (**F**) *or habitual action in the past* (**H**)?

   F   **1.** He already knew when the wedding would be and who would be invited.

_____ **2.** He just didn't know who the bride would be.

_____ **3.** Friends would repeatedly ask Weinlick when he was going to tie the knot.

_____ **4.** He would say he didn't know.

_____ **5.** Weinlick's sister added that it was important for her brother to marry someone who would fit in at family celebrations.

_____ **6.** Neither Weinlick nor Runze knew who would be chosen by his friends and family.

EXERCISE 2: Simple Past / Present Perfect

(Grammar Notes 1, 3)

Complete the story by circling the correct verb forms.

Ellen Rosetti and Mark Stevens (got married)/ have gotten married almost a year ago. Their
                                                              1.

marriage almost <u>didn't happen / hasn't happened</u>, though. They <u>got / have gotten</u> to know each other
                                    2.   **3.**

on a blind date. Then, a week later, Ellen's friend Alice <u>came / has come</u> up with two extra concert
                                                                    4.

tickets.

Ellen says, "On that second date, I <u>thought / 've thought</u>, 'He's the most opinionated man
                                                           5.

<u>I ever met / I've ever met</u>.' Then, a couple of weeks after the concert, Mark <u>called up / has called up</u>
   6.   **7.**

and <u>asked / has asked</u> me out. I <u>wanted / 've wanted</u> to say no, but something <u>made / has made</u> me
      8.   **9.**   **10.**

accept. After that, one thing <u>led / has led</u> to another." For his part, Mark says, "Ellen is unique. I
                                      11.

<u>never knew / 've never known</u> anyone even remotely like her."
       12.

Ellen says, "At first glance you might have trouble seeing how Mark and I could be married.

In certain ways, we're as different as night and day. I'm an early bird; he's a night owl.

He's conservative; I'm liberal. He <u>always loved / 's always loved</u> sports, and I
                                                              13.

<u>was never able / 've never been able</u> to stand them. I guess you might say, ultimately, that
        14.

we're a case of opposites being attracted to each other."

EXERCISE 3: *Used To / Would*

(Grammar Note 4)

Jim Garcia and Mark Stevens both got married fairly recently. Fill in the blanks in their conversation with the correct forms of **used to** *or* **would** *and the verbs in parentheses. Use* **would** *if possible. If* **would** *occurs with a pronoun subject, use a contraction.*

MARK: So, Jim, how does it feel to be an old married man? Been about six months, hasn't it?

JIM: Yep. It feels great. It's a lot different, though.

MARK: Yeah? How so?

JIM: Well, I guess I'd say I ____used to have____ a lot more freedom. Like on Saturdays, for
1. (have)

example. I _____ until 11:00 or even noon. Then, when I got up, my
2. (sleep)

buddies and I _____ out for breakfast at a restaurant. Now Jennifer and
3. (go)

I get up at 8:00 at the latest. She's really an early bird. And I either make her breakfast,

or she makes it for me. And then on Saturday nights I _____ out with the
4. (go)

guys and stay out till all hours of the night. Now it's just the two of us. Sometimes we go

out on Saturday night, and sometimes we don't.

MARK: Does that bother you?

JIM: You know, it doesn't. Life actually _____ kind of lonely. It's not anymore.
5. (be)

What about you? Have things really changed?

MARK: They sure have. For one thing, the neighborhood is totally different. Remember the

apartment I _____ in, right north of downtown? Well, Ellen and I just
6. (live)

bought a house in the suburbs. That's a trip, let me tell you.

JIM: I'll bet.

MARK: Yeah. My weekends _____ my own. I _____ all day
7. (be)   8. (spend)

Saturday working on my car or going mountain biking. Now I have to cut the grass and

take care of the yard.

JIM: So would you change anything?

MARK: Well, I've pondered that question. No, I sure wouldn't. You know how everyone says how

great it is to be single? Well, I _____ so too. Not now. Now I'd say "been
9. (think)

there, done that."

JIM: Me too. I wouldn't change a thing.

EXERCISE 4: Simple Past / Past Perfect

(Grammar Notes 1, 5)

Using the simple past and past perfect, complete the story of how Jim Garcia and Jennifer O'Leary got married. Combine each pair of sentences into one sentence. Begin the new sentence with the connecting word or phrase in parentheses. You can present the two clauses in either order.

1. Jim Garcia and Jennifer O'Leary graduated from high school. They knew each other for three years. (when)

   When they graduated from high school, Jim Garcia and Jennifer O'Leary had known

   each other for three years.

2. Jim completed four years of military service, and Jennifer graduated from college. They both returned to their hometown about a year ago. (by the time)

   _____

   _____

3. Jennifer started teaching, and Jim took a job as a computer programmer. They saw each other again. (by the time)

   _____

   _____

4. Neither went out on any dates. They ran into each other in a drugstore one morning. (when)

   _____

   _____

5. Jim drove to Olson's Drugstore. He woke up with a splitting headache. (because)

   _____

   _____

6. Jennifer's younger sister fell and hurt herself and needed medicine. Jennifer also went to Olson's. (because)

   _____

   _____

7. A week passed. Jim asked Jennifer out on a date. (when)

   _____

   _____

8. Jim and Jennifer dated for three months. They got married. (when)

   _____

   _____

EXERCISE 5: Weinlick / Runze Updated

(Grammar Notes 1–3, 7)

How are David and Elizabeth Weinlick doing some time after getting married? Read the update. Then answer the questions in complete sentences.

Eleven years after David Weinlick and Elizabeth Runze wed in a public ceremony at the Mall of America, their marriage was still going strong. As of May 31, 2009, David and Elizabeth are the parents of four children: daughter Emily, son Charlie, daughter Zoe, and son Zed.

David and Elizabeth say, "We've never regretted it. It sounds like a crazy thing to do, but there was instant chemistry—and we did our dating after we married." They have always stressed that commitment is the thing that makes a marriage work. The feelings came later, they say. "The day we got married we had no relationship. Zero. Nothing!" Elizabeth commented. Feelings of love developed after they got to know each other. Friends of the couple have noted that the Weinlicks are very much in love.

David and Elizabeth Weinlick in 2009

Interestingly, statistics show that "regular" marriages have approximately a 50 percent success rate, while about 85 percent of "arranged" marriages are said to succeed. There was no guarantee the Weinlicks' marriage would succeed, of course, but by all accounts it is doing well.

1. Where did the Weinlicks wed?

   They wed at the Mall of America.

2. What was the state of their marriage 11 years after the wedding?

   _____

3. How many children have they had in their 11 years of marriage?

   _____

4. What have they never regretted?

   _____

5. What have they always stressed about marriage?

   _____

6. What have friends noted about the Weinlicks?

   _____

7. There was no guarantee of what?

   _____

EXERCISE 6: Editing

Read Jennifer Garcia's journal entry. There are nine mistakes in the use of verb constructions. The first mistake is already corrected. Find and correct eight more.

May 20

                                                                        have been

I just had to write today. It's our six-month anniversary. Jim and I ~~are~~ married six months as of today. So maybe this is the time for me to take stock of my situation. The obvious question is whether I'm happy I got married. The answer is "Absolutely." When I remember what my life has been like before we were married, I realize now how lonely I've been before. Jim is a wonderful guy. Since we both work, we took turns doing the housework. He's really good about that. When we have been dating, I wasn't sure whether or not I'll have to do all the housework. But I wasn't having any reason to worry. Today we split everything 50 / 50. The only complaint I have is that Jim snored at night. When I tell him he does that, he only says, "Well, sweetie, you snore too." I don't believe it. But if this is our only problem, I guess we're pretty lucky.

    Well, I'd had a long and tiring day, but it's almost over. It's time to go to sleep.

STEP 4 COMMUNICATION PRACTICE

EXERCISE 7: Listening

A | *Listen to the news broadcast. In what country did the wedding take place?*

_____

B | *Read the questions. Listen again to the news broadcast. Answer each question in a complete sentence containing a past-time verb.*

1. What did Samantha Yang and Darrell Hammer hire Reverend Martinez to do?

   They hired him to marry them while they

   were parachute jumping from a plane.

2. To date, how many jumps have Samantha and Darrell each made?

   _____

   _____

3. How long have they been members of the jumping group?

   _____

   _____

4. How were they originally going to get married?

   _____

   _____

5. Why did they decide not to do this? (first reason)

   _____

   _____

6. Why did they decide not to do this? (second reason)

   _____

   _____

7. Had Reverend Martinez ever done this kind of wedding before?

   _____

   _____

8. Where did Reverend Martinez use to be a pastor?

   _____

   _____

Unusual Weddings

Do you take this woman to be your lawfully wedded wife?

I now pronounce you husband and wife.

EXERCISE 8: Pronunciation

A | *Read and listen to the Pronunciation Note.*

Pronunciation Note

In spoken English, auxiliary verbs in past verb forms are often contracted.

EXAMPLES: She**'s** recently been to see the doctor. (**'s** = **has**)
They**'ve** been to the theater several times. (**'ve** = **have**)
I**'d** been tired, so I took a nap. (**'d** = **had**)
In college, he**'d** spend hours studying. (**'d** = **would**)

B | *Listen and repeat the sentences. Underline the auxiliary in each sentence.*

EXAMPLE: Jack's just asked Nancy to marry him.

1. Nancy's agreed to marry Jack.

2. They've set the date for their wedding.

3. She never thought she'd marry so soon.

4. She'd planned to go to graduate school.

5. She expected she'd be in school for a long time.

6. Her life'd been predictable.

7. She'd go to class in the daytime and study at night.

8. Now she's totally changed her outlook.

C | *Listen and repeat the sentences. Underline the auxiliary in each sentence.*

EXAMPLE: Jack has just asked Nancy to marry him.

1. Nancy has agreed to marry Jack.

2. They have set the date for their wedding.

3. She never thought she would marry so soon.

4. She had planned to go to graduate school.

5. She expected she would be in school for a long time.

6. Her life had been predictable.

7. She would go to class in the daytime and study at night.

8. Now she has totally changed her outlook.

D | *PAIRS: Practice the sentences. One partner says a sentence with the contracted form. The other partner says the sentence with the full form.*

EXERCISE 9: Information Gap

A | *PAIRS: Complete the text. Each of you will read a version of the same story. Each version is missing some information. Take turns asking your partner questions to get the missing information.*

Student A, read the story about Jack Strait. Ask questions and fill in the missing information. Then answer Student B's questions.

Student B, turn to page 30 and follow the instructions there.

EXAMPLE: **A:** What kind of company did he use to work for?
B: He used to work for a company that . . . How long would he stay on the road?
A: He would stay on the road for . . .

Jack Strait's life is quite different now from the way it used to be. He used to work for a

company that _____. His job required him to do a lot of traveling.

He would stay on the road for two or three weeks at a time. It was always the same: As soon

as he pulled into a town, he would look for _____.

The next morning he'd leave his business card at a lot of different establishments, hoping

that someone would agree to see him. If he'd been lucky enough to arrange an appointment

in advance, he'd show them _____. Occasionally they would order a

carpet or some linoleum; most often they wouldn't.

Jack's marriage began to suffer. He missed his wife a lot, but there wasn't much he could

do about the situation. And when he was on the road, he hardly ever saw his children. He

would try to _____ if he had a spare moment. Usually, however, it

was so late that they had already gone to bed. They were growing up without him.

Finally, his wife laid down the law, saying, "Why should we even be married if we're never

going to see each other?" Jack decided she was right. He took a risk. He quit his job and

started his own business. Things were difficult at first, but at least the family was together.

That was five years ago. Things have changed a lot since then. Jack and his family used to

live in a small apartment. Now they own a house. Life is good.

B | *Compare your story with your partner's. Are they the same? Now discuss these questions: What did Jack's occupation use to be? Is it important to take risks in life as Jack did? Can you think of an example of a risk you have taken in your life?*

EXERCISE 10: Picture Discussion

PAIRS: Discuss the picture. Describe the situation. What is happening? Approximately how long do you think these people have been married? Do you think their relationship is less interesting or satisfactory than it used to be, or is it just different? Present your opinions to the class.

EXERCISE 11: Group Discussion

GROUPS: Talk about a significant change in each person's life. Each person says what has changed, what he or she was going to do, and what he or she is going to do now. Use the present perfect and future-in-the-past constructions. Choose from topics in the box or create your own topic. Report interesting examples to the class.

a move to another place   education plans   marriage   career plans

EXAMPLE: My career plans have changed. I wasn't going to attend college. I was going to . . .
Now I've decided to . . .

EXERCISE 12: Writing

A | *Write two or three paragraphs about the topic. Use the present perfect and future-in-the-past constructions.*

Describe a situation that has turned out differently from what you expected—for example, a marriage or other relationship, a job, college plans, a move, etc. First talk about what you thought would happen; then talk about what actually happened.

EXAMPLE: I've been happily married for some time now, but when I was introduced to the man who is now my husband, it never occurred to me that we would end up husband and wife. In fact, when I met Dave, I thought he was the most arrogant man I had ever met. Here's how it happened . . .

B | *Check your work. Use the Editing Checklist.*

Editing Checklist

Did you use . . . ?
☐ simple present correctly
☐ past perfect correctly
☐ present perfect correctly
☐ future in the past correctly

INFORMATION GAP FOR STUDENT B

Student B, read the story about Jack Strait. Answer Student A's questions. Then ask your own questions and fill in the missing information.

EXAMPLE: **A:** What kind of company did he use to work for?
B: He used to work for a company that sold carpets and flooring. How long would he stay on the road?
A: He would stay on the road for . . .

Jack Strait's life is quite different now from the way it used to be. He used to work for a company that sold carpets and flooring. His job required him to do a lot of traveling. He would stay on the road for _____. It was always the same: As soon as he pulled into a town, he would look for a cheap motel to stay in.

The next morning he'd leave _____ at a lot of different establishments, hoping that someone would agree to see him. If he'd been lucky enough to arrange an appointment in advance, he'd show them his samples. Occasionally they would order _____; most often they wouldn't.

Jack's marriage began to suffer. He missed his wife a lot, but there wasn't much he could do about the situation. And when he was on the road, he hardly ever saw his children. He would try to call them in the evenings if he had a spare moment. Usually, however, it was so late that they had already gone to bed. They were growing up without him.

Finally, his wife laid down the law, saying, "Why should we even be married if we're never going to see each other?" Jack decided she was right. He took a risk. He quit his job and started his own business. Things were difficult at first, but at least the family was together.

That was five years ago. Things have changed a lot since then. Jack and his family used to live _____. Now they own a house. Life is good.

B | *Compare your story with your partner's. Are they the same? Now discuss these questions: What did Jack's occupation use to be? Is it important to take risks in life as Jack did? Can you think of an example of a risk you have taken in your life?*

A | Complete the paragraph with simple past or present perfect forms of the verbs in parentheses.

Ever since Julio and Darla _____ married, they _____ a
                         1. (get)   **2. (do)**

lot of traveling. They _____ to six countries and plan to see another two this
                               3. (be)

summer. So far their favorite is Brazil, which they _____ twice. The first time
                                                4. (visit)

_____ in 2009. They _____ again last year. Darla says, "When I was
          5. (be)   **6. (go)**

a girl, I always _____ to marry a man who would take me to exotic places. Julio is
                      7. (want)

that man. I _____ anyone so adventurous."
           8. (never know)

B | Complete the paragraph with simple past and past perfect forms of the verbs from the box.

attend	be	invite	know	meet	propose

Julio and Darla _____ at a Travel Club meeting, which Darla
                   1.

_____ because a friend _____ her. It _____ a classic
    2.   **3.**   **4.**

case of love at first sight. They _____ each other for only two months by the time
                               5.

Julio _____ .
       6.

C | Circle the letter of the one underlined word or phrase in each sentence that is not correct.

1. When I <u>talked</u> to Jason, he <u>said</u> he <u>didn't</u> <u>used to be</u> a serious student.   **A B C D**
        A   **B**   **C**   **D**

2. When we <u>lived</u> in New York, we <u>would have</u> a lot more friends than we   **A B C D**
             A   **B**
   <u>did</u> when we <u>moved</u> to Chicago.
   C   **D**

3. I <u>am going to</u> <u>write</u> you as soon as I <u>got</u> home, but it <u>slipped</u> my mind.   **A B C D**
    A   **B**   **C**   **D**

4. Rosa and I <u>were going to</u> <u>have</u> dinner at a restaurant and then <u>go</u> to a   **A B C D**
               A   **B**   **C**
   movie, but we <u>did</u> after all.
            D

5. We <u>went</u> to the party, even though we <u>didn't know</u> who else <u>will</u> <u>be there</u>.   **A B C D**
      A   **B**   **C** **D**

6. Mary and Carlos <u>called</u> off their wedding, although they <u>had</u> <u>been</u> <u>planned</u>   **A B C D**
                   A   **B** **C** **D**
   it for months.

STEP 1 GRAMMAR IN CONTEXT

Before You Read

PAIRS: Look at the pictures and discuss the questions.

1. How can you prevent this problem when you travel?
2. Where do you like to travel?
3. Is it important to learn some of the language and culture of a place you'll be visiting?

Read

 *Read the article about getting the most out of a trip.*

Get the Most Out of It!

By Tammy Samuelson

So you**'re visiting** some new countries this year? You already have your tickets, and you **leave** in exactly four weeks. A month from now you**'ll be relaxing** in the sunshine or **visiting** famous landmarks. But are you prepared to maximize the enjoyment of your experience? In my capacity as *Times* travel editor, I've been journeying abroad since 1997, so I've learned a few things. In this week's column I**'m going to give** you suggestions in five areas that **will help** you get the most out of your trip.

FIRST TIP: Jetlag. If you've ever flown a significant distance away from your home time zone, you know lack of sleep is a problem. By the time you **arrive**, you**'ll have been flying** for eight to ten hours and **won't be able to keep** your eyes open. Then your entire body **will be** out of whack for days. Here's my suggestion: Take a late afternoon or evening flight, and make every effort to sleep on the plane, even if it's only for an hour or so. When you **land**, it **will** probably **be** late morning or early afternoon. Stay up until evening! Don't take a nap, no matter how excruciatingly tired and sleepy you feel. That way, you**'ll fall** into a new rhythm as naturally as possible. Your body **will adjust** much more quickly.

SECOND TIP: Tours. If you've been abroad before, I'd say go ahead and chart your own course. If you haven't, join a tour group. You can get excellent package deals that include accommodations and tours that hit the high points. Good tour leaders **will show** you the things you want to see. You**'ll make** new friends and **learn** a lot. Yes, it's true that tours can be hectic and intense. They're worth it, though.

THIRD TIP: Accommodations. Consider staying at bed and breakfasts. Package deals often don't allow you to choose your accommodations, but sometimes they set you up in B and B's. Bed and breakfasts are generally friendly places where small numbers of people stay, and they're often not that expensive. You**'ll meet** interesting people. The food is generally well prepared and nourishing.

FOURTH TIP: Money and valuables. Resist the temptation to carry your money, passport, or other valuables in a purse or wallet. Keep them in a money belt instead. Potential thieves **will be** out in force everywhere you go. They**'ll have** a lot more difficulty stealing from a money belt worn around your waist under your exterior clothing.

FIFTH TIP: Language and culture. Few things **will please** the inhabitants of the countries where you**'re going** more than your effort to learn something about them. Buy a phrasebook and start acquiring some of the basics of the language. Begin now and you**'ll have learned** enough to accomplish some basic communication by the time you **arrive**. Discover a bit of the history. Try to step out of your own mindset and put yourself into the shoes of the people who live there.

So there you have it. Take my advice. By the time you **get** home, you**'ll have acquired** some wonderful memories for your mental scrapbook. Make it the trip of a lifetime.

After You Read

A | **Vocabulary:** *Circle the letter of the best meaning for the* blue *words and phrases from the reading.*

1. You'll be relaxing or visiting famous **landmarks**.

   a. cities
   b. famous objects or structures
   c. statues
   d. museums

2. Are you prepared to **maximize** the enjoyment of your experience?

   a. make easy
   b. greatly decrease
   c. complicate
   d. greatly increase

3. Your entire body will be **out of whack** for days.

   a. not working properly
   b. ill
   c. wounded
   d. semiconscious

4. Don't take a nap, no matter how **excruciatingly** tired and sleepy you feel.

   a. pleasantly
   b. terribly
   c. interestingly
   d. boringly

5. Go ahead and **chart your own course**.

   a. take a cruise
   b. plan an auto trip
   c. make individual arrangements
   d. ask for help

(continued on next page)

6. Tours can be **hectic** and intense.

   a. full of hurried excitement   **b.** full of pleasure   **c.** full of danger   **d.** full of expense

7. Try to step out of your own **mindset**.

   a. culture   **b.** opinion   **c.** habitual mental attitude   **d.** educational background

8. You'll have acquired some wonderful memories for your mental **scrapbook**.

   a. photo album   **b.** health   **c.** allowance   **d.** record

B | **Comprehension:** *Refer to the reading and complete each statement with a single word.*

1. Jetlag is strongly influenced by _____ of sleep.

2. To avoid jetlag, you should stay up until _____ of the day you arrive.

3. The author recommends taking _____ if you haven't been abroad before.

4. Relatively small _____ of people stay in bed and breakfasts at a given time.

5. You may be victimized by _____ if you carry valuables in a wallet or purse.

6. To please the residents of countries you visit, you should buy and study a _____.

7. You'll understand them better if you put _____ in their shoes.

FUTURE TIME

Future Time: A Time in the Future

Simple Future
Will / Be going to + Base Form
You**'ll like** the hotel. You**'re going to like** the hotel.

Future Progressive
Will be / Be going to + Base Form + **-ing**
A week from now, you**'ll be relaxing** in the sun. A week from now, you**'re going to be relaxing** in the sun.

Simple Present
The tour **starts** tomorrow at 4:00 P.M.

Present Progressive
Be + Base Form + **-ing**
We**'re visiting** our friends later this summer.

Two Actions in the Future
I**'ll call** you as soon as we **land**.

Future Perfect
Will have + Past Participle
We**'ll have arrived** by 4:00 P.M.

Future Perfect Progressive
Will have been + Base Form + **-ing**
We **will have been flying** for hours by then.

GRAMMAR NOTES

1

Use **will** or **be going to** to say what you think will happen in the future.

BE CAREFUL! Use *will*, not *be going to*, to express a future action decided on at the moment of speaking.

NOTE: We most often use *be going to* to talk about a future situation that is planned or already developing.

- I think I**'ll enjoy** the trip.
  OR
- I think I**'m going to enjoy** the trip.

- Come by at noon. I**'ll change** my dentist's appointment.
  Not: I'm going to change my dentist's appointment.

- We**'re going to take** our vacation in June this year.
- Look at that sky! It**'s going to rain** for sure!

(continued on next page)

2	Use **will be** or **be going to be** + base form + *-ing* to describe an action that will be in progress at a certain time in the future. **USAGE NOTE:** We often use the **future progressive** informally to talk about a future intention.	• We**'ll be visiting** Florence on our Italy trip. • We**'re going to be spending** time in Rome too. • Next week at this time we**'ll be climbing** Kilimanjaro.
3	You can use the **simple present** to talk about a future action, state, or event that is part of a schedule or timetable.	• We **leave** on Saturday at 8:00 P.M. • The plane **arrives** in Rome at 8:30 A.M.
4	You can use the **present progressive** to talk about a future action or event that has already been arranged.	• We**'re traveling** to Japan in August. We already have our tickets.
5	To talk about two separate actions in the future, use **will** or **be going to** in the independent clause and the simple present in the dependent clause. **BE CAREFUL!** The verb in the dependent clause has the form of the simple present, but its meaning is future.	INDEPENDENT CLAUSE • We**'ll rent / 're going to rent** a car DEPENDENT CLAUSE when we **get** to Italy. Not: We'll rent a car when we ~~will~~ get to Italy. • We'll leave for the airport as soon as the taxi **gets** here.
6	Use the **future perfect** to show an action, state, or event that will happen **before** a certain time in the future. You can also use the future perfect in the **progressive**. **NOTE:** We often use the future perfect with *by* and *by the time*.	• By the end of our trip, we**'ll have seen** a lot of wonderful things. • By the end of the summer, we**'ll have been traveling** for several weeks. • **By the time** we finish our trip, we**'ll have visited** 10 countries.

REFERENCE NOTE

For definitions and examples of **grammar terms**, see Glossary on page G-1.

EXERCISE 1: Discover the Grammar

A | *These sentences from the reading express the future in several different ways. Underline the verbs showing future time and label the ways.*

1. So you're <u>visiting</u> some new countries this year?   *present progressive*

2. You leave in exactly four weeks.   _____

3. A month from now you'll be relaxing in the sunshine.   _____

4. I'm going to give you suggestions in five areas.   _____

5. The suggestions will help you get the most out of your trip.   _____

6. You'll have been flying for eight to ten hours.   _____

7. When you land, it will probably be late morning.   _____

8. By then you'll have acquired some wonderful memories.   _____

B | *Look at the sentences. Does the underlined verb refer to present time (**P**) or future time (**F**)?*

__F__ 1. So you're <u>visiting</u> some new countries this year?

_____ 2. You already <u>have</u> your tickets.

_____ 3. You <u>leave</u> in exactly four weeks.

_____ 4. When you <u>land</u>, it will probably be late morning or early afternoon.

_____ 5. You can get package deals that <u>include</u> accommodations and tours.

_____ 6. Package deals often <u>don't allow</u> you to choose your own accommodations.

_____ 7. Few things will please the inhabitants of the countries where you'<u>re going</u> more than learning something about them.

_____ 8. You'll have learned enough to accomplish some basic communication by the time you <u>arrive</u>.

_____ 9. Try to put yourself into the shoes of the people who <u>live</u> there.

_____ 10. So there you <u>have</u> it.

EXERCISE 2: Present Progressive Future

(Grammar Notes 1, 3–4)

Nancy Osborne is traveling in Europe. Complete her letter to her friend Evelyn with the correct future forms of the verbs in the box. Use the present progressive if possible.

arrive	leave	move	see	take
go	mind	not be able to use	~~shine~~	write

London Towers Hotel

Sunday, July 19
Hi Evelyn,

Well, I've been in London for three days now, and it hasn't stopped raining. Fortunately, the Internet says the sun

_____is going to shine_____ tomorrow. Hallelujah! I went to the British
       1.

Museum yesterday and had such a good time that I _____
                                                           2.

again this morning. In the afternoon I _____ a tour of the
                                                        3.

Tower of London.

I've been staying at a bed and breakfast that's really nice, but it's also

pretty expensive, so I _____ to a hostel tonight. I don't
                                          4.

think I _____ staying there, since I don't need luxury.
                                  5.

I've met some really nice people at the B and B, including a lady who gave

me a theater ticket she _____. So I _____
                                  6.   7.

a play at a West End theater on Friday night. On Saturday I

_____ for France at 6 P.M. via the Chunnel train. I
                8.

_____ in Paris at 5:30 A.M. Can you believe that?
                9.

That's it for now. Hope things are OK with you. I _____
                                                      10.

again soon.

Best,
Nancy

EXERCISE 3: Two Actions in the Future

(Grammar Note 5)

Complete the sentences about the rest of Nancy's trip to Europe. Use the correct form of the verbs in parentheses. Each sentence will describe two actions or events in the future.

1. As soon as Nancy _____*arrives*_____ in Paris, she _____*'ll find*_____ an inexpensive place
   (arrive)   **(find)**
   to stay.

2. She _____ her friend Carolyn the day after she _____.
      (meet)   **(arrive)**

3. Nancy and Carolyn _____ the Eiffel Tower, the Louvre, and the Palace of
                       (visit)
   Versailles before they _____ Paris.
                          (leave)

4. When they _____ touring Paris, they _____ a train to Rome.
               (finish)   **(take)**

5. They _____ Florence and Venice after they _____ Rome.
          (visit)   **(tour)**

6. Before they _____ back to the U.S., they _____ souvenirs.
                 (fly)   **(buy)**

EXERCISE 4: Personal Inventory (Future)

(Grammar Notes 1–6)

Answer each question in a complete sentence, according to your own experience.

1. What do you think your life occupation will be?

   _____

2. Where do you think you'll be living in five years?

   _____

3. What are you going to do this evening after dinner?

   _____

4. Where are you going on your next vacation?

   _____

5. What are you going to do as soon as you leave English class today?

   _____

6. What time does your next English class begin?

   _____

7. By when will you have finished your studies?

   _____

8. In a year's time, how long will you have been studying English?

   _____

EXERCISE 5: Editing

Read the travel log. There are eleven mistakes in the use of future verbs. The first mistake is already corrected. Find and correct ten more.

Travel Log

I am writing these words in English because I need the practice. At this moment I am on an airplane over the Pacific Ocean, on my way to a year of study at Columbia University in the United States. The plane left an hour ago. It's a 10-hour flight, so I hope I will have written a lot by the time we ~~will~~ land. I am looking forward to being there, but I am also a little afraid. What do I find when I will get to America? Will the Americans be arrogant and unfriendly? Will I make any friends? Am I happy? My best friend in Korea said, "You don't make any real friends when you'll be there." I am not so sure. I guess I find out.

* *

These were the words I wrote in my diary on the airplane last month. But I have been here for a month now, and I have found that things are a lot different from what I expected. The majority of people here are friendly. They go out of their way to help you if you need it, and my American friends invite me to go places. Soon I go hiking with a group from my dormitory.

Two of the ideas I had about the United States, however, seem to be true. One is that Americans don't pay much attention to rules. One of my best American friends says, in fact, "Rules are made to be broken." The other idea is about the American family. In Asia the family is very important, but some Asian people think the family means nothing in the United States. I don't know if this is true or not. But I think it might be true, since my American friends almost never mention their parents or their brothers and sisters. Anyway, I am going to have a chance to see a real American family. I go with my roommate Susan to spend Thanksgiving break with her family in Pennsylvania. When I will see her family, maybe I'm going to understand more.

EXERCISE 6: Listening

A | *The Fosters are traveling in Canada. Listen to their conversation. What city are they visiting?*

_____

B | *Read the sentences. Then listen again and write **T (True)** or **F (False)**.*

___T___ **1.** Tim is still in bed.

_____ **2.** The Fosters are going to the mall this morning.

_____ **3.** Amy and Tim want to go to the museum.

_____ **4.** Dad thinks the children can learn something at the museum.

_____ **5.** Tim thinks it's always important to learn new things.

_____ **6.** The Fosters are on the tour bus now.

_____ **7.** The Fosters will miss the bus if they don't hurry.

_____ **8.** Tim and Amy like tours.

_____ **9.** Amy and Tim would rather go to the museum by themselves than go on a tour.

_____ **10.** The Fosters are going to the mall before they go on the tour.

_____ **11.** The tour will end after 12:30.

EXERCISE 7: Pronunciation

A | *Read and listen to the Pronunciation Note.*

Pronunciation Note			
In spoken English, auxiliary verbs in future verb forms are often contracted.			
EXAMPLES: will	→	'll	He**'ll** be here in a few hours.
will not	→	won't	We **won't** go to the park tomorrow.
am	→	'm	I**'m** visiting Hong Kong this summer.
is	→	's	She**'s** taking Spanish next term.
are	→	're	They**'re** arriving on Friday.

B | *Listen to the sentences. Circle the future form you hear in each part of the sentences.*

1. I will not / (won't) be able to go with you tonight, but (I will) / I'll be able to go tomorrow night.

2. I'm / I am not going to attend college this fall, but I'm / I am going to attend in the spring.

3. I will / I'll be able to help you tomorrow; unfortunately, I will not / won't be able to help you today.

(continued on next page)

4. We <u>will not / won't</u> be traveling in Asia in July, but <u>we will / we'll</u> be there in August.

5. They <u>will not / won't</u> be moving to a new house in September, but <u>they will / they'll</u> be moving in November.

6. <u>We're not / We are not</u> leaving this weekend, but <u>we are / we're</u> leaving next weekend.

7. We <u>won't have / will not have</u> visited every South American country by the end of our trip, but we <u>will have / we'll have</u> seen most of them.

C | *PAIRS: Practice the sentences.*

EXERCISE 8: Pair Discussion

A | *Check (✓) the things that you believe will happen in the next 25 years. Add your own item in the last row.*

B | *Talk about each item with your partner.*

C | *Report your predictions to the class.*

Event	You	Your Partner
Take vacations in space		
Eliminate poverty		
End offshore oil drilling		
Stop climate change		

EXAMPLE: **A:** I think we'll be taking vacations in space within 25 years.
B: Really? I don't think we will. There won't be enough resources.

EXERCISE 9: Group Discussion

A | *GROUPS: Read the short paragraph about world traveler John Clouse.*

Indiana attorney John Clouse was the first person to see all 317 of the world's officially recognized countries. Clouse, who died in June 2008, had the following comment about people around the world:
"I don't believe there are evil empires and evil people. Yes, there are some bad leaders in the world, but seeing people as individuals has taught me that they are all basically alike. You can be in some terrible places and someone will extend hospitality to you."

B | *Discuss the ideas in Clouse's statement, giving examples from your own experience to support your viewpoint. Touch on the following questions in your discussion:*

- Are there evil empires and evil people?
- Are people all basically alike?
- Will people always extend hospitality to you, wherever you are?

EXAMPLE: **A:** I disagree with Clouse. I believe there are evil empires and evil people. Maybe there aren't many, but there are some.
B: What's an example of an empire you think is evil?

C | *Report your group's conclusions to the class.*

EXERCISE 10: Writing

A | *Write two or three paragraphs on one of the following topics, making sure to use future constructions.*

- What is your response to the quote by Clouse in Exercise 9? Give examples from your own experience to support your viewpoint.
- Imagine you're going on your dream vacation next week. Describe the vacation.

EXAMPLE: For most of my life, my idea of a dream vacation has been to visit China. This dream is finally going to come true. I leave next Friday for a two-week trip to China with a group from work. We're going to visit Beijing, Shanghai, and the Great Wall. We're even going to . . .

B | *Check your work. Use the Editing Checklist.*

Editing Checklist

Did you use . . . ?
- ☐ future with **will** correctly
- ☐ future with **be going to** correctly
- ☐ simple present correctly
- ☐ present progressive correctly

Check your answers on page UR-1.

Do you need to review anything?

A | Complete the telephone message with correct forms of the verbs from the box.

| be | call | get | have to | let | stop by |

Hi, Mary. This is Bill. I _____ work late tonight, so I _____ late
                                 1.   **2.**

for dinner. I _____ you as soon as the boss _____ me leave. I
                          3.   **4.**

_____ the store and pick up dessert before I _____ there. Bye.
       5.   **6.**

Love you.

B | Complete the email with the correct forms of the verbs in parentheses. More than one
answer is possible in some items.

Dear Andy,

   Sam and I are _____ our vacation in Australia this year! Our plane _____
                         1. (take)   **2. (leave)**

tonight and arrives in Tokyo tomorrow. Then there's a 10-hour flight to Sydney. By the time we

_____ there, we _____ for over 24 hours. We _____
       3. (get)   **4. (fly)**   **5. (be)**

exhausted, but it will certainly be worth it. We _____ two and a half weeks in
                                                         6. (spend)

Australia. We _____ you a postcard as soon as we _____ settled in our
                     7. (send)   **8. (be)**

bed and breakfast in Sydney. Stay tuned!

Martha

C | Circle the letter of the one underlined word or phrase in each sentence that is not correct.

1. <u>Call</u> me when you <u>get</u> to town; maybe <u>I'm going to</u> <u>be</u> free.   **A B C D**
   A   B   C   D

2. <u>As soon as</u> <u>I'll hear</u> from Mandy, <u>I'll let</u> you know when <u>she's coming</u>.   **A B C D**
       A   B   C   D

3. I just <u>heard</u> the weather report; <u>according to</u> the forecast, <u>it's raining</u>   **A B C D**
              A   B   C

   tonight, but tomorrow <u>it will be</u> sunny and warm.
                              D

4. The boss <u>calls</u> you <u>as soon as</u> she <u>knows</u> if there <u>will be</u> a job.   **A B C D**
                  A   B   C   D

5. <u>We'll</u> <u>have been</u> <u>traveled</u> for over a month by the time we <u>return</u>.   **A B C D**
       A   B   C   D

6. <u>By the time</u> the summer <u>is</u> over, <u>I'll have</u> <u>visiting</u> 10 new countries.   **A B C D**
        A   B   C   D

From Grammar to Writing
THE SENTENCE: AVOIDING SENTENCE FRAGMENTS

You can strengthen your writing by writing complete sentences and avoiding sentence fragments. A complete sentence must have:

- a subject
- at least one verb that shows time
- at least one independent clause
- initial capitalization and end punctuation

These word groups are fragments, not sentences:

Sherry sitting and writing a letter. (no verb showing time)

Were taking the train to Barcelona. (no subject)

Such an exciting year. (no subject, no verb showing time)

As soon as they could. (not an independent clause)

We can change these fragments into sentences by doing the following:

Sherry was sitting and writing a letter. (adding a verb showing time)

The girls were taking the train to Barcelona. (adding a subject)

The year 2011 was such an exciting year. (adding a subject and a verb showing time)

They decided to return to Barcelona as soon as they could. (adding an independent clause)

1 | *Read the paragraph. There are eight sentences and eight fragments. The first sentence is already underlined. Find and underline seven more.*

In late December. <u>Sherry, Akiko, and Lisa took a one-day trip to Barcelona.</u> Not knowing anyone there. They stayed in a youth hostel for a very reasonable price. On their one day in the city. They visited the Sagrada Familia, Gaudí's famous church. All three girls were impressed by the church's beauty. And decided to climb to the top instead of taking the elevator. Nearing the top, Akiko began to feel dizzy and had to start down again. Sherry and Lisa continued climbing. However, even Sherry, who had done a great deal of mountain climbing in Canada. Felt nervous and unprotected at the summit. Both she and Lisa agreed that the view was magnificent. And the climb well worth it. The three decided to return to Barcelona. As soon as they could.

On your own paper, rewrite the paragraph, changing all the fragments to sentences by combining them appropriately.

3 | *Read the paragraph. There are 16 sentences with mistakes in initial capitalization and end punctuation. The first mistake is already corrected. Find and correct 15 more. Do not add or eliminate any commas.*

> *L*
> ~~l~~ast summer when my wife and I were traveling in Morocco, we had one of the most interesting bargaining experiences ever. we were in an open-air market in Rabat, and I really wanted to buy a Moroccan *jellaba,* a long, heavy, ankle-length garment there were several different shops where jellabas were sold, but Heather and I were drawn to one shop in particular I tried one jellaba on it fit perfectly, and I knew it was the one I wanted, so I asked the merchant how much it was he said it was $100 now I've always been uncomfortable about bargaining, so I was ready to pay his price Heather took me aside, however, and said that was too much and that he expected me to bargain when I said I couldn't bargain, she told me that bargaining was part of the game and that I should offer him less I sighed, tried to swallow the lump in my throat, and suggested $25 he smiled and asked for $75, whereupon I offered $35 he looked offended and shook his head Heather grabbed my hand, and we started walking away I thought that was going to be the end of the experience, but then the merchant came running after me, saying he'd accept $50 I ended up buying the jellaba for that amount, and I still have it since then I've developed courage and gained self-confidence, so, as they say, travel is indeed broadening.

4 | *Before you write . . .*

1. We often say, "Travel is broadening." Think of a time when you learned something significant during a travel experience. How did your behavior or thinking change because of your experience?
2. Describe the experience to a partner. Listen to your partner's experience.
3. Answer questions about your experience. Ask your partner about his or her experience. For example: *Where and when did it happen? Why did you . . . ? How did you feel? How has this experience changed you?*

5 | *Write a draft of a short composition (one or two paragraphs) about a travel experience in which you learned something significant. Follow the model. Include information that your partner asked about.*

I love to travel / often travel / recently traveled.

_____

_____

_____

Several months ago, / A couple of years ago, / In 2011,

_____

_____

_____

_____

_____

_____

Now _____

_____

_____

_____

_____

_____

6 | *Exchange compositions with a different partner. Complete the chart.*

1. The writer wrote complete sentences and avoided fragments.   **Yes** ☐   **No** ☐

2. What I liked in the composition:

   _____

   _____

   _____

3. Questions I'd like the writer to answer about the composition:

   Who _____?

   What _____?

   When _____?

   Where _____?

   Why _____?

   How _____?

   (Your own question) _____?

7 | *Work with your partner. Discuss each other's chart from Exercise 6. Then rewrite your own composition and make any necessary changes.*

MODALS AND OTHER AUXILIARIES

Modals to Express Degrees of Necessity
CULTURAL DIFFERENCES

Before You Read

PAIRS: Look at the picture on page 51 and discuss the questions.

1. What are the people doing? Is this a practice in your culture?
2. What are some things that should and shouldn't be done in your culture? Make a short list.

Read

Read the article about cultural differences.

What We Should and Shouldn't Have Done

Recently my wife and I had a cross-cultural experience that taught us about some things we **should have done** differently. My company sent me to work at our branch office in Japan. My Japanese co-workers have been friendly and gracious, and last week one of them invited us for dinner. We were honored, and the food was delicious. But though Masayuki and Yukiko, his wife, were most polite and friendly, we felt a bit uncomfortable about the evening. I asked my friend Junichi about it. He's lived in Japan and the United States, so he knows the cultural differences. He gave me several pointers. Now we know what we **should** and **shouldn't have done**.

The first tip was about shoes. We knew you**'re supposed to take** them **off** in a Japanese home. We didn't know you**'re supposed to arrange** them to point toward the door so when you leave you can put them on without turning around. But this wasn't a big mistake, Junichi said.

The second pointer was about gifts. We knew we **should take** a gift. Masayuki and Yukiko seemed a little shocked, though, when we pulled a CD out of a plastic bag and said, "We thought you'd like this rock and roll CD." Junichi chuckled and said, "Well, you **should have wrapped** the CD. It's OK to bring it in a plastic bag, but the gift **has to be wrapped**. And you **mustn't say** anything about it. Just give it to your hosts. The main problem, though, was the gift itself. A rock and roll CD isn't really appropriate."

What We Should and Shouldn't Have Done

"Well, what **should** we **have taken**?"

"A box of chocolates. Or you **could have taken** some flowers."

Then I told Junichi about what happened before dinner. Masayuki and Yukiko offered us some tea and snacks. The tea was delicious, but we had trouble finishing the raw sushi. Masayuki and Yukiko seemed perplexed. Junichi chuckled again and said, "In Japan it's considered impolite to leave half-eaten food on a plate."

"You mean you**'ve got to eat** everything that's offered?" I asked.

"You **don't have to**. But if you take something, you **must finish** it."

After dinner, Helen asked Yukiko if she **could help** in the kitchen. This is normal in the United States, but Junichi said you**'re not to do** this in Japan. Visitors **aren't allowed to go** into the kitchen.

Another thing you **shouldn't do**, he said, is praise an object in the house. If you do, your Japanese hosts might feel they **have to give** you the object. Fortunately, we didn't do that.

At evening's end, Masayuki offered us another drink. Not wanting to be impolite, we accepted. Finally we felt we absolutely **had to leave**, so when we were offered another drink, I said, "Thanks, we**'d better get going**; we **have to get up** early." Masayuki and Yukiko seemed relieved. Junichi said, "That's what you **should have done** in the first place. When you're offered a drink at the end of the evening, you **should decline** gently. Leaving earlier would have been fine."

I asked what we **might do** to rectify the situation. "**Shall** we **invite** them to our apartment?"

"Yes, I think you **ought to have** them **over**. But don't have an informal, Western-style party. Just make it a simple dinner for the four of you."

Good advice, I thought. What really struck me is how much we all have to learn about other cultures.

After You Read

A | Vocabulary: *Complete the definitions with the correct word or phrase from the box.*

chuckle	gracious	perplexed	praise
decline	have someone over	pointer	rectify

1. To be _____ is to be polite, kind, and pleasant.

2. A _____ is a suggestion, tip, or piece of advice.

3. To _____ is to laugh quietly.

4. To feel _____ is to be confused, puzzled, or troubled.

5. To _____ something or someone is to express admiration.

6. To _____ something is to refuse it.

7. To _____ is to invite a person or persons to your home.

8. If you _____ a situation, you improve or fix it.

B | Comprehension: *Circle the letter of the correct answer.*

1. The author and his wife _____.
   a. followed exactly the Japanese custom of taking your shoes off
   b. should have left their shoes pointing toward the door, but didn't

2. In Japan, it's a good idea to _____.
   a. bring something like a rock and roll CD as a house gift
   b. wrap a gift instead of just bringing it in the original bag

3. In Japan, it's wrong to _____.
   a. talk about a gift when you give it to your host
   b. bring a wrapped gift in a plastic bag

4. An appropriate gift to take to a Japanese home would be _____.
   a. a CD
   b. flowers

5. When you are offered something to eat in a Japanese home, you _____.
   a. shouldn't take something unless you are sure you can finish it
   b. don't have to worry about eating all of it

6. According to their Japanese friend, the author and his wife should _____.
   a. ask Masayuki and Yukiko to join them for a quiet dinner party
   b. ask Masayuki and Yukiko to a typical Western-style party

MODALS TO EXPRESS DEGREES OF NECESSITY (RANGING FROM OBLIGATION TO NO OBLIGATION)

Necessity
100%

Obligation (Necessity)								
You	must have to have got to	call	them.	You	must not can't are not allowed to	call	them.
You	had to	call	them.	You	weren't allowed to	call	them.

Advice								
You	had better should ought to	leave	early.	You	had better not shouldn't	leave	early.
You	should have ought to have	left	early.	You	shouldn't have	left	early.

Expectation								
You	are supposed to are to	take	a gift.	You	are not supposed to are not to	do	this.
You	were supposed to were to	take	a gift.	You	were not supposed to were not to	do	this.

Suggestion				No Obligation (No Necessity)			
You	could might	give	roses.	You	don't have to	call	them.
You	could have might have	given	roses.	You	didn't have to	call	them.

0%

GRAMMAR NOTES

1

Modals are auxiliary verbs. The modals are *can, could, may, might, shall, should, will, would, must, ought to,* and *had better.* Each modal has only one form for all persons.

- I / You / He / She / We / They **could take** some flowers.

Use **simple modals** (modal + base form) to show degrees of necessity in the present and the future.

- We **should invite** Jim to the party tonight.

Use **perfect modals** (modal + *have* + past participle) to show degrees of necessity in the past.

- We **should have invited** Jim to last week's party too.

Modals show speakers' attitudes toward the actions they are describing. Modals are used to talk about obligations, advice, expectations, and suggestions.

- You **could invite** them **over**.
- You **should leave** early.

2

Some **modal-like expressions** have meanings equivalent to or similar to meanings of modals:

must	*have to, have got to*
should	*ought to*
may	*be allowed to*

- You **must / have to / have got to finish** everything on your plate.
- You **should / ought to take** a gift.
- Visitors **may not / are not allowed to help** in the kitchen.

3

Use *must*, *have to*, and *have got to* to show strong necessity. They are similar in meaning.

- You **must / have to / have got to arrive** on time.

USAGE NOTES

Use *must* in more formal English to show a very strong obligation that can't be escaped.

A: You mean you **must eat** everything they offer you?

Use *have to* in all forms and situations, formal and informal.

B: No, you **don't have to**.

Use *have got to* in conversation and informal writing. It is rarely used in the negative. Use *don't have to* instead.

- We**'ve got to get going**.

Use *will have to* to show future necessity.

- We**'ll have to invite** them **over**.

BE CAREFUL! Use *had to* + base form to show past necessity. Don't use *must have* + past participle.

- We **had to leave.**
  Not: We ~~must have left~~.

4	Use **must not** to say that it is **necessary not** to do something (*that it is prohibited*).	• You **must not smoke** here.
	Use **don't / doesn't have to** + base form to say that something is **not necessary**.	• You **don't have to take** everything offered to you.
	In the past, use **didn't have to** + base form to say that something **was not necessary**.	• You **didn't have to bring** a gift.
	BE CAREFUL! Although *must* and *have to* have similar meanings, *must not* and *don't have to* have very different meanings.	• We **mustn't miss** the flight. Not: We ~~don't have to~~ miss the flight.
5	Use **should** or **ought to** to offer advice. They mean "it would be a good idea if . . ." or "it's the right thing to do" and are basically the same in most situations. We normally use *should*, not *ought to*, in questions and negatives.	• You **should / ought to decline** gently. **A: Should** I **invite** a guest? **B:** No, you **shouldn't**.
	Use **should have / ought to have** + past participle to express advice about past situations. *Should have* and *ought to have* suggest that the action did not happen. *Shouldn't have* and *ought not to have* suggest that it did.	• You **should / ought to have done** that the first time. • You **shouldn't / ought not to have mentioned** your gift.
	NOTE: We sometimes use **shall** in questions to ask for advice or direction. In this meaning, *shall* is used only with *I* or *we*. When it is used with *we*, it is often followed by a sentence with *let's*. In this meaning, *shall* is similar to *should*.	**A: Shall** we **get** them some flowers? **B:** Yes, **let's do** that.
6	**Had better** is like *should* and *ought to* but stronger.	• We**'d better get going**, or we'll be late.
	Use **had better** to give a warning that something bad or negative will happen if advice isn't followed.	• **Hadn't you better avoid** talking about politics during dinner?
7	Use **be supposed to** to show an expectation. Use it only in the present and the past. In the past, the affirmative suggests that the action didn't happen. The negative suggests that the action did happen.	• You**'re supposed to take off** your shoes when you enter a Japanese home. • We **were supposed to take** flowers. • We **weren't supposed to mention** the gift we'd brought.
	You can use **be to** + base form in more formal English to express a strong expectation.	• All employees **are to attend** the company office party. • You**'re not to ask** any personal questions.

(continued on next page)

8	Use *could* or *might* + base form to make polite, not-too-strong suggestions about the present or future.	• You **could / might take** them some chocolates.
	Use *could have / might have* + past participle to make polite suggestions about a past opportunity. In this meaning, *might have* and *could have* mean that the action didn't happen.	• You **could have / might have taken** some flowers.

STEP 3 FOCUSED PRACTICE

EXERCISE 1: Discover the Grammar

Read the sentences. Circle the letter of the choice that best explains the meaning of the sentence.

1. We knew that you're supposed to take off your shoes when you enter a Japanese home, so we did.

   a. Japanese people expect guests to remove their shoes.

   b. It doesn't matter whether or not you wear your shoes in a Japanese home.

2. Well, you should have wrapped the CD.

   a. You wrapped the CD, and that was the right thing to do.

   b. You didn't wrap the CD, and that was a cultural mistake in Japan.

3. And you mustn't say anything about the gift.

   a. It's not a good idea to say anything about the gift.

   b. It's wrong to say anything about the gift.

4. Or you could have taken some flowers.

   a. Flowers are an acceptable gift in Japan, but you didn't take any.

   b. You made a cultural mistake by not taking flowers.

5. According to the rules of Japanese culture, visitors aren't allowed to go into the kitchen.

   a. The Japanese expect visitors to stay out of the kitchen.

   b. It's OK for visitors to go into a Japanese kitchen.

6. If you praise an object, your Japanese hosts might feel they have to give the object to you.

   a. Japanese hosts might feel a strong obligation to give the object to you.

   b. Japanese hosts might feel they can choose not to give the object to you.

7. When a Japanese host invites you to have a drink at the end of the evening, you should decline gently.

   a. It's an obligation to decline gently.

   b. It's a good idea to decline gently.

8. Yes, you ought to do that.

   a. It doesn't matter whether you do that.

   b. That would be the right thing to do.

9. Junichi says you are not to do this in Japan.

   a. People won't care if you do this in Japan.

   b. It's a cultural mistake to do this in Japan.

10. Shall we have them over?

    a. Do you think they will come to our house?

    b. Do you think we should ask them to come to our house?

EXERCISE 2: Modals

(Grammar Notes 3, 6–8)

Read the conversation between Fumiko, a visiting exchange student, and her American friend Jane. Complete the conversation with items from the box.

~~are you supposed to leave~~	ought to have given	supposed to do
could have left	should we have left	were supposed to leave
don't have to leave	should you leave	you're supposed to do
had to worry	should you tip	

JANE: Hi, Fumiko. How are things going?

FUMIKO: Really well. But I need some pointers about something.

JANE: Sure. What?

FUMIKO: Tipping. I just don't understand it. _____Are you supposed to leave_____ a tip everywhere
                                                                    1.

you eat? This is really bothering me. I've never _____
                                                                    2.

about this before. We don't tip in Japan.

JANE: You don't?

FUMIKO: No. You're not really _____ that. It's all included in the
                                                      3.

service charge.

JANE: Tell me more. Have you had a problem with this?

FUMIKO: Yeah. Last week a Chinese friend of mine and I had dinner at a restaurant. We knew we

_____ a tip, but we didn't know how much.
                    4.

JANE: How much did you leave?

FUMIKO: About 25 percent. _____ more?
                                              5.

JANE: Wow! Twenty-five percent. That's quite a bit. The service must have been really good.

FUMIKO: Actually, it wasn't. The waiter was pretty rude . . . and slow.

JANE: If you're not satisfied with the service, you _____ anything.
                                                                          6.

FUMIKO: So how much _____ the waiter if you're satisfied?
                                        7.

JANE: Between 15 and 20 percent. Fifteen is the usual.

FUMIKO: Hmmm. OK. Now here's another question. I'm confused about what

_____ if you're sitting at a lunch counter instead of at a
                    8.

table. _____ anything for the person behind the counter?
                    9.

JANE: It's a nice gesture. Why do you ask?

FUMIKO: Yesterday I had lunch at a cafeteria counter. The waitress was really nice and polite. I felt

like I _____ her something.
                                   10.

JANE: Did you?

FUMIKO: No.

JANE: Well, you _____ something. Maybe 5 to 10 percent.
                                      11.

FUMIKO: Oh. OK. Next time I will.

EXERCISE 3: *Must / Have To / Should / Be Supposed To*   (Grammar Notes 3–4, 6–7)

A | *Read the short essay about the treatment of babies in two different cultures.*

An American woman was spending a month teaching on the Indonesian island of Bali. She was staying at the home of a Balinese family, and late one afternoon the woman of the house was obliged to leave home for a time. When she came back, her eight-month-old son was lying on a large bed, crying loudly. "What is happening with my son?" asked the Balinese woman. "Oh," said the American teacher, "I don't think there's anything wrong with him. I just thought it would be good for him to crawl on the floor for a bit. I put him down to let him crawl, but he didn't seem to like it and started crying. I thought maybe it would be a good idea if he just cried to let his frustration out."

A discussion followed. The Balinese woman told the American that in Bali it is not considered a good thing to let babies cry. Since Balinese culture is characterized by the strength of the extended family, there is almost always someone available to pick children up if they start crying and carry them around. In fact, there is even a "putting down" ceremony that occurs when the child is ready to walk and may be put down on the ground for the first time. Further, the Balinese mother said, their children are not expected to crawl because that activity is seen as too much like what animals do.

The American was fascinated with what her Balinese host had told her. She pointed out that in the United States the extended family is not nearly as prevalent as in Bali, so there is often no one around to help with children. In many families, both mother and father work, so at the end of the day both are too tired to carry children around for long periods. Many also feel that it doesn't hurt babies to allow them to cry for a time. As for crawling, said the American woman, most American parents are delighted when their children learn to crawl, feeling that it is essential for them to develop that skill in order to gain muscular strength and prepare for walking.

Both women learned a great deal that day about the other's culture.

B | *Complete the sentences, using modals or modal-like expressions. Make some sentences negative if necessary.*

1. The incident happened because the Balinese woman _____*had to*_____ leave home for a time.

2. The American woman thought the baby _____ crawl around a bit on the floor.

3. In Bali, parents believe that babies _____ be picked up and held most of the time, especially if they are crying.

4. The Balinese mother no doubt felt that her American guest _____ put the baby down.

5. In Bali, children _____ crawl since that is too much like what animals do.

6. Most American parents believe that their children _____ crawl in order to develop muscular strength and prepare for walking.

EXERCISE 4: *Should Have / Could Have*   *(Grammar Notes 6, 8)*

Look again at the opening reading. Write six sentences about what the American couple should have done and shouldn't have done. Then write four sentences about what they could or might have done.

1. *They should have wrapped the CD.* _____

2. _____

3. _____

4. _____

5. _____

6. _____

7. _____

8. _____

9. _____

10. _____

EXERCISE 5: Editing

Read the letter from Tong-Li, an international exchange student in Australia, to her friend Masako in Singapore. There are nine mistakes in the use of modals or modal-like expressions. The first mistake is already corrected. Find and correct eight more.

Dear Masako,

    Sorry it's taken me so long to write. I ~~shouldn't~~ *should* have gotten to this weeks ago, but I've been so busy. I'm really looking forward to the holidays and seeing all you guys again. School is going well. It's tough but really interesting, and I'm sure I should be studying even more than I have been. Part of the problem is that I'm taking too many classes. You're only suppose to take five a term, but I'm taking six.

    Anyway, I've gotten to know a lot of new people, including several Australians. I have this one really good friend, a girl named Jane. She invited me to her house last week for a party. Actually, it was my birthday, but I didn't know she knew that. I thought it was a party like any other. I figured I better take some kind of gift, but I couldn't decide what it should be. Finally, I came up with the idea of a bouquet of flowers. As soon as I got to the party, I gave it to Jane, and she was really happy to get it. But then the funniest thing happened. I guess I ought to expect something was up from the mysterious way Jane was acting, but I didn't. This was a surprise party–for me! As soon as I took off my coat and sat down, a lot of people jumped up from behind sofas and other places where they'd been hiding and shouted, "Surprise! Happy birthday!" I was embarrassed, but I must not have been because everyone was really friendly, and pretty soon I forgot about my embarrassment. Then they gave me presents. I was about to put them away, but Jane said, "Aren't you going to open them?" I was perplexed and didn't know what to do. In China you shouldn't have opened gifts right when you get them, but apparently you are supposed to in Australia. So I opened them. The nicest gift was a new blouse from Jane. She told me I must have gone and try it on immediately, so I did. It's beautiful. Anyway, what a party! I thought I knew all about Australian culture, but I guess I'm not as familiar with it as I thought. The custom of opening up presents in front of the gift giver is a strange one to me.

    The weather is kind of chilly. How is it back in Singapore? Nice and warm? I shall bring you something special from Australia when I come?

    Well, Masako, I'm running out of space, so I got to sign off. Write soon.

                             Best,

                             Tong-Li

EXERCISE 6: Listening

A | *Listen to the telephone conversation. Where are Dad and Ray, and why?*

_____

B | *Read the questions. Then listen again. Write complete answers, using modals or modal-like expressions.*

1. Why do Dad and Ray need to get home as soon as possible?

   Mom's surprise party is supposed to start in 15 minutes.

2. What is Bev's opinion about delaying Mom's present, and why?

   _____

3. What does Dad say when Bev reminds him about not putting things off till the last minute?

   _____

4. What is Dad's opinion about Bev's camera suggestion?

   _____

5. What is Bev's opinion about a dress?

   _____

6. What does Dad say about Bev's blouse suggestion?

   _____

7. What is Bev's scarf suggestion?

   _____

8. What does Bev say about getting home as soon as possible, and why?

   _____

EXERCISE 7: Pronunciation

A | *Read and listen to the Pronunciation Note.*

Pronunciation Note

In conversation and in rapid speech, modals and modal-like auxiliaries are often reduced.

EXAMPLES:

should / could / might + have	→	should've, could've, might've
have to	→	hafta
has to	→	hasta
supposed to	→	sposta
had better	→	'dbetter

B | *Listen and repeat the sentences with reduced forms of modals and modal-like auxiliaries.*

1. We have to take a gift to the party.
2. We should have had them over for dinner.
3. We're supposed to have dinner at their house on Monday.
4. You could have declined their offer to have a drink.
5. We had better leave now.
6. You might have gotten them some flowers.
7. He wasn't supposed to be here until Monday.
8. The gift has to be wrapped.

C | *PAIRS: Practice the sentences. One partner says a sentence with a full form. The other partner responds with the reduced form.*

EXERCISE 8: Information Gap

PAIRS: Complete the story. Each of you will read a version of the same story. Each version is missing some information. Take turns asking your partner questions to get the missing information.

Student A, read the story. Ask questions and fill in the missing information. Then answer Student B's questions.

Student B, turn to page 67 and follow the instructions there.

> EXAMPLE: **A:** Where were they supposed to stay?
> **B:** They were supposed to stay at . . . What should they have gotten?
> **A:** They should have gotten . . .

A married couple was traveling in Europe and had just entered a new country. They had been having a wonderful time, but now everything was going wrong. The first problem was finding accommodations. They were supposed to stay at _____, but when they got to the hotel there was no record of their reservation. The wife said they should have gotten a confirmation number. They hadn't, unfortunately, so they had to spend the night _____. The next day they finally found a room at a hotel far from the center of town. There were two rooms available: a large one and a tiny one. Since they were on a tight budget, they decided they had better take the tiny one.

The second problem was communication. They were starving after spending hours looking for accommodations, so they went into a restaurant. A waiter brought them a menu, but they couldn't understand it. The husband said they should have _____. They hadn't done that, though, so they didn't know what to order.

Time passed. Other people were being served, but they weren't. Frustrated, they decided they had to do something. But what? They noticed that a boy about 11 years old seemed to be listening to their conversation. Soon the boy came over to their table. "Excuse me," he said. "You have to _____. Then they'll take your order." The husband and wife were both astonished but grateful. The wife said, "You speak our language very well. Did you study it somewhere?" The boy said, "I lived in Australia for three years. I learned English there." He asked, "Shall I help you order? I can translate the menu."

When the couple got back home, their friends asked them what they had liked best about the trip. The wife said, "Well, the best part was visiting that country where everything went wrong until that boy rectified the problem. At some point, everybody should _____. You don't have to be miserable, but you need a challenge. That's when you learn things. Maybe that's what people mean when they say travel is broadening."

EXERCISE 9: Discussion

A | *SMALL GROUPS: Decide individually whether each of the behaviors in the chart is required, advised, allowed, or unimportant in your culture or another culture you are familiar with. Check (✓) the appropriate boxes. Then discuss the results with the other members of your group.*

B | *Report your results to the rest of the class.*

EXAMPLE: **A:** When you're invited to dinner in your culture, are you supposed to take a gift?
B: Absolutely. You must take a gift. And it has to be wrapped. What about in your culture?
A: It's pretty much optional. You should take a gift if it's a birthday party, but . . .

	Must	Should	Mustn't	Shouldn't	Don't Have To	Doesn't Matter
1. take a gift when invited somewhere						
2. ask how old someone is						
3. smoke without asking permission						
4. hug friends when you see them						
5. shake hands when you meet someone						
6. remove your shoes at someone's house						

(continued on next page)

Modals to Express Degrees of Necessity   **65**

	Must	Should	Mustn't	Shouldn't	Don't Have To	Doesn't Matter
7. offer to pay your share at a restaurant						
8. ask how much someone weighs						
9. ask what someone's occupation is						
10. leave a tip in a restaurant						
11. call people by their first name						

EXERCISE 10: Writing

A | *Write two or three paragraphs about a past situation that you feel you should have handled differently. Tell what you should or could have done to rectify the situation (past) and what you should, could, or might do in a similar future situation.*

EXAMPLE: Two years ago my husband and I were traveling on a train in Europe. It was the middle of the night, and we were the only travelers in a sleeping car. We were both deeply asleep when suddenly our compartment door was loudly opened and several young people came in and began looking for their beds. They were talking very loudly and did not settle down and go to sleep. For a while we tolerated this and tried to go back to sleep but couldn't. Finally, my husband got very angry and started to yell at them. He shouldn't have done this, because they just laughed at him. Instead of this, he should have . . .

B | *Check your work. Use the Editing Checklist.*

> **Editing Checklist**
>
> Did you use . . . ?
> ☐ *should*, *could*, or *might* correctly
> ☐ *should have* correctly
> ☐ *could have* correctly

Student B, read the story. Answer Student A's questions. Then ask your own questions and fill in the missing information.

EXAMPLE: **A:** Where were they supposed to stay?

        B: They were supposed to stay at the Grand State Hotel. What should they have gotten?

        A: They should have gotten . . .

A married couple was traveling in Europe and had just entered a new country. They had been having a wonderful time, but now everything was going wrong. The first problem was finding accommodations. They were supposed to stay at the Grand State Hotel, but when they got to the hotel there was no record of their reservation. The wife said they should have gotten

_____. They hadn't, unfortunately, so they had to spend the night at the train station. The next day they finally found a room at a hotel far from the center of town. There were two rooms available: a large one and a tiny one. Since they were on a tight budget, they decided they had better _____.

The second problem was communication. They were starving after spending hours looking for accommodations, so they went into a restaurant. A waiter brought them a menu, but they couldn't understand it. The husband said they should have brought along a phrasebook. They hadn't done that, though, so they didn't know what to order.

Time passed. Other people were being served, but they weren't. Frustrated, they decided

_____. But what? They noticed that a boy about 11 years old seemed to be listening to their conversation. Soon the boy came over to their table. "Excuse me," he said. "You have to pay for your meal first. Then they'll take your order." The husband and wife were both astonished but grateful. The wife said, "You speak our language very well. Did you study it somewhere?" The boy said, "I lived in Australia for three years. I learned English there." He asked, "_____? I can translate the menu."

When the couple got back home, their friends asked them what they had liked best about the trip. The wife said, "Well, the best part was visiting that country where everything went wrong until that boy rectified the problem. At some point, everybody should experience difficulty. You don't have to _____, but you need a challenge. That's when you learn things. Maybe that's what people mean when they say travel is broadening."

Check your answers on page UR-1.

Do you need to review anything?

A | *Circle the correct modal or modal-like expression to complete each sentence.*

1. You <u>weren't supposed to / were supposed to</u> mention the gift. Now it won't be a surprise!

2. She <u>had to / didn't have to</u> bring food. We have a lot left over from the party.

3. Bill <u>might not have / shouldn't have</u> told Ai about it! Now everyone will know.

4. You <u>could / should</u> take some flowers. Or a box of chocolates would be good.

5. We <u>shouldn't / 'd better not</u> discuss anything political. Sam loses his temper easily.

6. You <u>must have / should have</u> your passport with you. You'll be deported if you don't.

7. Chie <u>should / 's got to</u> pay her rent by Saturday. She'll be evicted if she doesn't.

8. You <u>aren't allowed to / don't have to</u> go into a Japanese kitchen. It's just not done.

9. Sami <u>should have / could have</u> given them a CD. They like flowers too.

10. <u>Hadn't we better / Aren't we supposed to</u> get going? The play starts in 20 minutes.

B | *In the blank after each sentence, write a single modal with a meaning similar to the underlined modal-like auxiliary.*

1. You <u>have to</u> be there by 10 A.M. sharp. _____

2. We <u>ought to</u> invite Hana over for dinner. _____

3. We <u>aren't allowed to</u> smoke in the office. _____

4. Ken <u>has</u> simply <u>got to</u> study harder. _____

5. <u>Are</u> you <u>supposed to</u> leave a tip here? _____

C | *Circle the letter of the one underlined word or phrase in each sentence that is not correct.*

1. We <u>ought</u> <u>look into</u> a tour if we <u>can find</u> one that <u>won't bankrupt</u> us.   **A B C D**
     A   B   C   D

2. All <u>is to</u> <u>attend</u> the party on Saturday and <u>should</u> <u>bring</u> a gift.   **A B C D**
     A   B   C   D

3. I <u>ought to</u> <u>take</u> extra cash along, and I <u>don't have to</u> <u>forget</u> my passport.   **A B C D**
     A   B   C   D

4. You <u>had better</u> <u>to set</u> your alarm, or you <u>might not</u> <u>wake up</u> on time.   **A B C D**
       A   B   C   D

5. <u>I'd invited</u> Bob to dinner Monday, but he <u>must</u> <u>decline</u> because he's sick.   **A B C D**
  A   B   C   D

Modals to Express Degrees of Certainty
PUZZLES

STEP 1 GRAMMAR IN CONTEXT

Before You Read

PAIRS: Discuss the questions.

1. When people say, "Columbus discovered the New World," what do they mean?
2. What theories have you heard regarding who might have "discovered" the New World?

Read

Read the article about the discovery of America.

Who *Really* Discovered America?

A well-known school rhyme goes like this: "In fourteen hundred and ninety-two, Columbus sailed the ocean blue"—and then discovered America. However, Columbus **may not have been** the first non-Native American to visit the Western Hemisphere. So many other potential discoverers have been nominated that the question **might** almost **be rephrased** as "Who *didn't* discover America?" What does history show? Who *really* discovered the New World? Those suggested include the Vikings, the Japanese, the Chinese, the Egyptians, the Hebrews, the Portuguese, and some Irish monks.

The Vikings are the best-known contenders. Evidence suggests that Leif Erickson and cohorts visited the New World about the year 1000, almost 500 years before Columbus. Viking records and New World artifacts indicate they arrived at a place they named "Vinland the Good"—the land of grapes. Scholars originally thought Vinland **must have been** Newfoundland, but today it is believed Vinland **couldn't have been** that island since it is too far north for grapes to grow. **Could** the climate **have been** warmer in Erickson's day? Perhaps. However, current thought is that Vinland **may have been** the New England coast.

The Japanese are more recent candidates. Pottery fragments discovered in 1956 on the coast of Ecuador date back about 5,000 years. These fragments resemble Japanese pottery of the same era, but it has been established that there was no native pottery in Ecuador in 3000 B.C.E. **Could** the Japanese **have introduced** it? Smithsonian Institute scholars conclude that individuals **may have sailed** from Japan across

Christopher Columbus

(continued on next page)

the Pacific to Ecuador, or Japanese fishermen **might have been swept** out to sea and **carried** 10,000 miles across the ocean. This theory **may sound** unlikely and **may** eventually **be disproved,** but the pottery evidence **must mean** something.

One interesting theory stems from the story of St. Brendan, a sixth-century Irish monk who made many voyages to establish monasteries. A sixth-century document suggests that Brendan made a journey far out into the Atlantic, reports of which **may have influenced** Columbus to believe that there really was a New World. Brendan and his fellow monks saw "sea monsters," "crystals rising up into the sky," and "a rain of bad-smelling rocks." In 1976, British navigation scholar Tim Severin decided to see if Brendan and his companions **could** really **have accomplished** this voyage. Using the specifications described in the St. Brendan text, they built a curragh, an Irish leather boat, and attempted the journey. On the way, they passed Greenland and wintered in Iceland, where they saw whales, a volcano, and icebergs. They theorized that Brendan's sea monsters **might have been** whales, the ice crystals icebergs, and the bad-smelling rocks volcanic debris. Severin's group did eventually get to Newfoundland, proving that a curragh **could have made** the journey to North America. Religious artifacts and stone carvings bearing vocabulary and grammatical constructions from Old Irish have been found in Virginia. This suggests that other missionaries **could have gone** to the New World after Brendan's return. Thus the story **may be** true.

But back to the original question: Who really "discovered" the New World? Future research **should get** us closer to an answer. Columbus did not, of course, really *discover* America. The real finders were the Native Americans who migrated across the Bering Strait more than 10,000 years ago.

The claim about Columbus really means that he started two-way communication between the Old World and the New. In that sense Columbus's reputation is still safe.

Could this boat have made it across the Atlantic?

After You Read

A | Vocabulary: *Match the blue words and phrases on the left with their meanings on the right.*

_____ **1.** So many other **potential** discoverers have been nominated . . .

_____ **2.** Those suggested include the Vikings, the Japanese, . . . and some Irish **monks**.

_____ **3.** The Vikings are the best-known **contenders**.

_____ **4.** Leif Erickson and **cohorts** visited the New World about the year 1000.

_____ **5.** New World **artifacts** indicate the Vikings arrived at a place they named Vinland the Good.

_____ **6.** One interesting theory **stems from** the story of St. Brendan.

_____ **7.** Brendan made many voyages to establish **monasteries**.

_____ **8.** The bad-smelling rocks may have been volcanic **debris**.

a. originates with

b. remains of an explosion

c. religious residences

d. possible

e. likely candidates

f. human-made objects

g. companions

h. members of an all-male religious group

B | Comprehension: *Circle **T (True)** or **F (False)**. Correct the false statements.*

1. Schoolchildren are often taught that Columbus discovered America.   **T**   **F**

2. Scholars originally theorized that Vinland was probably Newfoundland.   **T**   **F**

3. Scholars currently believe that Vinland couldn't have been Newfoundland because the island is too far south for grapes to grow.   **T**   **F**

4. Pottery fragments found in Ecuador date from the year 5000 B.C.E.   **T**   **F**

5. The story of St. Brendan almost certainly caused Columbus to believe that there was a New World.   **T**   **F**

6. St. Brendan and his companions could have gotten to America in a curragh.   **T**   **F**

7. The ice crystals seen by Brendan and his companions must have been icebergs.   **T**   **F**

8. Columbus didn't discover America, but he had a great deal to do with promoting contact between the Old World and the New.   **T**   **F**

MODALS TO EXPRESS DEGREES OF CERTAINTY

Speculations about the Present							
It	must has (got) to	be	true.	It	can't / couldn't must not	be	true.
It	may / might could	be	true.	It	may not might not	be	true.

Speculations about the Past							
It	must have had to have	been	true.	It	can't have couldn't have must not have	been	true.
It	may have might have could have	been	true.	It	may not have might not have	been	true.

Speculations about the Future							
We	should ought to	solve	it soon.				
We	may might could	solve	it soon.	We	may not might not	solve	it soon.

GRAMMAR NOTES

1

We use **modals** and **modal-like expressions** to express different degrees of certainty. With these modals we speculate based on logic and facts.

- The story **must** be true.
  (approximately 90% certain)
- The story **might** be true.
  (approximately 50% certain)

Remember that we use modals with progressive as well as simple forms.

- He **may** be planning another trip.

When we want to state a fact we are absolutely— 100%—sure of, we don't use modals.

- That story is true.
- He was planning another trip.

2	Use **must / have to / have got to** + base form when you are speculating about the present and are almost certain.	• The evidence **must / has to / has got to mean** something.
	To make a negative speculation, use **can't / couldn't** + base form.	• That theory **can't / couldn't be** right.
	Use **must not** + base form when you are slightly less certain.	• It **must not be** right. • The explorer **must not be** famous.
	NOTE: We normally don't contract *must not* in this meaning of *must*.	Not: The explorer ~~mustn't~~ be famous.
	In questions, use **could / couldn't** + base form.	• **Could** that **be** the case? • **Couldn't** that **be** the explanation?
3	Use **may / might / could** + base form when you are speculating about the present and are less certain.	• We **may / might / could know** the answer soon.
	Use **may not / might not** + base form in the negative.	• They **may not / might not have** any evidence.
	BE CAREFUL! We usually do not contract *might not*, and we never contract *may not*.	Not: They ~~mayn't~~ have any evidence.
	In questions, use **could / might** + base form.	• **Could / Might** that **be** correct?
4	Use **must have / had to have** + past participle when you are speculating about the past and are almost certain.	• They **must have / had to have visited** America.
	In the negative, use **can't have / couldn't have** + past participle to suggest impossibility.	• That **can't / couldn't have happened**.
	Use **must not have** + past participle when you are slightly less certain.	• He **must not have made** the trip.
	In questions, use **can have / could have** + past participle.	• **Can / Could** that **have been** the reason?

(continued on next page)

5	When you are speculating about the past and are less certain (about 50%), use **may have / might have / could have** + past participle.	• They **may / might / could have reached** the New World.
	BE CAREFUL! **Could have** + past participle has two meanings.	• He **could have gone**. I don't know for sure. *(It's a possibility—a degree of certainty)* • He **could have gone** but didn't. *(a missed opportunity)*
	In the negative, use **may not have / might not have** + past participle.	• They **may / might not have found** what they were looking for.
	In questions, use **might have / could have** + past participle.	• **Might / Could** they **have had** trouble?
6	Use **should / ought to** + base form when you are almost certain about a future action or event.	• Continued research **should / ought to get** us closer to an answer.
7	Use **may / might / could** + base form when you are less certain about a future action or event.	• We **may / might / could know** the answer soon.
	In the negative, use **may / might + not / never** + base form.	• However, we **may / might never know** the answer.

STEP 3 FOCUSED PRACTICE

EXERCISE 1: Discover the Grammar

Read the sentences. Circle the letter of the choice that best explains the meaning of the sentence.

1. Columbus may not have been the first to visit the Western Hemisphere.

   a. He might not have been the first.

   b. He could not have been the first.

2. It must have been about the year 1000 when Leif Erickson visited the New World.

   a. I'm almost certain it was about the year 1000.

   b. I think maybe it was about the year 1000.

3. The assumption is that Vinland couldn't have been Newfoundland.

   a. It must not have been Newfoundland.

   b. It can't have been Newfoundland.

4. How could the voyage have happened?

  a. I'd like an explanation of how the voyage was impossible.

  b. I'd like an explanation of how the voyage was possible.

5. Individuals may have sailed from Japan to Ecuador.

  a. It's possible they did it.

  b. It's almost certain they did it.

6. The pottery evidence must mean something.

  a. I'm almost sure it means something.

  b. I strongly doubt it means something.

7. Other missionaries could have gone to the New World after Brendan's return.

  a. It's possible that they went.

  b. They had the opportunity to go but didn't.

8. Continued research should get us closer to an answer.

  a. It's possible that it will.

  b. It's almost certain that it will.

EXERCISE 2: Affirmative Modals

(Grammar Notes 1–3, 6)

Read the conversation. Complete it with modal constructions from the box.

could be working	might be	must have been visiting
~~could have gotten~~	might be meeting	should be
may have had to	must have	

BLAKE: I wonder what's keeping Harry. He's usually on time for office parties. I suppose he

_____ *could have gotten* _____ stuck in traffic.
                    1.

SAMANTHA: Yeah, that's a possibility. Or he _____ work late. I've
                                                      2.

never known him to be late for a party.

BLAKE: You know, I've always felt there's something a little puzzling—or even mysterious—about

Harry.

SAMANTHA: What makes you say that?

BLAKE: Well, he never says much about his past. He's an interesting guy, but I don't know much

about him. For all I know, he _____ an international spy
                                              3.

who works with mysterious cohorts.

(continued on next page)

SAMANTHA: I think I know what you mean. Or he _____ as a
_4._

government agent.

BLAKE: This is potentially a case of *cherchez la femme.*

SAMANTHA: What does that mean?

BLAKE: It means "look for the woman." I figure he _____ a
_5._

girlfriend that he doesn't want us to know about.

SAMANTHA: Yeah, maybe so. You know, now that I think of it, he always leaves work early on Friday

afternoons. I see him go to the parking garage about 4:00, and it always seems like he's

trying not to be seen. He _____ his secret love.
_6._

(The doorbell rings.)

BLAKE: Oh, wait a minute. There's the doorbell. Everyone else is here. That

_____ him.
_7._

HARRY: Hi, folks. Sorry I'm late. Had some business to take care of.

SAMANTHA: Business, huh. You mean romantic business?

HARRY: Romantic business? What are you talking about?

BLAKE: We figure you _____ your lady love. After all, we see you
_8._

leave early every Friday afternoon.

HARRY: Pretty funny. Well, there is a lady, and I love her. But it's not what you think.

SAMANTHA: What is it, then?

HARRY: My mother. She's 88 years old, and she lives in a retirement home. I go to see her

every Friday.

EXERCISE 3: Affirmative / Interrogative Modals

(Grammar Notes 3–5)

Read the article about past cultures. Complete the sentences with past and present modal verbs, using the words in parentheses.

World Review

Where do we draw the line between myth or legend and reality? What happens to cultures when they disappear? We at *World Review* decided to explore these questions in this month's issue.

Let's first consider the ancient Pueblo people of the U.S. Southwest. Scholars think that these people, called the Anasazi or "ancient ones" by the Navajo,

_____*may have settled*_____ about 100 c.e. in the Four Corners
　　1. (may / settle)

area, where today the states of Arizona, Utah, Colorado, and New Mexico come together. We know from the evidence of artifacts and ruins that the Anasazi developed agriculture and built impressive cities and cliff dwellings. About the year 1300, however, something happened. The Anasazi abandoned their dwellings and migrated to the Rio Grande Valley in New Mexico and the White Mountains in Arizona. What _____ this?
　　　　　　　　　　　　　　　　　　　　　　　　　　2. (could / cause)

Today many anthropologists assume that today's Pueblo peoples in the Southwest

_____ the descendants of the Anasazi. However, questions remain: What
　3. (must / be)

_____ an end to their flourishing culture? Drought? Warfare? Are certain
　4. (might / bring)

present-day Native Americans really descendants of the Anasazi? Or _____

the Anasazi actually _____?
　　　　　　　　5. (could / disappear)

Let's next turn our attention to Atlantis, the famed "lost continent" said to have existed in the Atlantic Ocean west of Gibraltar thousands of years ago. Is Atlantis a myth, or

_____ it _____? Plato wrote about Atlantis in two dialogues,
　　　　　　　　6. (could / exist)

describing it as a fabulous island, larger than Libya and Turkey. He believed that Atlantis

(continued on next page)

_____ about 9,000 years before his time. The Atlanteans were reputed to
  7. (had to / exist)

have conquered many lands around the Mediterranean and, he thought,

_____ evil and greedy in the process. Their island or continent was
  8. (must / become)

supposed to have sunk into the sea after being hit by earthquakes. _____
                                                                      9. (Could / there really / be)

an Atlantis? Certain writers think the present-day Basques _____
                                                             10. (might / be)

descendants of survivors of the catastrophe, if there was one. Is the Atlantis story just an

entertaining legend invented by Plato? Or, if Atlantis was real, is the problem simply that it

existed so long ago that traces of its memory are all that remain? A contending theory is

that reports of a disaster on the island of Thíra _____ the Atlantis legend.
                                                     11. (may / influence)

Thíra, in the Mediterranean Sea north of Crete, was destroyed about 1500 B.C.E. by

volcanic eruptions and earthquakes that covered the area with debris and devastated

civilization on nearby Crete. Perhaps the Atlantis legend stems from the Thíra disaster.

Perhaps the descendants of Atlanteans _____ among us. At this point, we
                                          12. (might / still / walk)

simply don't know.

EXERCISE 4: Personal Inventory (Future)   *(Grammar Notes 6–7)*

*Write 10 sentences about things you might accomplish in the next 10 years. Write two
sentences each with* **should, ought to, may, might,** *and* **could.** *Then compare your sentences
with a partner's.*

> EXAMPLES: I **might get** married within 10 years.
>   I **should finish** my college education by 2015.

EXERCISE 5: Editing

Read the student essay. There are eight mistakes in the use of modals. The first mistake is already corrected. Find and correct seven more.

WHY WE ITCH

One ~~must~~ *might* think that with all the scientific progress made in the last century, researchers would be able by now to answer this very simple question: Why do we itch? Unfortunately, scientists can't answer this question with any certainty. They simply don't know.

There are some clear cases involving itching. If a patient goes to her doctor and complains of terrible itching, and the doctor finds hives or some other kind of rash, the doctor will probably say that she must eat something she was allergic to—or that she must not have been stung or bitten by some insect. Scientists can easily explain this kind of case. Most itching, however, does not have an obvious cause.

Here's what scientists do know: Right under the surface of the skin there are sensory receptors that register physical stimuli and carry messages to the brain. These receptors detect pain and let the brain know about it. If there is a high level of physical stimulation to the body, the sensory receptors might carried a message of pain to the brain. If the level of physical stimulation is low, the sensors might be report it as itchiness.

There has been a lot of speculation about the function of itching. Some researchers think the function of itching may to warn the body it is about to have a painful experience. Others theorize that early humans might developed itching as a way of knowing they needed to take insects out of their hair. Still others believe that itching could be a symptom of serious diseases such as diabetes and Hodgkin's disease.

One of the most interesting aspects of itching is that it may have be less tolerable than pain. Research has shown, in fact, that most of us tolerate pain better than itching. Many people will allow their skin to be painfully broken just so they can get rid of an itch.

EXERCISE 6: Listening

A | *Listen to a discussion in a biology class. In what college class did the professor first hear a recording of his voice?*

_____

B | *Now listen to statements made during the discussion. Then circle the letter of the sentence that gives the same information.*

1. **a.** It's almost impossible that it was me.

   b. It's possible that it was me.

2. **a.** There must be some mistake.

   b. There's possibly some mistake.

3. **a.** It's possible that all of you have had this experience before.

   b. It's almost certain that all of you have had this experience before.

4. **a.** You have probably figured out the answer.

   b. You will probably be able to figure out the answer.

That can't be my voice!

5. **a.** It's got to be because we hear the sound in a different way.

   b. It's possibly because we hear the sound in a different way.

6. **a.** It's possibly because the sound travels through different substances.

   b. It's almost certainly because the sound travels through different substances.

7. **a.** It's certain that it's a combination of the two things.

   b. It's possible that it's a combination of the two things.

8. **a.** It's almost certain that the sound others hear is the real sound.

   b. It's unlikely that the sound others hear is the real sound.

9. **a.** The sound we heard was probably the real sound.

   b. The sound we hear is probably the real sound.

10. **a.** It's certain that internal hearing is more accurate than external hearing.

    b. It's almost certain that internal hearing is more accurate than external hearing.

EXERCISE 7: Pronunciation

A | *Read and listen to the Pronunciation Note.*

Pronunciation Note
In modal verb constructions, the word **to** is often reduced to /tə/. The word **have** is often reduced to /əv/.

B | *Listen to the conversations. In each conversation, a certain word is reduced in one sentence but not in the other. Circle the word that is reduced.*

1. **A:** Let's call Mary. She ought (to) be home by now.

   B: Yeah, she really ought to.

2. **A:** Bill should have gotten the package already.

   B: Yeah, he should definitely have it by now.

3. **A:** He's got to solve that problem before things get worse.

   B: You're right. He's got to.

4. **A:** We should have that job done professionally.

   B: Probably. Actually, I should have done it myself.

5. **A:** Do I have to finish this today?

   B: You don't have to, but it would be nice.

6. **A:** Nancy had to have her own way.

   B: Yes, but the situation had to have been tough on her.

C | *PAIRS: Practice the sentences. Take turns using unreduced and reduced forms.*

EXERCISE 8: Pair Discussion

A | *Work with a partner to solve the puzzles. Using modals of certainty, suggest several possible solutions to each puzzle, write them down—from most likely to least likely— and label them accordingly. Include a modal verb construction in each sentence.*

1. On November 22, 1978, an 18-year-old thief broke into a lady's house and demanded all her money. She gave him all she had: $11.50. The thief was so angry that he demanded she write him a check for $50. Two hours later, the police caught the thief. How?

   EXAMPLE: There **may have been** a security camera in the bank building.

2. A dog owner put some food in a pan for her cat. Then, because she didn't want her dog to eat the cat's food, she tied a six-foot rope around his neck. Then she left. When she came back, she discovered that the dog had eaten the cat's food. What happened?

3. Two monks decided to ride their bicycles from their monastery to another monastery in a town 6 miles away. They rode for a while and then reached a crossroads where they had to change direction. They discovered that the sign with arrows pointing to different towns in the area had blown down. They didn't know which road was the right one. Nevertheless, they were able to figure out which road to take. What do you think they did?

4. Roy Sullivan, a forest ranger in Virginia, had several experiences in his life in which he was struck by a powerful force. Two times his hair was set on fire. He had burns on his eyebrows, shoulder, stomach, chest, and ankle. Once he was driving when he was hit and was knocked 10 feet out of his car. What do you think happened to him?

B | *Report your answers to the class.*

EXERCISE 9: Group Discussion

A | *GROUPS: Look again at the story of Atlantis in Exercise 3. Which explanation do you think is the most likely? Which do you like best? Discuss your opinions with your partners.*

B | *Report your opinions to the class.*

    EXAMPLE: **A:** Which explanation do you like best about Atlantis?
                B: Well, the one I like best is that the Basques are descendants of the Atlanteans. But I don't think it's the most likely explanation.
                A: What is it, then?
                B: I think it must have been . . .

EXERCISE 10: Writing

A | *Write three or four paragraphs about an interesting world mystery you have heard of. Using present and past modals of certainty, speculate on the causes and possible explanations. Use one of the following topics or choose your own:*

- How were the great pyramids in Egypt built?
- Are humans really to blame for the melting of the ice in Greenland and Antarctica?
- Does the Loch Ness monster really exist?
- How did the great statues get to Easter Island?

EXAMPLE: Does the Loch Ness monster really exist? I've always wanted to believe it does, and for years I did believe that. Recently, however, I've come to a different conclusion. Reports of seeing the monster might be from people's imaginations. Or they could just be tricks. So the legend can't be true. Here's why I think this . . .

B | *Check your work. Use the Editing Checklist.*

Editing Checklist

Did you use . . . ?
- ☐ present modals of certainty correctly
- ☐ past modals of certainty correctly
- ☐ speculations about the future correctly

UNIT 5 Review

Check your answers on page UR-1.
Do you need to review anything?

A | Circle the correct word or phrase to complete each sentence.

1. That <u>must / may</u> be the answer to the mystery. All evidence points to it.

2. Ellen <u>might / will</u> be here later, but I don't know for sure.

3. A monk <u>must / might</u> have made the trip, but the evidence isn't conclusive.

4. It <u>couldn't / shouldn't</u> have been Newfoundland, which is too far north.

5. We <u>should / may</u> find out what really happened later today. Louis says he knows.

6. You <u>may not / ought not to</u> have trouble solving the problem—you're good at math.

7. They <u>had to / might</u> have been home—I heard their music.

8. She <u>might be / 's got to be</u> the one who took it. No one else had access to it.

9. They <u>had to be / must have been</u> away last week. Their car was gone.

10. There <u>must / might</u> be a key around here somewhere. Dad said he had one.

B | In the blank after each sentence, write a modal or modal-like expression of certainty with a meaning similar to the underlined phrase.

1. <u>It's possible that Jeremy</u> had to work late. _____

2. <u>It's very likely that Mari</u> missed her flight. _____

3. <u>It's impossible that they</u> heard the news. _____

4. <u>It's likely that we'll</u> know the answer soon. _____

5. <u>You had the opportunity to get</u> a scholarship. _____

C | Circle the letter of the one underlined word or phrase in each sentence that is not correct.

1. <u>Might</u> she <u>have forgotten</u>, or <u>could she had</u> <u>had to</u> work?　　　A　B　C　D
　　　A　　　　　　B　　　　　　　C　　　　D

2. I <u>think</u> Ed <u>isn't</u> here because he <u>should</u> <u>be</u> sick.　　　A　B　C　D
　　　A　　　B　　　　　　　　　　C　　D

3. Al <u>can't</u> <u>get</u> here by 7:00, but he <u>shouldn't</u> <u>make</u> it by 8:00.　　　A　B　C　D
　　　　A　　B　　　　　　　　　　　　C　　　D

4. I suppose they <u>couldn't</u> <u>be working</u> late at the office, but Amy　　　A　B　C　D
　　　　　　　　　A　　　　B

　 <u>didn't mention</u> it, and neither <u>did</u> Mary.
　　　　C　　　　　　　　　　　　　D

5. I'm sorry; I <u>could</u> <u>had</u> called to say <u>I'd be</u> late, but I <u>forgot</u>.　　　A　B　C　D
　　　　　　　A　　B　　　　　　　　C　　　　　　D

From Grammar to Writing
TOPIC SENTENCES

An important way to strengthen your writing is to provide a **topic sentence** for each paragraph. A topic sentence is a general sentence that covers the paragraph's content. All the supporting examples and details of the paragraph must fit logically under this sentence, which usually comes first.

EXAMPLE: **For me, a dog is a better pet than a cat.** When I come home from work, for example, my dog comes to meet me at the door. He is always glad to see me. My cat, on the other hand, couldn't care less whether I'm at home or not, as long as I keep filling her food dish. Another good thing about a dog is that you can teach him tricks. Cats, however, can't be bothered to learn anything new. The best thing about a dog, though, is that he's a great companion. I can take my dog on hikes and walks. He goes everywhere with me. As we all know, you can't take a cat for a walk.

The topic sentence for this paragraph tells the reader what to expect in the paragraph: some reasons why the writer considers a dog a superior pet.

1 | *Each of the word groups is a fragment but is also a potential topic sentence. Make necessary additions to each.*

EXAMPLE: Reasons why the legal driving age should be raised. (not an independent clause)
Correction: There are several reasons why the legal driving age should be raised.

1. A city where exciting and mysterious things happen.

_____

2. Reasons why college isn't for everybody.

_____

3. Wild animals not making good pets.

_____

4. Regular exercise and its benefits.

_____

2 | *Look at the following paragraphs containing supporting details but no topic sentences. For each set of details, write an appropriate topic sentence.*

1. _____

    a. For one thing, there's almost always a traffic jam I get stuck in, and I'm often late to work.

    b. Also, there's not always a parking place when I do get to work.

    c. Worst of all, I'm spending more money on gas and car maintenance than I would if I took public transportation.

(continued on next page)

2. _____

    a. One is that I often fall asleep when watching the TV screen, no matter how interesting the video is.

    b. Another is that watching movies is basically a social experience, and I'm usually alone when I watch videos.

    c. The main reason is that the TV screen, no matter how large it is, diminishes the impact that you get when watching a movie on the big screen.

3. _____

    a. First, nothing spontaneous usually happens on a guided tour, but I've had lots of spontaneous experiences when I planned my own vacation.

    b. Second, tour guides present you with what *they* think is interesting, but when you are in charge of your own vacation, you do what *you* think is interesting.

    c. Most importantly, individually planned vacations can often be less expensive than guided tours.

4. _____

    a. First of all, cats don't bark and wake up the neighbors or bite the letter carrier.

    b. Second, dogs have to be walked at least two times a day, but cats handle their own exercise.

    c. Finally, cats eat a lot less than dogs.

3 | Before you write . . .

1. When we get to know people from other cultural backgrounds, we often learn a great deal about other cultures and about ourselves. Think about a significant experience you had involving someone from another culture. What did you learn? How did your behavior or thinking change because of your experience?

2. Describe the experience to a partner. Listen to your partner's experience.

3. Ask and answer questions about your experiences. For example: When did it happen? Why did you . . . ? Where were you when . . . ? How did you feel? What do you do or think now that is different from before?

4 | Write a draft of a two- or three-paragraph composition about your cross-cultural experience. Follow the model. Include information that your partner asked about.

Where, when, with whom the experience occurred . . .

_____

_____

_____

The events that happened . . .

_____

_____

_____

Changes in you and your behavior since the experience happened . . .

_____

_____

_____

5 | *Exchange compositions with a different partner. Complete the chart.*

1. The writer provided an appropriate topic sentence for each paragraph. **Yes** ☐ **No** ☐

2. What I liked in the composition:

   _____

   _____

   _____

3. Questions I'd like the writer to answer about the composition:

   Who _____?

   What _____?

   When _____?

   Where _____?

   Why _____?

   How _____?

   (Your own question) _____?

6 | *Work with your partner. Discuss each other's chart from Exercise 5. Then rewrite your own composition and make any necessary changes.*

III

NOUNS

Before You Read

PAIRS: Discuss the questions.

1. What are the most important health issues today?
2. How important is exercise for health? Do you exercise a lot, a little, or not at all?

Read

Read the transcript of part of a TV program about health.

Concerned about Health?
ASK THE EXPERT

HEALTH QUESTIONS
WITH DR. MEL BRAND

Miranda Olson:	Good **afternoon**. Welcome to Ask the **Expert**. I'm Miranda Olson. My **guest** today is Dr. Mel Brand, and we're going to devote today's entire **program** to your **questions** about **health**. So let's get right to it. . . . Tell us your **name** and where you're from.
Sally Matthews:	Hi, Dr. Brand. I'm Sally Matthews from San Diego, California. We hear a lot of negative **stuff** about fast **food**, but my **husband** and **kids** love **hamburgers** and **fries** and **sodas**. How bad is it?
Dr. Mel Brand:	Sally, it's OK in **moderation**—but I wouldn't make a **habit** of it. Most fast **food** is full of **salt**, **sugar**, **cholesterol**, and lots of **calories**. An occasional **trip** to a fast **food place** won't hurt you, especially if you order healthy **salads** or **sandwiches**. But I wouldn't make it more than once or twice a **week**.
Miranda Olson:	OK. Next **question**?

Concerned about Health? ASK THE EXPERT

Bob Gonzales:	Dr. Brand, I'm Bob Gonzales from Tampa, Florida. I'm 25 years old, and my **question** is about **sun**. My lovely **wife** is a wonderful **woman**, but she's also a **member** of the **sunblock police**. She won't let me go out the **door** without putting **sunblock** on. I've always been able to get a good **tan**, so is this really necessary? It's a **drag**.
Dr. Brand:	Bob, I've got to side with your **wife**. The **sun** makes us feel wonderful, and we love its **warmth**, but it has its **dangers**. I've treated **patients** with **skin cancer**. The most telling **example** was an older **man** who hiked for 40 years and refused to wear a **hat**. He developed **skin cancer** and eventually died of it. I'm not trying to scare you, but you should wear **sunblock** if you're going out in the **sun** for more than a few **minutes**. And you should definitely wear a brimmed **hat** that protects your **face** and your **neck**. And that's all of us, not just fair-skinned **people**.
Miranda Olson:	OK. Next **question**?
Martina Smith:	Dr. Brand. I'm Martina Smith from Toronto, Ontario. My **question** is about **weight**. My **husband** is 5 **feet** 11 **inches** tall and weighs about 250. He used to be in good **shape** when he was a **tennis champ**, but now he doesn't get any **exercise**. When I try to get him to go to the **gym**, he either says he's too tired or he doesn't have **time**. Any **suggestions**?
Dr. Brand:	Martina, tell your **husband** he's way too heavy. Have you heard of **body mass index**? Anyone with a **BMI** more than 25 is considered overweight. Your **husband** would have a **BMI** of about 35, which puts him in the obese **category**. He's got to start exercising and taking off the **pounds**. Have him start slowly and build up to at least three **times** a **week**. Get him to play a **game** of **tennis** with you. But don't delay.
Miranda Olson:	All right. Another **question**?
Frank Lee:	Hi, Dr. Brand. I don't know if this is a **health question** or not, but is there a **cure** for **baldness**? I've been losing my **hair** since I was 35, and . . .

A | Vocabulary: *Complete the definitions with the correct word or phrase from the box.*

BMI	champ	drag	obese	sunblock
brimmed	devote	in moderation	side with	telling

1. To _____ someone is to agree with that person.

2. A(n) _____ example or argument is one that is very effective.

3. Someone who is _____ is very much overweight.

4. One's _____ is a numerical measurement of body fat.

5. A person who has won competitions is a(n) _____.

6. Something dull, tedious, or uninteresting is called a(n) _____.

7. When we act within reasonable limits we do things _____.

8. A hat with an edge that gives protection or shade is said to be _____.

9. We _____ our time or attention to an activity when we focus on it completely.

10. _____ is a cream or oil for your skin that prevents sunburn.

B | Comprehension: *Circle the letter of the correct answer.*

1. According to Dr. Brand, consuming fast food is _____ OK.
   a. usually   **b.** occasionally   **c.** never   **d.** always

2. Dr. Brand suggests that too much _____ in food is not beneficial.
   a. protein   **b.** calcium   **c.** fiber   **d.** cholesterol

3. Dr. Brand says _____ should wear sunblock if they spend time in the sun.
   a. fair-skinned   **b.** dark- skinned   **c.** people over 40   **d.** everyone
   people   people

4. Exposure to the sun _____ cause skin cancer.
   a. will   **b.** shouldn't   **c.** can   **d.** won't usually

5. Anyone with a BMI exceeding _____ is considered overweight.
   a. 40   **b.** 35   **c.** 25   **d.** 20

6. Dr. Brand believes exercise is of _____ importance to someone overweight.
   a. no significant   **b.** great   **c.** some   **d.** minimal

NOUNS

Proper Nouns
Mel Brand is a physician.

Common Nouns
The **doctor** is an **expert**.

Count and Non-Count Nouns

Count Nouns			
Article or Number	Noun	Verb	
A One	**snack**	is	refreshing.
The Two	**snacks**	are	

Non-Count Nouns		
Noun	Verb	
Rice	is	nourishing.
Nutrition		important.

Nouns with Count and Non-Count Meanings

Count Meaning
There's **a hair** in my soup!
A chicken escaped from the henhouse.
How many **times** did you eat out?
Please bring us **two coffees**.
Brie is **a soft cheese**.
I see **a light** in the window.

Non-Count Meaning
Sandra has black **hair**.
We had **chicken** for dinner.
It takes **time** to prepare a good meal.
I'd like some **coffee**.
Cheese is produced in France.
The sun provides **light**.

Non-Count Nouns Made Countable

Non-Count Noun
You need **advice**.
Let's play **tennis**.
There's not enough **salt** in the soup.
I like **bread** with my meal.
It's unhealthy to eat **meat** every night.
Please put more **paper** in the printer.

Made Countable
Let me give you **a piece of advice**.
Let's play **a game of tennis**.
Add **one spoonful of salt**.
Please get **a loaf of bread** at the store.
The recipe takes **three pounds of meat**.
Two packages of paper are all we have.

GRAMMAR NOTES

1

Nouns name persons, places, and things. There are two types of nouns: **proper** nouns and **common** nouns.

Proper nouns name particular persons, places, or things. They are usually unique and are capitalized in writing.

- Dr. Brand, Ichiro Suzuki, São Paulo, China, the Empire State Building, Harrod's

Common nouns refer to people, places, or things but are not the names of particular individuals.

- scientist, athlete, city, country, building, department store

2

There are two types of **common nouns**: count nouns and non-count nouns.

Count nouns refer to things that you can count separately. They can be singular or plural. You can use *a* or *an* before count nouns.

- one **woman**, eight **planets**
- I'd like **a sandwich**.
- Some **vegetables** are tasty.
- That's **an** interesting **question**.

Non-count nouns refer to things that you cannot count separately. They usually have no plural form. We usually do not use *a* or *an* with non-count nouns, though they are often preceded by *some* or *the*.

- You should avoid **cholesterol**.
  Noт: You should avoid ~~a cholesterol~~.
- Let me give you **some advice**.
  Noт: Let me give you ~~an advice~~.

We normally use a **singular verb** with a non-count noun. We use a **singular pronoun** to refer to the noun.

- **Rice feeds** millions.
- **It** feeds millions.

3

Notice the following categories and examples of **non-count nouns**:

Abstractions
Diseases
Food and Drink
Natural phenomena
Particles
Others

- chance, energy, honesty, love
- AIDS, cancer, influenza, malaria
- bread, coffee, fish, meat, tea, water
- electricity, heat, lightning, rain, sun
- dust, pepper, salt, sand, sugar
- equipment, furniture, money, news, traffic

4	Many nouns have both a non-count and a count meaning.	• **Experience** is a great teacher. • College was **a** wonderful **experience**.
		• We eat **fish** twice a week. • My son caught **a fish** yesterday. • I want to be a professor of **history**. • I read **a history** of the Civil War.
		• Is **space** really the final frontier? • There's **an** empty **space** in that row.
		• People say **talk** is cheap. • We had **a** good **talk** last night.
		Other examples are *cuisine*, *film*, *rain*, *reading*, *work*, and *spice*.

5	We can **make certain non-count nouns countable** by adding a phrase that gives them a form, a limit, or a container. We use these phrases when we want to be more precise or emphatic.	**NON-COUNT NOUN** **MADE COUNTABLE**
		furniture a piece of furniture lightning a flash / bolt of lightning meat a piece of meat rice, sand a grain of rice / sand tennis a game of tennis water, rain a drop of water / rain equipment a piece of equipment
	NOTE: All of these nouns are commonly used with **some** or **any**. Phrases such as *a piece of*, *a grain of*, and *a bolt of* sometimes sound more formal and are commonly found in writing.	• Can I give you **some advice**? *(more conversational)* • Can I give you **a piece of advice**? *(more formal)*

| 6 | We can use many **non-count nouns** in a **countable sense** with *a / an* or in the plural to mean *kind / type / variety of*. | • In Italy, I tasted **a** new **pasta**.
• That shop sells many different **teas**.
• Many tasty **cheeses** are produced in France. |
| | *A / an* and plurals can also be used to indicate discrete amounts. | • I drank **a soda**.
• Please bring us two **orange juices**. |

(continued on next page)

7 Some nouns are irregular:

a. A few **non-count nouns** end in **-s**.

- news, mathematics, economics, physics

b. A few **count nouns** have **irregular plurals**.
- *criterion, criteria*
- *stimulus, stimuli*
- *phenomenon, phenomena*

- Thunder is **an** atmospheric **phenomenon**.
- Thunder and lightning are atmospheric **phenomena**.

c. The count nouns *people* and *police* are plural, not singular. They take a plural verb.

- People are funny.
  NOT: ~~People is~~ funny.
- The police are coming.
  NOT: The ~~police is~~ coming.

In the singular, we generally use *person* and *police officer*.

- He's **an energetic person**.
- She's **a police officer**.

REFERENCE NOTES

For a list of **non-count nouns**, see Appendix 5 on page A-4.
For a list of phrases for **counting non-count nouns**, see Appendix 6 on page A-5.
For a list of **irregular noun plurals**, see Appendix 4 on page A-3.

STEP 3 FOCUSED PRACTICE

EXERCISE 1: Discover the Grammar

Read the sentences based on the opening reading. Underline the count nouns. Circle the non-count nouns.

1. We're going to devote the entire program to your questions about health.

2. It's OK in moderation, but I wouldn't make a habit of it.

3. Most fast food is full of salt, sugar, cholesterol, and calories.

4. We love its warmth, but it has its dangers.

5. I've treated patients with skin cancer.

6. You should wear sunblock if you're going out in the sun for more than a few minutes.

7. He used to be in good shape when he was a tennis champ, but now he doesn't get any exercise.

8. Your husband would have a BMI of about 35, which puts him in the obese category.

9. Is there a cure for baldness?

10. I've been losing my hair for several years.

EXERCISE 2: Count / Non-Count Senses

(Grammar Notes 4, 6–7)

Interactive websites on the Internet give people information about entertainment, cultural events, and the weather. Fill in the blanks in the bulletin board messages, choosing the correct count or non-count form in parentheses.

[Follow-Ups]   [Post a Reply]   [Message Board Index]

Community Bulletin Board for August 26, 2012

Poet Jefferson Jung will give _____*a reading*_____ of his poetry tonight in the Burlington Civic
1. (reading / a reading)

Center. He describes his latest book of poems as _____ in progress.
2. (work / a work)

Community Bulletin Board for August 27, 2012

On Monday afternoon at 4 P.M. at City Hall, Professor Helen Hammond, who has written

_____ of the space program, will give _____ on the exploration
3. (history / a history)   **4. (talk / a talk)**

of _____ in the 21st century at _____ when we seem to be
5. (space / a space)   **6. (time / a time)**

running out of funds for the space program. Professor Hammond will focus on several of the

government's _____ for suggesting budget cuts.
7. (criterion / criteria)

Community Bulletin Board for August 28, 2012

If you have not made reservations for the annual Labor Day picnic, _____ is
8. (time / a time)

running short. _____ on the remodeling of Patton Pavilion, where the picnic will
9. (Work / A work)

be held, is complete. All residents of Burlington are invited, but you must have a ticket, which

will cover the price of dinner. The menu will include _____, meat, and pasta as
10. (fish / a fish)

main courses. _____ and _____ are free.
11. (Soda / A soda)   **12. (milk / a milk)**

Community Bulletin Board for August 29, 2012

On Wednesday evening at 8:00 P.M. in the Civic Auditorium, Professor Mary Alice Waters will

present a program on the Hmong, an ethnic group of China and Laos. Professor Waters, a

professor of _____ at the university, will show _____ about
13. (history / a history)   **14. (film / a film)**

marriage customs of the Hmong and other peoples of eastern Asia.

EXERCISE 3: Non-Count Nouns Made Countable

(Grammar Note 5)

Complete the pairs of sentences. In the sentences on the left, use **some** or **any**. In the sentences on the right, use a phrase that makes the non-count noun countable.

More Conversational

1. **a.** When we moved to the new office, we lost _____*some*_____ equipment.

2. **a.** Look! I just saw _____ lightning in the sky.

3. **a.** We didn't play _____ tennis after all.

4. **a.** Let me give you _____ advice: Don't buy that item.

5. **a.** There hasn't been _____ rain here for over a month.

6. **a.** There wasn't _____ rice left on the plate.

7. **a.** I had _____ meat for dinner.

8. **a.** We bought _____ furniture at the mall.

More Formal

1. **b.** When we moved to the new office, we lost _____*a piece of*_____ equipment.

2. **b.** Look! I just saw _____ lightning in the sky.

3. **b.** We didn't play _____ tennis after all.

4. **b.** Let me give you _____ advice: Don't buy that item.

5. **b.** There hasn't been _____ rain here for over a month.

6. **b.** There wasn't _____ rice left on the plate.

7. **b.** I had _____ meat for dinner.

8. **b.** We bought _____ furniture at the mall.

EXERCISE 4: Personal Inventory (Past)

(Grammar Notes 3–7)

Using your own personal experience, write a sentence for each of the prompts. Use the present perfect in each sentence.

EXAMPLE: best / time / had / in the last month
The best time I've had in the last month was my sister's wedding.

1. two best / films / seen / in the last year

_____

2. two funniest people / ever met

_____

3. best / advice / ever had

_____

4. most enjoyable work / ever done

_____

5. most beautiful work of art / ever seen

_____

6. best / news / heard / this month

_____

7. worst / traffic / ever seen

_____

8. most interesting experience / had / in the last year

_____

EXERCISE 5: Editing

Read the letter. There are nine mistakes in the use of count and non-count nouns. The first mistake is already corrected. Find and correct eight more.

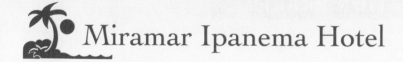 Miramar Ipanema Hotel

Dear kids,

Your mom and I are having‚ wonderful time in Brazil. We landed in Rio de Janeiro on Tuesday as scheduled and made it to our hotel without any problems. On Wednesday we walked and sunbathed on Copacabana and Ipanema beaches. The only problem was that I didn't put on any sunblock and got bad sunburn. There's a good news, though; it's better today. Actually, there's one other problem: We don't have enough furnitures in our hotel room. There's no place to put anything. But everything else has been great. We went to a samba show, and even though it was intended for tourists, it was a lot of fun.

The Brazilian people is very friendly and helpful. On Friday we had a flight to São Paulo scheduled for 9:00 A.M., and we missed the bus and couldn't get a taxi. But we were saved by one of the hotel employees, who gave us a ride to the airport. We got there just in time. Now we're in São Paulo. It's an exciting place, but I can't get over the traffic. It took two hours to get from our hotel to the downtown area. Yesterday we had lunch at a famous restaurant where they serve feijoada, a typical Brazilian food. It had so many spice in it that our mouths were on fire, but it was delicious. Tonight we're going to have dinner at a very famous restaurant where they serve every kind of meats you can think of.

(continued on next page)

The other thing about Brazil that's really interesting is the amount of coffees the Brazilians drink. They have little cups of coffee several times a day-called caffezinho. We tried it; it's very strong and sweet.

That's all for now. Your mom hasn't had a time to go shopping yet, which is good. You know how much I hate shopping.

Love,
Dad

STEP 4 COMMUNICATION PRACTICE

EXERCISE 6: Listening

A | *Listen to the conversation. Why is Joe Smith at the doctor's office?*

_____

B | *Listen again. Answer each question with a complete sentence.*

1. What did the TV speaker say Joe needs to do?

   He said that he needs to lose weight.

2. What is his cholesterol level?

   _____

3. Which meal does Joe skip daily?

   _____

4. Why?

   _____

5. How much exercise does he get?

   _____

6. Where does he eat his midday meal?

   _____

7. What is Joe at high risk for?

   _____

8. Why isn't the doctor going to put Joe on a diet?

_____

9. What will Joe still be able to eat?

_____

10. How many times a week will Joe need to exercise at the beginning?

_____

EXERCISE 7: Pronunciation

A | *Read and listen to the Pronunciation Note.*

> **Pronunciation Note**
>
> In fast speech, the word **of** in noun phrases is sometimes reduced to /ə/ before words beginning with a consonant. The pronunciation /əv/ is maintained before words beginning with a vowel.
>
> **EXAMPLES:** a lot **of** people = a lot**ə** people
> a lot **of** advice = a lot**əv** advice
>
> **Note:** This reduction sometimes happens in fast speech. It is perfectly correct to pronounce **of** as /əv/ in all situations.

B | *Listen and repeat the sentences. Circle* **of** *where it is reduced to* /ə/. *Underline* **of** *where it maintains the pronunciation* /əv/.

1. I ate a lot of doughnuts for lunch.

2. Mary gave me an important piece of advice.

3. There were a lot of new people in class today.

4. We bought a new piece of furniture for the living room.

5. We lost a piece of equipment when we changed offices.

6. Can you pour me a glass of orange juice?

7. I had a delicious piece of meat for supper.

8. There was a large group of engineers at the convention.

9. I bought my fiancée a bouquet of flowers.

10. There was a basket of eggs on the kitchen table.

C | *PAIRS: Practice the sentences. Take turns.*

EXERCISE 8: Discussion

A | *Look again at the sentences you wrote in Exercise 4. Share your answers with the other members of your group.*

> EXAMPLE: **A:** What's the best advice you've ever had?
> **B:** The best advice I've ever had was to go to college.

B | *Report interesting examples to the entire class.*

EXERCISE 9: Personal Inventory

A | *Complete the survey by circling the answers that best apply to you.*

1. In general I'd say I'm _____.

  a. in excellent health   **b.** in good health   **c.** in fair health   **d.** not concerned about my health

2. The drink I like the best is _____.

  a. water   **b.** soda   **c.** milk   **d.** other

3. The best exercise for me is _____.

  a. running   **b.** swimming   **c.** walking   **d.** other

4. My absolute favorite food is _____.

  a. meat   **b.** pasta   **c.** dessert   **d.** other

5. I never miss _____.

  a. a meal   **b.** a social experience   **c.** exercising   **d.** watching my favorite TV show

6. My most challenging health issue is _____.

  a. losing weight   **b.** gaining weight   **c.** avoiding stress   **d.** other

7. I'm _____ ill.

  a. often   **b.** sometimes   **c.** seldom   **d.** never

B | *CLASS: Discuss your answers. What trends do you see?*

EXERCISE 10: Writing

A *Write three or four paragraphs about one of these topics:*

- the single most important health issue in society today
- the single most important thing I can do to improve my health

Use both count and non-count nouns.

EXAMPLE: The single most important thing I can do to improve my health is to reduce my stress level. For several years now stress has been a problem in my life. I think the way to accomplish this is to do fewer things and do them better. I know I am involved in too many things, but somehow I can't help it. For example . . .

B *Check your work. Use the Editing Checklist.*

Editing Checklist

Did you use . . . ?
- ☐ articles correctly
- ☐ count nouns correctly
- ☐ non-count nouns correctly

A | Identify the boldfaced word as a count noun (**C**) or a non-count noun (**NC**).

1. Jack Sanderson describes his latest novel as a **work** in progress. _____

2. Let me give you some **advice**: Don't drop out of college. _____

3. My favorite dinner is fried **chicken** and mashed potatoes. _____

4. We saw an interesting new **film** at our local cinema last night. _____

5. I don't care much for potatoes, but I do like **rice**. _____

6. My favorite professor is giving a **talk** tonight. _____

7. In my view, **reading** is one of the most beneficial activities. _____

B | Complete each sentence in two ways: first in a more conversational way and second in a more formal way.

1. **a.** There hasn't been _____ rain here for three months.

   b. There hasn't been _____ rain here for three months.

2. **a.** We bought _____ furniture at a discount store.

   b. We bought _____ furniture at a discount store.

3. **a.** There wasn't _____ rice left in the bowl.

   b. There wasn't _____ rice left in the bowl.

4. **a.** We played _____ tennis before dinner.

   b. We played _____ tennis before dinner.

C | Circle the letter of the underlined word or phrase in each sentence that is not correct.

1. Ralph is in <u>the intensive care unit</u> of <u>the city hospital</u> after being   **A B C D**

               A   B
   struck by <u>a lightning</u> on <u>a camping trip</u>.

          C   D

2. Her son dislikes <u>cauliflower</u>, <u>carrots</u>, <u>beans</u>, and most other <u>vegetable</u>.   **A B C D**

                  A   B   C   D

3. At the yard sale we bought <u>some</u> garden <u>equipment</u> and <u>a</u> new <u>furniture</u>.   **A B C D**

                      A   B   C   D

4. <u>People</u> who <u>lives</u> in glass <u>houses</u> shouldn't throw <u>stones</u>.   **A B C D**

   A   B   C   D

5. It takes <u>a</u> <u>work</u> to prepare <u>a</u> nutritious <u>meal</u>.   **A B C D**

    A B   C   D

STEP 1 GRAMMAR IN CONTEXT

Before You Read

PAIRS: Discuss the questions.

1. What is an example of a serious environmental problem?
2. Do you think people exaggerate the seriousness of hazards to the environment? If so, what would be an example?
3. How can serious environmental problems be remedied?

Read

Read the article about an environmental disaster.

The Real Mystery of EASTER ISLAND

There are two mysteries about Easter Island. One is this: Who built its gigantic statues, and how were they moved? **The** other, greater **mystery** is what changed **the island** so drastically?

Easter Island, settled about **the year** 900 by Polynesians, lies in **the South Pacific** about 2,300 miles west of Chile, **the country** to which it belongs. If you go to Easter Island today, you'll see about 500 statues in various stages of disrepair— many toppled over. You'll also see more

This area was once a subtropical forest.

than 100 enormous platforms on which **the statues** stood.

Easter Island was discovered by Dutch explorer Jacob Roggeveen on April 5, 1722— Easter Sunday. On landing, Roggeveen saw **the island** much as it is today: **a** rather desolate **place** covered mostly by grassland, with no trees taller than 10 feet. However, Easter Island was once much different: Most of it was **a** subtropical **forest**. At one time, **the island** was home to as many as 15,000 people,

(continued on next page)

while today there are only about 200. What occurred to cause such drastic changes?

The two **mysteries** are closely connected. It is believed today that **the Easter Islanders** built and moved **the statues** themselves. But how could they have done this? **The wheel** had been invented long before, but **the Easter Islanders** didn't have access to it, nor did they have cranes, metal tools, or large animals. **A** convincing **explanation** is that they devised canoe rails—ladders with parallel wooden logs connected by crosspieces—which they used to drag **the statues**. But large trees would have been required to build **the rails**, along with other kinds of trees to provide bark to make rope to pull **the statues**. Had such trees ever existed there?

Botanist John Flenly and anthropologist Paul Bahn believe they had. Studies have established that **the island** was once covered with forests. One of **the** principal **trees** was **the Chilean wine palm**, which grows as high as 65 feet and as wide as 3 feet. **The trunks** of **the wine palm** were presumably used to lift and move **the statues**, with **the bark** of other trees used to make rope for hauling. But what happened to **the trees**? Today **the deforestation** of Easter Island can be seen as one of **the** greatest environmental **disasters** of all time. No one knows for sure how or why it happened, but **the island** apparently experienced **a decline** several hundred years after being settled. It is thought that 11 ruling chiefs constructed **the statues** as competitive demonstrations of their power. As **the population** increased, **the rivalry** became fiercer. More land was cleared to grow crops, and more trees cut down for firewood and for moving **the statues**. This deforestation led to **the drying** of **the land**, **the loss** of nutrients in **the soil**, and eventually less and less rainfall. In effect, **the climate** was changed.

Why did **the Easter Islanders** allow **the disaster** to happen? Did they simply not recognize there was **a problem**, or was it too late to do anything when they figured it out? Perhaps more significantly, are there parallels for us today? Are we acting as **the Easter Islanders** did, but on **a** global **scale**? For example, does **the push** to cut down trees in **the name** of jobs and economic development make environmental sense? Are we overfishing **the ocean** in **an** ostrich-like **belief** that **the supply** of seafood is limitless? Are future catastrophes in **the works**? We mustn't shy away from these questions.

After You Read

A | **Vocabulary:** *Match the blue words and phrases on the left with their meanings on the right.*

_____ **1.** The greater mystery is what changed the island so **drastically**.

_____ **2.** You'll see about 500 statues in disrepair, many **toppled over**.

_____ **3.** The island today is a rather **desolate** place.

_____ **4.** The trees provided **bark** to make rope for pulling the statues.

_____ **5.** The **trunk** of the wine palm was used to lift and move the statues.

_____ **6.** The bark of other trees was used to make rope for **hauling**.

_____ **7.** As the population increased, the **rivalry** became fiercer.

_____ **8.** Do we have an **ostrich-like** belief that the supply of seafood is limitless?

a. pulling

b. competition

c. a tree's main stem

d. overturned

e. suddenly and severely

f. refusing to face reality

g. appearing deserted

h. a tree's outer covering

B | **Comprehension:** *Circle* **T** *(True) or* **F** *(False). Correct the false statements.*

1. Easter Island was settled about the year 900 by Chileans.   **T**   **F**

2. When the island was settled, much of it was a subtropical forest.   **T**   **F**

3. The population of Easter Island today is much less than it once was.   **T**   **F**

4. The Easter Islanders used wheels to move their statues.   **T**   **F**

5. The island declined apparently because of political competition among chiefs. **T**   **F**

6. The climate of Easter Island changed a great deal over the years.   **T**   **F**

7. Deforestation led to the island becoming wetter.   **T**   **F**

INDEFINITE AND DEFINITE ARTICLES

A / *An*: Indefinite Article		
	Non-Specific	**Generic**
SINGULAR COUNT NOUNS	He saw **a statue** at **an exhibition**.	**A statue** is **a** three-dimensional **figure**.

Zero Article (No Article)		
	Non-Specific	**Generic**
PLURAL COUNT NOUNS	Easter Island has impressive **statues**.	**Statues** are made in all shapes and sizes.
NON-COUNT NOUNS	The statues are made of **stone**.	**Stone** is an important building material.
PROPER NOUNS	**Ms. Johnson** spent a year on **Easter Island**. She worked in **Egypt** and **Hawaii**. She now lives in **New York City**.	

The: Definite Article		
	Specific	**Generic**
SINGULAR COUNT NOUNS	He finally got a computer. **The computer** he got is good. It's **the best computer** in **the world**.	**The computer** is a great invention.
PLURAL COUNT NOUNS	**The rain forests** in South America are being cut down.	**The rain forests** are in danger everywhere.
NON-COUNT NOUNS	**The stone** from that quarry is very soft.	
PROPER NOUNS	She crossed **the Sahara**, visited **the Pyramids**, and sailed down **the Nile**.	

GRAMMAR NOTES

1	Speakers use **indefinite** (non-specific / generic) nouns when they do not have a particular person, place, or thing in mind. Use the indefinite article, *a / an*, with indefinite **singular count nouns**.	• He wants to buy **a statue**. • She wants to be **an anthropologist**.
2	A noun is often **indefinite** the first time a speaker mentions it. It is usually **definite** after the first mention.	• I heard of **an** interesting **mystery**. • **The mystery** is about Easter Island.
3	Use **zero article** (no article) with indefinite plural count nouns, indefinite non-count nouns, names of people, names of most countries, and habitual locations.	• The island used to have tall **trees**. • **Platinum** and **gold** are valuable minerals. • **Mr. Flenly** is a botanist. • Many statues have been found in **Egypt**. • People spend most of their time at **work**, at **school**, or at **home**.

4 A noun is **generic** when it represents all members of a class or category of persons, places, or things—generic nouns talk about things in general.

Three common ways to use nouns generically are

a. Indefinite article + count noun

b. Zero article + plural count noun

c. Zero article + non-count noun

NOTE: You can also make a generic statement with the definite article + adjective. A noun such as *people* is implied. The adjective is plural in meaning and takes a plural verb.

- **A computer** is **a machine** that does calculations and processes information.
- **Computers** are **machines** that do calculations and process information.
- **Water** is essential for survival.

- **The rich** are fortunate. They need to help **the poor**, who **are** not so fortunate. (= *the rich people, the poor people*)

5 A noun is **definite** when the speaker and listener know which particular person, place, or thing is being talked about. Use the definite article, *the*, with non-count nouns and singular and plural nouns that are definite for you and your listener.

NOTE: A noun or noun phrase is normally definite if you can ask a *which* question about it. Nouns of this type are often followed by a phrase with *of*.

- **The food** we had for lunch was terrible.
- **The island** used to be covered by forests.
- **The statues** were made by tribal chiefs.

- **The population** of Easter Island has declined a great deal.
- The population **of which island** has declined a great deal?

6 Use the **definite article** with nouns that describe something unique.

An adjective can often make a noun represent something unique. Examples are *first*, *last*, *only*, *right*, *wrong*, and the comparative and superlative forms of adjectives.

- **The sun** gives us light and heat.

- It was **the worst disaster** in the country's history.

7 You can use the **definite article** generically to talk about inventions, musical instruments, living things, and parts of the body.

- **The wheel** was invented thousands of years ago.
- She plays **the harp**.
- **The wine palm** grew on Easter Island.
- **The brain** is the seat of intelligence.

(continued on next page)

8 Note these other uses of the **definite article** with nouns:

a. With public places
• the bank, the post office, the library

b. With the names of many geographical regions or features
• the Grand Canyon, the Colorado River, the Pacific Ocean, the Bahamas, the Gulf Coast

c. With the names of a few countries
• the Netherlands, the United States, the Dominican Republic

d. With the names of ships
• the *Titanic*, the *Queen Mary*

REFERENCE NOTE

For more complete lists of **nouns used with the definite article**, see Appendices 7–9 on pages A-5 and A-6.

STEP 3 FOCUSED PRACTICE

EXERCISE 1: Discover the Grammar

A | *Read the sentences based on the opening reading. For each sentence, identify the underlined word or phrase as non-specific (N), definite (D), or generic (G).*

_N_ **1.** We've become aware of <u>an even greater mystery</u>.

_____ **2.** Chile is <u>the country</u> to which Easter Island belongs.

_____ **3.** There are gigantic <u>platforms</u> all over the island.

_____ **4.** At one time <u>the island</u> was home to as many as 15,000 people.

_____ **5.** <u>The wheel</u> had been invented long before.

_____ **6.** <u>Canoe rails</u> are <u>ladders</u> with parallel wooden logs connected by crosspieces.

_____ **7.** <u>The Chilean wine palm</u> grows as high as 65 feet.

_____ **8.** Did they simply fail to recognize <u>an eventual problem</u>?

_____ **9.** Are we overfishing <u>the ocean</u>?

_____ **10.** Is <u>the supply</u> of seafood limitless?

B | *Read the sentences based on the reading. Then circle the letter of the choice that best explains the meaning of the sentence.*

1. Who built the statues there?

 a. Who built some of the statues there?

 (b.) Who built all of the statues there?

2. The island was settled by Polynesians.

 a. Some of the Polynesians settled the island.

 b. All of the Polynesians settled the island.

3. One of the principal trees in the forest was the Chilean wine palm.

 a. There was one Chilean palm tree in the forest.

 b. There were many Chilean palm trees in the forest.

4. But what happened to the trees on the island?

    a. What happened to all of the trees on the island?

    b. What happened to some of the trees on the island?

5. Trees were cut down to provide firewood.

    a. All of the trees were cut down.

    b. Some of the trees were cut down.

EXERCISE 2: Articles

(Grammar Notes 1–3, 5–6, 8)

Read the descriptions of two notable environmental disasters that have occurred in recent years. Fill in the blanks with the correct article in parentheses ("—" means no article is needed).

HURRICANE KATRINA: THE COSTLIEST EVER

On August 23, 2005, _____ Hurricane Katrina formed over
    1. (— / The)

_____ Bahamas and promptly moved westward along _____
2. (— / the)   **3. (a / the)**

Gulf Coast of _____ United States, causing very great destruction. At first
    4. (— / the)

_____ Katrina was only _____ Category 1 hurricane, but by the
5. (— / The)   **6. (a / the)**

time it reached New Orleans it had become a Category 3. In terms of damage, it is considered

one of _____ five worst hurricanes in _____ American history,
    7. (a / the)   **8. (— / the)**

largely because of _____ failure of New Orleans's levee system. Eighty percent of
    9. (— / the)

_____ city was flooded, and at least 1,836 people died. There was great criticism
10. (a / the)

of _____ way the government handled _____ crisis.
  11. (a / the)   **12. (— / the)**

DEVASTATING EARTHQUAKE IN HAITI

On _____ afternoon of January 12, 2010, _____ country
    13. (a / the)   **14. (— / the)**

of Haiti was struck by _____ devastating earthquake that registered 7.0 on
    15. (a / the)

_____ Richter Scale. _____ epicenter of _____
16. (a / the)   **17. (An / The)**   **18. (— / the)**

quake was near Leogane, _____ town approximately 16 miles west of Port-
    19. (a / the)

au-Prince, _____ country's capital. According to _____ Haitian
    20. (— / the)   **21. (a / the)**

government, at least 230,000 people were killed, 300,000 injured, and 1,000,000 left homeless.

There was _____ extremely severe damage to _____ infrastructure
    22. (— / an)   **23. (an / the)**

of Port-au-Prince. Many nations responded with humanitarian aid.

EXERCISE 3: Articles

(Grammar Notes 1–2, 4–6, 8)

*Read the two excerpts from the article "Earthweek: A Diary of the Planet." Fill in the blanks
with the articles needed. Leave a blank if no article is necessary.*

Permafrost Warning

_____The_____ melting of permafrost in Sweden's subarctic region due to
1.

global warming is believed to be releasing vast quantities of the greenhouse gas methane

into _____ atmosphere. _____ research team, led by
2.   3.

_____ GeoBiosphere Science Center at Lund University, said its research shows
4.

that _____ part of _____ soil that thaws during summer has
5.   6.

become deeper since 1970, and the permafrost has disappeared entirely in some locations. "This

has led to significant changes in the vegetation and to _____ subsequent increase
7.

in emission of the greenhouse gas methane," the team announced. The team added that methane

is 25 times more damaging to _____ atmosphere than _____
8.   9.

carbon dioxide and often is overlooked in the discussion of greenhouse gases.

Plastic Pollution

_____ German magazine *Geo* published _____ report saying
10.   11.

that _____ plastic trash has created _____ environmental
12.   13.

hazard that stretches across _____ Pacific from California to Hawaii, resulting
14.

in more plastic than plankton on _____ water's surface. _____
15.   16.

March issue quotes biologist Charles Moore of the Algalita Marine Research Foundation as

saying, "Most plastic floats near _____ sea surface where some is mistaken
17.

for _____ food by birds and fishes." The masses of plastic find their way
18.

into _____ Pacific from _____ western United States and
19.   20.

_____ Canada after storms flush the debris downstream and ultimately into
21.

_____ ocean. Maritime observers have witnessed areas of floating plastic that
22.

stretch as far as the eye can see in _____ central Pacific.
23.

EXERCISE 4: Generic Nouns

(Grammar Notes 4, 8)

Write two sentences about each invention or instrument. In the first sentence, write about the item's characteristics. In the second sentence, use the definite article to say when the item was invented.

EXAMPLE: computer / electronic device / process information and perform high-speed calculations / 1944

A computer is an electronic device that processes information and performs high-speed calculations. / Computers are electronic devices that process information and perform high-speed calculations.

The computer was invented in 1944.

1. TV set / electronic device / receive electromagnetic waves, convert waves into images, display them on a screen / 1920s by Farnsworth and Zorinsky

   _____

   _____

2. wheel / circular device / turn around central point / 5,000 to 6,000 years ago

   _____

   _____

3. clarinet / woodwind instrument / use a reed / around 1700

   _____

   _____

4. guitars / stringed instruments / typically have six strings / in the 1400s in Spain

   _____

   _____

5. automobiles / self-powered traveling vehicles / 1874 by Siegfried Marcus in Vienna

   _____

   _____

6. telephones / communication devices / convert sound signals into waves and reconvert them into sounds / 1878 by Alexander Graham Bell

   _____

   _____

Read the student composition about nuclear power. There are nine mistakes in the use of articles. The first mistake is already corrected. Find and correct eight more.

Nuclear Power

Many people today are against ~~the~~ nuclear power. I disagree with them for several reasons. First, we need the additional power sources. We are running out of the petroleum. Many environmentalists say we need to develop the use of geothermal and wind energy. I am certainly not against these sources, and we should work on developing them. But they can't do everything. Then there's the suggestion of hydroelectric power. Many say that even though there are the problems with it, it is better than going nuclear. I am big supporter of hydroelectric power, but it can't provide all the power we need either.

Second, many are against nuclear plants because they believe they are unsafe. They always mention the accidents at Chernobyl and Three-Mile Island as examples. Yes, these were serious problems, but we have learned from them. There haven't been the major problems with nuclear reactors for many years now. We can make nuclear power safe if we develop the strict controls and inspections. France produces about 77 percent of its power from nuclear energy. The French have had the issue of getting rid of nuclear waste, but they are working on it. If the French can do it, other countries can too.

Third, once a device is invented or a process is developed, it can't really be abandoned. Willy Brandt, a former German chancellor, said, "We cannot return to the age of nuclear innocence." We don't live in perfect world. There are potential dangers of using nuclear energy, but there are potential dangers in everything. As far as I am concerned, nuclear power will be necessity in the future.

EXERCISE 6: Listening

A herd of elk

Wolves

A | *Listen to the conversation between a husband and a wife. The conversation is about reintroducing wolves into what places?*

_____

B | *Read the statements. Then listen again to the conversation. Circle the letter of the correct answer.*

1. According to the husband, the newspaper is on the side of _____.
   a. the ranchers and hunters   **b.** the environmentalists

2. Whose point of view does he think is not considered?
   a. the ranchers' and hunters'   **b.** the environmentalists'

3. The husband supports the point of view of _____.
   a. the ranchers and hunters   **b.** the environmentalists

4. The husband _____ a hunter.
   a. is   **b.** is not

5. The husband thinks _____ are dangerous creatures.
   a. wolves in general   **b.** some wolves

6. The wife thinks the husband's idea about wolves killing people is _____.
   a. a stereotype   **b.** basically true

7. The wife supports the point of view of _____.
   a. the ranchers and hunters   **b.** the environmentalists

8. Before 1995, there were too many _____ in Yellowstone.
   a. elk   **b.** wolves

9. According to the wife, some of the _____ elk have been killed off.
   a. old and sick   **b.** young and strong

10. The wife thinks _____ are intelligent and helpful.
    a. some wolves   **b.** wolves in general

EXERCISE 7: Pronunciation

A | *Read and listen to the Pronunciation Note.*

Pronunciation Note
The definite article *the* has two pronunciations: It is pronounced /ðə/ before words beginning with a consonant sound, as in "the statue." It is pronounced /ði/ before words beginning with a vowel sound, as in "the environment."

B | *Listen to the sentences. Underline uses of* **the** *pronounced as* /ðə/. *Circle uses of* **the** *pronounced as* /ði/.

1. (The) environmentalists are from <u>the</u> local college.

2. The inhabitants of Easter Island built the statues themselves.

3. The climate of the area was changed.

4. The forests that used to cover the island are gone.

5. The sad truth is that the Earth's resources are limited.

6. Fortunately, that's not the end of the story.

7. The 11 ruling chiefs were responsible for the problem.

8. Are we overfishing the ocean in the mistaken belief that the supply of seafood is unlimited?

C | *PAIRS: Practice the sentences. Take turns.*

EXERCISE 8: Picture Discussion

GROUPS: Form small groups and discuss the picture. Identify some of the items you see. Then discuss the situation. How can we dispose of items we no longer need or want? What solutions are there to this problem?

> **EXAMPLE:** **A:** I see a lot of plastic bags and cardboard boxes.
> **B:** How do you think we should dispose of things like those?
> **C:** We could recycle as much as possible . . .

EXERCISE 9: Game

*TEAMS: Two teams take turns asking a **who** or **what** question about each answer in the chart. Your teacher directs the game and awards points. Each question can earn two points, one for the correct question and one for correct use of the article.*

> EXAMPLE: A: Answer: The country that owns Easter Island.
> B: Question: What is Chile?

Answers				
The type of tree that used to grow on Easter Island	The ship that sank in the Atlantic in 1912 on its first voyage	The place in a city or town where one keeps one's money	The home country of the first European to see Easter Island	The name of the people who settled Easter Island
The animals that have been reintroduced in national parks	The circular object that was not used in moving the Easter Island statues	The outer covering of a tree	The body of water in which Easter Island is located	The people in a particular circumstance who have a great deal of money
The material from which the Easter Island statues are made	A form of precipitation that is necessary for crops to grow	A form of energy that involves the use of radioactive material	The device invented by Easter Islanders to move their statues	A liquid substance used to produce gasoline
The place in a city or town where one can mail letters	A type of natural phenomenon that devastated the country of Haiti in 2010	The part of the human body that is the seat of intelligence	The nation over which Hurricane Katrina formed	The electronic device invented in 1944 by Farnsworth and Zorinsky
A type of animal killed by wolves in Yellowstone National Park	A woodwind instrument that uses a reed and was invented about 1700	The people in a particular circumstance who are badly off economically	A polluting material in the ocean that birds and fish mistake for food	In the Arctic and subarctic region, the part of the soil that doesn't thaw in the summer

EXERCISE 10: Writing

A | *GROUPS: Choose an environmental issue from the list or develop your own idea. Write three to four paragraphs about the topic you select. Say why you think the issue is important and what should be done about it.*

Possible Issues

- saving endangered animals
- improving air quality
- building nuclear power plants
- disposing of garbage
- ensuring the supply of clean water

EXAMPLE: Laws against air pollution have been in effect for decades now, but we haven't seen much progress in reducing air pollution. Actually, air pollution has gotten worse in many areas. If we want to make real progress, we need stricter laws, and we need to enforce them. There are three areas where we can improve: pollution from automobiles, factories, and the burning of forests. Let's look at each of these separately.

    The automobile . . .

B | *Check your work. Use the Editing Checklist.*

Editing Checklist

Did you use . . . ?
- ☐ definite articles correctly
- ☐ indefinite articles correctly
- ☐ zero articles correctly

A | *Identify each boldfaced word or phrase as non-specific (N), definite (D), or generic (G).*

1. **The clarinet** was invented around the year 1700. _____

2. My parents bought me **a trumpet** when I started band in middle school. _____

3. **The moon** is Earth's only satellite. _____

4. **Water** is an extremely valuable commodity in desert areas. _____

5. In my view, we need to help **the poor** in whatever way we can. _____

6. **The man** who is giving the lecture is my next-door neighbor. _____

7. The ship was hit by **an iceberg** on its maiden voyage. _____

8. There's **water** all over the kitchen floor. _____

B | *Fill in the blanks with **a**, **an**, or **the** where necessary. Leave a blank if no article is needed.*

Disaster at Sea: Many Lives Lost

April 16, 1912. _____ *Titanic*, _____ British steamer, sank in _____ North
          1.   **2.**   **3.**
Atlantic last night after hitting _____ iceberg, disproving its builders' claims that it
                                   4.
couldn't be sunk. _____ ship was on its maiden voyage from Southampton, England, to
                  5.
_____ New York City. More than 1,500 people perished, in large part because _____
  6.   **7.**
lifeboats were felt to take up too much deck space, and there were only 20 of them.

C | *Circle the letter of the underlined word or phrase in each sentence that is not correct.*

1. One of <u>the most famous inventions</u> in <u>the</u> <u>human history</u> is <u>the wheel</u>.   A B C D
                      A   B   C   D

2. <u>The CEO</u> of <u>the company</u> lives in <u>big house</u> in <u>the suburbs</u>.   A B C D
      A   B   C   D

3. <u>Journey</u> is <u>a three-hour trip</u> if <u>the traffic</u> and <u>the weather</u> are OK.   A B C D
      A   B   C   D

4. <u>The plan</u> to build <u>a extensive monorail system</u> is <u>a citizen-initiated proposal</u>.   A B C D
      A   B   C   D

5. <u>The extinction</u> of <u>the dinosaurs</u> is still <u>a matter of debate</u> in   A B C D
        A   B   C
<u>scientific community</u>.
        D

8 Quantifiers
MONEY

STEP 1 GRAMMAR IN CONTEXT

Before You Read

PAIRS: Discuss the questions.

1. Do you pay for most things with cash, with credit cards, or by some other means?
2. What would be the advantages and disadvantages of living in a cashless society?

Read

Read the article about money.

BUSINESS AND YOU · AUGUST 6, 2012 · BUSINESS TODAY

What's Happening to CA$H?

How did money originate, and where? The Babylonians were the first to develop actual "money" when they started to use gold and silver about 2500 B.C.E. In the succeeding centuries, **many** other **items** came to be used as currency, e.g., jewelry, land, and even cattle.

In the last **two centuries**, however, the movement has been away from the physical and toward the abstract. **One example** is fiat money, i.e., paper currency issued by a government. Fiat money isn't based on gold or silver; it has value only because the government says it does. Perhaps the most abstract type of money involves the electronic transfer of funds from **one** bank **account** to another. **No** actual **money** is transferred. The balance in **one account** is simply increased, and the balance in the other decreased correspondingly.

Does this mean that cash no longer has **any advantages**? Not at all. Suppose you're walking down a street and remember you need to buy **some flowers**. You see a vendor

and decide this is the time to buy **a dozen roses**. Do you write a check or pull out your bank card? At this writing, **few** street **vendors** take checks, and even **fewer** take plastic. **Most of them** prefer cash. You

DO YOU TAKE ANY CREDIT CARDS?

What's Happening to CA$H?

simply hand the vendor **a few bills** and happily walk away with your flowers. Pretty easy, huh? It wouldn't be that easy without cash.

Or suppose you'd like to give **a little money** as a gift. It's a lot more personal and pleasing to receive **a few** crisp **bills** in a birthday card than a check. Suppose you're at a food fair and want **a couple of hot dogs**. It's much easier to pull out cash to pay for them. In restaurants these days, it's common to pay with a credit or debit card and include a tip. Sometimes, though, you might want to make a better emotional connection by leaving your server **some** actual **cash** in appreciation of good service.

So cash has its advantages. Of course, it has **a number of disadvantages** as well. You might be robbed. Carrying **a lot of coins** can make holes in your pockets. It's inconvenient to take **a great deal of money** with you to pay for large purchases; imagine trying to carry **enough cash** to pay

for a house or a car—or even a sofa. Besides that, cash has been handled by **many** different **people** and is covered with germs.

Then there's the matter of paying bills. Traditionally, **most people** in North America have used checks, but the trend is to pay electronically. In Japan, payment for such things as heat, electricity, and water is handled by automatic deduction from a bank account. It's much easier than writing out **several checks** to different agencies. And since it's automatic, people don't have to worry about remembering to pay their bills.

There are **a number of disadvantages** to electronic money, however. Some people have **little use** for credit cards, saying that using them encourages us to live beyond our means. Others say using electronic money places too **much control** of our personal finances in the hands of strangers. Mistakes are easily made and hard to correct.

The jury is still out on whether the trend toward **less and less use** of cash is good or bad. What seems clear is that it's definitely growing.

After You Read

A | **Vocabulary:** *Match the blue words and phrases on the left with their meanings on the right.*

_____ **1.** In the **succeeding** centuries, many other items came to be used as currency.

_____ **2.** Many other items came to be used as currency, **e.g.**, jewelry, land, and cattle.

_____ **3.** **Fiat** money isn't based on gold or silver.

_____ **4.** The balance in the other account is **correspondingly** decreased.

_____ **5.** At this writing even fewer vendors **take plastic**.

_____ **6.** It's more personal to receive a few **crisp** bills than a check.

_____ **7.** Some say using credit cards encourages us to **live beyond our means**.

_____ **8.** **The jury is still out** on whether the trend toward less use of cash is good or bad.

_____ **9.** One example is fiat money, **i.e.**, paper currency issued by a government.

a. live a lifestyle we can't afford

b. the evidence isn't yet conclusive

c. in a parallel manner

d. specially authorized

e. following

f. firm or fresh

g. for example

h. that is

i. accept credit cards for payment

B | Comprehension: *Refer to the reading and complete each sentence with a single word.*

1. In recent years money has become less physical and more _____.

2. Fiat money has value only because a _____ says it has value.

3. Most street vendors would rather have _____ than take a check or credit card.

4. We often leave a server a tip to show appreciation for good _____.

5. It's inconvenient to use cash to pay for large _____.

6. Since many people have used physical money, it may be covered with _____.

7. The trend in bill paying is to pay _____.

8. With electronic money, _____ can exert control of our personal finances.

STEP 2 GRAMMAR PRESENTATION

QUANTIFIERS

Quantifiers	With Count Nouns	With Non-Count Nouns
One	**One store** is open.	Ø*
Each	**Each coin** is valuable.	Ø
Every	**Every bank** is closed.	Ø
Two	**Two stores** are open.	Ø
Both	**Both stores** are nearby.	Ø
A couple of	She bought **a couple of gifts**.	Ø
Several	She bought **several gifts**.	Ø
Few	They have **few investments**.	Ø
A few	She has **a few investments**.	Ø
Many	Does he own **many buildings**?	Ø
A great many	He owns **a great many buildings**.	Ø
A number of	He owns **a number of buildings**.	Ø
Little	Ø	They have **little money**.
A little	Ø	She has **a little money**.
Much	Ø	Does he have **much property**?
A great deal of	Ø	He owns **a great deal of property**.
No	They have **no bonds**.	They have **no insurance**.
Any	They don't have **any bonds**.	They don't have **any insurance**.
Some	They have **some stocks**.	They have **some cash**.
Enough	You have **enough stocks**.	You have **enough cash**.
A lot of / Lots of	He has **a lot of / lots of clients**.	He has **a lot of / lots of patience**.
Plenty of	He has **plenty of clients**.	He has **plenty of patience**.
Most	**Most banks** are safe.	**Most work** is useful.
All	**All banks** are insured.	**All work** is tiring.

*Ø: quantifier not used

GRAMMAR NOTES

1	**Quantifiers** state the number or amount of something. Quantifiers can be single words or phrases.	• I bought **a dozen tulips**. • There's **some money** in my account.
	Quantifiers are used with both nouns and pronouns.	• **A lot of people** vacation in the summer. • **Most of us** are going on the trip.
	Quantifiers are often used alone if the noun or pronoun has just been mentioned, as in a question.	**A:** Have you made **many friends** here? **B:** Yes, I've made **a lot**.

2	**Quantifiers** are used with different types of nouns: **a.** with singular count nouns: *one, each, every*, etc.	• I took **each item** back to the store. • We were able to solve **every problem**.
	b. with plural count nouns: *two, both, a couple of, a dozen, several, few, a few, many, a great many, a number of*, etc.	• We visited **a couple of countries**. • We bought **a few souvenirs**.
	c. with non-count nouns: *a little, little, much, a great deal of, a great amount of*, etc.	• I only make **a little money** at that job. • She earns **a great deal of money**.
	d. with both plural count nouns and non-count nouns: *no, any, some, enough, a lot of / lots of, plenty of, most, all*, etc.	• She has **no plans** to travel. • We took **no cash** on the trip.

3	Use *a few / few* with count nouns and *a little / little* with non-count nouns.	• Mary has **a few investments**. • She has saved **a little money**.

	Note the difference between *a few* and *few* and between *a little* and *little*. *A few* and *a little* are used to give a statement a positive sense. They mean "some—not a great number or amount but enough to be satisfactory."	• I have **a few** good **friends**.
		  (= some; enough to satisfy)
		• We have **a little food** at home.
		  (= some; enough to satisfy)

	Few and *little* are used to give a statement a negative sense. They mean "hardly any" or "not much at all—not enough to be satisfactory."	• Jerry has **few friends**.
		  (= not enough to be satisfactory)
		• Mary has **little self-confidence**.
		  (= not enough to be satisfactory)

	NOTE: If we add the word **only** to *a few* or *a little*, the positive sense disappears.	• I have **only a few** friends. *(= I would like more.)* • I have **only a little** money. *(= I would like more.)*
	BE CAREFUL! In comparison, use **fewer** with count nouns and **less** with non-count nouns. Use **more** with both count and non-count nouns.	• I have **fewer problems** than I used to. • I earn **less money**, though. • I have **more friends**. • I also have **more self-confidence**.

(continued on next page)

4 Use *many* with count nouns and *much* with non-count nouns.

- He doesn't have **many friends**.
- I don't have **much trouble** getting to work.

Use *a great many* with count nouns and *a great deal of* with non-count nouns. These quantifiers are rather formal and used more in writing than in speech.

- The government has **a great many responsibilities**.
- Presidents are under **a great deal of stress**.

BE CAREFUL! *Much* is not often used in affirmative sentences, especially in speech. It is usually replaced by *a lot of* or *lots of*.

- We spend **a lot of money** on rent.
- There's **lots of construction** going on.

However, *much* is common in questions, negative statements, and in combination with the adverb *too*.

- Did they spend **much money**?
- She doesn't watch **much TV**.
- I ate **too much** for dinner.

Use *number* with count nouns and *amount* with non-count nouns.

- The **number of students** attending college has increased.
- The **amount of stress** in people's lives seems to be increasing.

5 Use *some* and *any* with count nouns and non-count nouns.

- Did you make **some / any purchases**?
- Do you have **some / any cash** with you?

Use *some* in affirmative statements.

- Bill bought **some souvenirs**.
- He borrowed **some money** from me.

Use *any* in negative statements.

- Alice didn't take **any trips**.
- She didn't have **any money**.

Use both *some* and *any* in questions. In general, use *some* in offers and *any* in negative questions.

- Did you buy **some / any clothes**?
- Would you like **some soda**?
- Didn't you send **any postcards**?

BE CAREFUL! Don't use two negatives in the same simple sentence.

- Jack **didn't** understand **anything**.
  Not: Jack didn't understand nothing.

6 Many **quantifiers** appear in phrases with the preposition *of*. Use *of* + *the* or another determiner when you are specifying particular persons, places, things, or groups.

- **Most of the EU countries** are using the euro.
- We saw **many of her films**.

We generally use quantifiers without *of* when we have no particular person, place, thing, or group in mind.

- **Most people** don't understand the economy.
- **Many restaurants** take credit cards.

BE CAREFUL! Quantifiers with *of* can be used only with plural count nouns and non-count nouns.

- **Most of the coins** were very old.
- **Most of the gold** was pure.
  Not: <s>Most of</s> the coin was very old.

NOTE: Quantifiers such as *most of* and *many of* can be followed by a singular or a plural verb, depending on the noun that follows *of*.

- Most of the **food has** been eaten
  (non-count noun + singular verb)
- Most of the **people have** arrived.
  (plural noun + plural verb)

REFERENCE NOTE
For more information on **count and non-count nouns**, see Unit 7.

STEP 3 FOCUSED PRACTICE

EXERCISE 1: Discover the Grammar

Look at the sentences based on the opening reading. Could they be rewritten using the words in parentheses without changing the basic meaning or creating an incorrect sentence? Write Y (Yes) or N (No).

___N___ **1.** This is a trend that has been developing for *many* years now. (much)

_____ **2.** Are there still *any* advantages to cash? (some)

_____ **3.** You suddenly remember you need to buy *some* flowers. (any)

_____ **4.** At this writing, *few* flower vendors take checks. (a few)

_____ **5.** *Few* vendors take plastic. (little)

_____ **6.** Suppose you'd like to give *a little* money as a gift. (little)

_____ **7.** It's *much* easier to pull out cash to pay for them. (a lot)

_____ **8.** Cash has *some* disadvantages as well. (any)

_____ **9.** Cash has been handled by *many* different people. (a lot of)

_____ **10.** *Most* people have paid their bills with checks. (a great deal of)

_____ **11.** It's easier than writing out *several* checks. (a little)

_____ **12.** Some people have *little* use for credit cards. (a little)

EXERCISE 2: Quantifiers

(Grammar Notes 2–5)

Complete the sentences by choosing the correct quantifier. The sentences are connected in a story.

1. We just got back from our second trip to Europe. This time we visited _____*fewer*_____

    countries. (less / fewer)

2. We didn't visit _____ of the Scandinavian countries this time. (some / any)

3. We spent _____ money this time too. (less / fewer)

4. We did buy _____ wonderful souvenirs, though. (some / any)

5. The last time we rented a car and were amazed by the _____ cars on the roads.

    (amount of / number of)

6. This time we traveled by train. We expected _____ people to be traveling that

    way. (much / a lot of)

7. However, there weren't very _____. (much / many)

8. We had _____ problems finding seats in the railroad cars. We never had to

    stand. (few / a few)

9. That's a good thing. My husband has _____ patience when it comes to

    competing with other passengers for places to sit. (little / a little)

10. The trip was so economical that we had _____ extra money at the end. (little /

    a little).

EXERCISE 3: Quantifiers

(Grammar Notes 2–6)

Ron and Ashley Lamont are trying to save money for a trip to South America. They are examining their budget. Complete their conversation with quantifiers from the box, using each expression once.

$50	a lot of	every	less	much
a couple of	both of	few	more	one of
a few	enough	fewer	most of	some

ASHLEY: Ron, we're still spending _____*a lot of*_____ money on things we don't really need. After
                                         1.

I pay the bills this month, we're going to have even _____ cash left over than
                                                         2.

we did last month. We're supposed to be saving for the trip to South America, remember?

We're not saving _____ money. If we don't start saving _____,
                         3.   **4.**

we won't be able to go.

RON: What have we bought that we don't need?

ASHLEY: That exercise machine, for one thing. We've only used it _____ times. We

        5.

        could get a year's membership at the gym for what it cost and still have something left over.

RON: You mean _____ us could get a membership, don't you?

        6.

ASHLEY: No, _____ us could. That's what I'm saying. The machine cost $500, and

        7.

        memberships are $200 each. Let's sell the thing and go to the gym.

RON: Hmm. Maybe you're right. What else?

ASHLEY: Well, we're spending about _____ extra a month on those premium cable

        8.

        channels. We'd have _____ channels to choose from if we went back to the

        9.

        basic coverage, but we don't watch _____ TV anyway.

        10.

RON: Yeah, you're right . . . And you know, I'd say we could get rid of call waiting on the phone.

        We've used it *very* _____ times, and _____ my friends say they

        11.   12.

        hate it when they call, and then another call comes in while we're talking.

ASHLEY: Uh-huh. Let's cancel it, then. And here's one more suggestion. We should start taking a bag

        lunch to work _____ times a week instead of going out at noon. If we did

        13.

        these four things, we'd have _____ money left _____ month

        14.   15.

        that could go into our trip fund.

RON: Oh no! Not my lunches with the boys! Lunchtime is when I get to see them.

ASHLEY: Invite them over to play volleyball. Then think of Rio de Janeiro.

EXERCISE 4: Numbers

Look at the chart. Then complete each sentence with the appropriate quantifier from the box.
Use one quantifier twice.

Note: The figures are approximations.

	The World in 1960	The World in 2003–2009
Population	3,020,100,000	6, 829,360 (2009)
Birth rate per thousand people	31.2	19.86 (2009)
Death rate per thousand people	17.7	8.37 (2009)
Female life expectancy at birth	51.9 years	68.07 years (2009)
Male life expectancy at birth	48.6 years	64.29 years (2009)
Electricity use per person	1,445 kilowatt hours	2.596 kilowatt hours (2005)
TV sets per thousand people	112.8	215.5 (2003)
Gross domestic product per person	$2,607	$10,386 (2009)

a great deal of	fewer	more		the number of
~~a great many~~	less	the amount of		

1. ___A great many___ people were born between 1960 and 2009.

2. There were _____ births per thousand people in 2009 than in 1960.

3. There were _____ deaths per thousand people in 1960 than in 2009.

4. The life expectancy of men is _____ than that of women.

5. On the average, _____ females lived to be older than 52 or males older than 49

   in 1960 than today.

6. There was _____ growth in the use of electricity between 1960 and 2005.

7. There was a big increase in _____ TV sets in the world between 1960 and 2003.

8. _____ gross domestic product in 2009 was almost four times that of 1960.

EXERCISE 5: Editing

Read the excerpt from a president's speech. There are eight mistakes in the use of quantifiers. The first one is already corrected. Find and correct seven more.

THE WHITE HOUSE
WASHINGTON

My fellow citizens: We are at a time in our history when we need to make some real

                                          a great many

sacrifices. Recent presidents have made ~~a great deal of~~ promises they didn't keep. Tonight

you deserve to hear the truth. On the economy, we've made little progress, but we still have

a great many work to do, so I'm proposing several measures. First, I want to raise taxes on

the very wealthy because a few of them really pay their share. Second, many members of

the middle class are carrying an unfair tax burden, so I'm asking for a tax cut for them. If

I'm successful, most of you in the middle class will pay 10 percent less in taxes next year,

though a few of you in the higher-income group may see your taxes rise little. Third, there

are much loopholes in the current law that allow some people to avoid paying any taxes at

all; I want to close these loopholes.

    Further problems are that we have very few money available for health care reform, and

we've made a little progress in reducing pollution and meeting clean air standards.

Therefore, as my final measure, I am asking for a 50-cent-a-gallon tax on gasoline, which

will result in many more people using public transportation and should create additional

revenue. Thus, we will have enough money to finance our new health care program and

will be helping the environment at the same time.

EXERCISE 6: Listening

A | *Listen to the conversation in a restaurant. Who chose the restaurant?*

_____

B | *Read the questions. Then listen again and circle the letter of the correct answer.*

1. Which restaurant has fewer menu choices?

   (a.) this restaurant   **b.** the last restaurant

2. At which restaurant does the food cost less?

   a. this restaurant   **b.** the last restaurant

3. How much money does Steve have?

   a. none at all   **b.** a few dollars

4. Does Steve have enough money to pay the bill?

   a. yes   **b.** no

5. How much is the bill?

   a. $75   **b.** $45

6. How many credit cards does Steve have?

   a. one   **b.** none at all

7. Do Mary and Steve have enough money together to pay the bill?

   a. yes   **b.** no

8. Are there any ATM machines nearby?

   a. Yes, there are.   **b.** No, there aren't.

EXERCISE 7: Pronunciation

A | *Read and listen to the Pronunciation Note.*

Pronunciation Note

Remember that a vowel in an unstressed syllable normally takes **the schwa /ə/ sound**. Using the schwa sound correctly in unstressed syllables is important for being understood and for improving one's accent. For example, in the word *thousand*, the first vowel, represented by *ou*, is stressed. The second vowel, represented by *a*, is unstressed and has a schwa sound.

B | *Listen to the sentences. Then listen again and repeat. Circle the syllables that have no stress and in which the vowel assumes a schwa sound. The number in parentheses indicates the number of such syllables in the sentence.*

1. (A) lot (of) peo(ple) vaca(tion) here. (4)

2. I have fewer problems than I used to. (2)

3. She doesn't watch much television. (3)

4. Presidents are under a great deal of stress. (4)

5. We are facing a great many challenges today. (4)

6. The amount of money I earn is minimal. (4)

7. The number of students in colleges is growing. (6)

8. I took each item back to the store. (3)

C | *PAIRS: Practice the sentences. Take turns.*

EXERCISE 8: Game

TEAMS: Form two teams. Each team uses its prompts to construct eight questions about world facts, using quantifiers. Then each team creates two questions of its own, for a total of 10 questions. The other team tries to answer each question correctly, using a complete sentence. For answers, see page G-AK2.

> **EXAMPLE:**   country / more / people / China / India
> **A:** Which country has more people, China or India?
> **B:** China has more people.

Team A's Prompts
1. country / fewer / people / Canada / Mexico
2. country / more / land area / Canada / the United States
3. country / produce / less / oil / Venezuela / Mexico
4. country / no / snowfall / Somalia / Tanzania
5. country / fewer / rivers / Libya / Nigeria
6. country / smaller number / people / Monaco / Cyprus
7. country / produce / large amount / gold / Nigeria / South Africa
8. city / less / rainfall / Aswan, Egypt / Athens, Greece
9. _____
10. _____

(continued on next page)

1. country / fewer / people / Great Britain / Spain
2. country / more / land area / Australia / Brazil
3. country / produce / less / oil / the United States / Saudi Arabia
4. country / no / military / Colombia / Costa Rica
5. country / fewer / rivers / Yemen / Turkey
6. country / smaller number / people / San Marino / Kuwait
7. country / use / larger amount / nuclear energy / the Netherlands / France
8. city / less / rainfall / Antofagasta, Chile / Nairobi, Kenya
9. _____
10. _____

EXERCISE 9: Personal Inventory

A | *Compare your life now to your life five years ago. Write eight sentences, using each of the quantifiers from the box.*

a few	a little	a lot	fewer	less	many	more	much

EXAMPLE: I have **more friends** now than I did five years ago.

B | *PAIRS: Discuss the changes in your life with your partner.*

C | *CLASS: Report interesting examples to the entire class.*

EXERCISE 10: Writing

A | *Write three or four paragraphs about an interesting experience you have had with money. Choose one of the topics or create your own topic. Use quantifiers where appropriate.*

- a time when you ran out of money
- a time when you tipped too much or too little
- a time when you lost your wallet or purse

EXAMPLE: The most interesting experience I've had with money was when I was visiting New York. I had gone to a restaurant and ordered an expensive meal. I thought I had enough money to pay for the meal, but I had a big surprise. Here's how it happened . . .

B | *Check your work. Use the Editing Checklist.*

Editing Checklist

Did you use . . . ?
☐ quantifiers with count nouns correctly
☐ quantifiers with non-count nouns correctly

Check your answers on page UR-1.
Do you need to review anything?

A | Circle the correct word or phrase to complete each sentence.

1. Most / Most of people enjoy eating a well-cooked meal.

2. The number of / amount of traffic on the freeway today is astounding.

3. I'd like to help you, but I don't have some / any time today.

4. My son Ali earned a lot of / much money at his part-time job.

5. Can you please get me a couple / a couple of candy bars at the store?

6. The number of / The amount of patients has increased.

7. About how much / many people live in your home town?

8. Bobby's problem is that he has little / a little motivation to get a job.

9. We have plenty / plenty of glasses and plates, so don't bring any.

10. We have any / no money left after our night on the town.

B | In the blank after each sentence, write a quantifier with a meaning similar to the underlined word or phrase.

1. We have made a lot of friends in our new neighborhood.   _____

2. I don't have a lot of work to finish this afternoon.   _____

3. He has a great deal of money in the bank.   _____

4. Andrea has some problems in her new job.   _____

5. We have many disagreements with your plan.   _____

6. Each person in the class earned a good score.   _____

C | Circle the letter of the underlined word or phrase in each sentence that is not correct.

1. There's just too <u>much</u> traffic on the road today; the <u>amount</u> of people   **A B C D**
                A   **B**
    driving is incredible, and I've never seen this <u>many</u> cars in <u>one</u> place.
                                          C   **D**

2. I have <u>less</u> money and <u>fewer</u> friends, but <u>a little</u> stress and <u>no</u> complaints.   **A B C D**
         A   **B**   **C**   **D**

3. <u>Many of</u> <u>my co-workers</u> work hard, but <u>a few</u> don't do <u>nothing</u>.   **A B C D**
    A   **B**   **C**   **D**

4. <u>A great deal of</u> the <u>people who work</u> in our office have <u>a lot of</u>   **A B C D**
        A   **B**   **C**
    experience but <u>less</u> training than I would expect.
                   D

9 Modification of Nouns
EXPECTATIONS

STEP 1 GRAMMAR IN CONTEXT

Before You Read

PAIRS: Discuss the questions.

1. What is the difference between hoping for something to happen and expecting it to happen? Discuss this with your classmates.

2. In your experience, does what you expect to happen usually happen? Give an example.

3. How can expectations be a negative force? How can they be a positive force?

Read

Read the article about expectations.

POCKET DIGEST

THE EXPECTATION SYNDROME
I Hope for It, but I Don't Expect It
by Jessica Taylor

Picture the scene: It's the **29th Summer** Olympics in Beijing, China. The **Women's** Marathon is about at the **halfway** point when a **Romanian** runner, Constantina Dita, suddenly surges to the front of the pack. Most viewers probably expect her to hold the lead for a **short** time before relinquishing it to the favorites, who include **Kenyan** runner Catherine Ndereba and **Chinese** runner Zhou Chunxiu. Few if any expect Dita to win the **gold** medal—but win she does. As she enters the stadium, Dita begins to slow a bit, but the **roaring** crowd reenergizes her and enables her to win the race with a time of two hours, 26 minutes, a **22-second** lead over the **silver** medalist. The **38-year-old** Dita, who managed only a **20th-place** finish in the **2004 Athens** Olympics, becomes the **oldest women's marathon** champion.

Now picture another situation: Your **film-buff** friends have seen the **Academy Award-winning** *Avatar*. They rave about its **superb color** photography, its **fantastic computer-generated** scenes of **strange-looking, otherworldly** creatures, and its **awesome special 3-D** effects. They praise its **serious** but **heartwarming** treatment of the **age-old** conflict between exploiters and those they exploit. They say it's the **best English-language** movie in **recent** years. When you see it, though, you're disappointed. You don't find it as excellent as everyone has been saying. In fact, you feel it's a **predictable**, rather **tedious** movie—basically just another **special-effects fantasy** film.

THE EXPECTATION SYNDROME

These situations illustrate what we might call "the **expectation** syndrome," a condition in which events do not turn out as we feel they will or should. Sometimes children do not meet their **parents' career** expectations of them; athletes do not win the contests people expect them to win; **great** literature doesn't live up to its reputation. I asked psychiatrist Robert Stevens whether expectations can actually make things turn out negatively, or whether we're merely talking about an **unpleasant**, **frustrating** irony of the **human** condition.

RS: Well, the mind has **immense** power to control outcomes. For example, there's a **medical** condition called "**focal** dystonia"—an **abnormal muscle** function caused by **extreme** concentration. Somehow, when athletes are concentrating too hard, **certain brain** functions are affected. They miss the basket, don't hit the ball, or lose the race. In effect, they're letting their expectations control them.

JT: Have you ever experienced this phenomenon in your **everyday** life?

RS: Yes. Here's a **personal** example from skiing that shows that the mind has **tremendous** power to control things. There are days when, as a **cautious intermediate** skier, I stand at the top of a **steep**, **icy** slope, plotting my **every** move down the course, fearing I'll fall. Sure enough, I do fall. Other days I feel different. My expectations are miles away. I forget about myself, ski well, and don't fall. When we focus excessively on goals, our expectations can take over and place us outside the process. On the other hand, when we concentrate on the process instead of the goal, we're usually more successful. Have you heard the phrase "trying too hard"? That's what people often do.

JT: Very interesting. What's your recommendation about expectations, then?

RS: Just that it's better to hope for things than to expect them.

After You Read

A | Vocabulary: *Match the blue words and phrases on the left with their meanings on the right.*

_____ 1. We see the Romanian runner suddenly **surge** to the front of the pack.

_____ 2. Most viewers probably think she will soon **relinquish** the lead in the race.

_____ 3. Dita is the oldest women's **marathon** champion.

_____ 4. Your film-**buff** friends have seen *Avatar*.

_____ 5. The film has many scenes of **otherworldly** creatures.

_____ 6. The film is about people who **exploit** others.

_____ 7. These situations illustrate "the expectation **syndrome**."

_____ 8. Great literature doesn't always **live up to** its reputation.

_____ 9. Are we talking about a frustrating **irony** of the human condition?

_____ 10. It's a predictable, rather **tedious** movie.

a. boring, and continuing for a long time

b. extraterrestrial

c. condition opposite to what is expected

d. set of physical or mental conditions that show you have a problem

e. person interested in and knowledgeable about something

f. move forward powerfully

g. equal

h. give up

i. take unfair advantage of someone

j. footrace of 26 miles, 385 yards (42.2 kilometers)

B | Comprehension: *Circle* **T (True)** *or* **F (False)**. *Correct the false statements.*

1. Constantina Dita takes the lead about three-fourths of the way through the marathon.   **T**   **F**

2. Dita is the favorite to win the marathon.   **T**   **F**

3. Most spectators expect Dita to win the gold medal.   **T**   **F**

4. Dita is energized when she enters the stadium to complete the race.   **T**   **F**

5. Dita won a medal in the 2004 Athens Olympics.   **T**   **F**

6. To date, Dita is the oldest woman to win the marathon.   **T**   **F**

7. Among other things, *Avatar* is about people who take advantage of others unfairly.   **T**   **F**

8. The expectation syndrome occurs when events do not turn out as we want.   **T**   **F**

9. The human mind often controls outcomes of situations.   **T**   **F**

10. Expectations take over when we don't focus enough on goals.   **T**   **F**

MODIFICATION OF NOUNS

	Adjective Modifier	Noun Modifier	Head Noun
I remember the		Summer	Olympics.
	wonderful		athletes.
	amazing	volleyball	games.
	unexpected	Romanian	victory.

Order of Adjective Modifiers								
	Opinion	Size	Age	Shape	Color	Origin	Material	
I saw a	great		new			French		movie.
I met its	fascinating		young			Chinese		director.
She had		large		round			jade	earrings.
She wore a		long			red		silk	dress.

Several Adjective Modifiers	
Different Modifier Categories	Same Modifier Category
A **great new epic** movie	A **serious**, **profound**, and **heartwarming** movie
	A **serious**, **profound**, **heartwarming** movie
	A **heartwarming**, **profound**, **serious** movie

Compound Modifiers		
The movie has lots of	**computer-generated**	scenes.
	strange-looking	creatures.
The main character is a	**10-year-old**	girl.
	long-haired, short-legged	boy.

GRAMMAR NOTES

1 Nouns can be modified both by adjectives and by other nouns. **Adjective** and **noun modifiers** usually come before the noun they modify. The noun that is modified is called the head noun.

ADJECTIVE MODIFIERS   NOUN MODIFIER
• Yao Ming is a **famous Chinese basketball**

HEAD NOUN
player.

2 **Noun modifiers** usually come directly before the nouns they modify.

When there are both adjective and noun modifiers, the noun modifier comes closer to the head noun.

• **Milk chocolate** is chocolate made with milk.
• **Chocolate milk** is milk with chocolate in it.

ADJ. MOD. NOUN MOD. HEAD NOUN
• Pelé is a **famous soccer player**.

(continued on next page)

3 Two common types of **adjective modifiers** are present participles and past participles (also called **participial adjectives**).

- It was a **boring** movie.
- The **bored** viewers left.

Remember that participial adjectives that end in *-ing* describe someone or something that causes a feeling.

- The result of the game was **shocking**.
- The news is **exciting**.

Participial adjectives that end in *-ed* describe someone who experiences a feeling.

- We were **shocked** by the result.
- Everyone is **excited** by the news.

4 When there is **more than one modifier** of a noun, the modifiers generally occur in a **fixed order**. The following list shows the usual order of common adjective and noun modifiers. The order can be changed by the emphasis a speaker wants to give to a particular adjective.

NOTE: Avoid using more than three adjective modifiers before a noun.

Position	Category of Modifier	
1	Opinions	• ugly, beautiful, dull, interesting
2	Size	• big, tall, long, short
3	Age or temperature	• old, young, hot, cold
4	Shapes	• square, round, oval, diamond
5	Colors	• red, blue, pink, purple
6	Origins, nationalities, or social classes	• computer-generated, Brazilian, Chinese, middle-class
7	Materials	• wood, cotton, denim, silk, glass

5 When a noun has **two or more modifiers** in the **same category**, separate the adjectives with a comma. If the modifiers are in different categories, do not separate the adjectives with a comma.

- He is a **serious, hardworking** student.
- I bought a **beautiful denim** shirt.

NOTE: The order of adjectives in the same category can vary.

- He is a **serious, hardworking** student.
- He is a **hardworking, serious** student.

6 Compound modifiers are constructed from more than one word. Here are four common kinds:

a. number + noun

- I work in a **10-story** building.

b. noun + present participle

- It's a **prize-winning** film.

c. noun + past participle

- It's a **crime-related** problem.

d. adjective + past participle

- The actor plays a **long-haired, one-armed** pirate in the movie.

When compound modifiers precede a noun, they are generally hyphenated.

BE CAREFUL! Plural nouns used as modifiers become singular when they come before the noun.

- Her daughter is 10 years old.
- She has a **10-year-old** daughter.
  NOT: She has a ~~10-years-old~~ daughter.

7 **BE CAREFUL!** In written English, avoid having more than two noun modifiers together. Using too many noun modifiers in sequence can be confusing. Look at the example: Is Jerry a student who won an award for painting portraits? Is Jerry a painter who won an award for painting students? Is the award given by the students?

- Jerry Gonzales won the **student portrait painter** award.

To avoid confusing sentences like this, break up the string of noun modifiers with prepositional phrases or rearrange the modifiers in some other way.

- Jerry Gonzales won the award for painting portraits of students.
  OR
- Student Jerry Gonzales won the award for painting portraits.

STEP 3 FOCUSED PRACTICE

EXERCISE 1: Discover the Grammar

Read the sentences based on the opening article. Circle all head nouns that have noun or adjective modifiers before them. Underline adjective modifiers once and noun modifiers twice.

1. It's the 29th Summer (Olympics).

2. The Women's Marathon is about at the halfway point when a Romanian runner surges to the head of the pack.

3. Dita finishes the race with a 22-second lead over the silver medalist.

4. The 38-year-old Dita managed only a 20th-place finish in the 2004 Athens Olympics.

(continued on next page)

5. Your film-buff friends have seen the Academy Award–winning *Avatar*.

6. They love its strange-looking creatures and awesome special effects.

7. They admire its serious but heartwarming treatment of the age-old conflict between exploiters and those they exploit.

8. Children sometimes do not meet their parents' career expectations of them.

9. "Focal dystonia" is an abnormal muscle function caused by extreme concentration.

10. I stand at the top of a steep, icy slope, plotting my every move down the course.

EXERCISE 2: Multiple Modifiers   *(Grammar Notes 4–5)*

Bill and Nancy are dressing for a party being thrown by Nancy's new boss. Nancy isn't sure what is expected and is very worried about making a good impression. Unscramble the modifiers in their conversation. Place commas where they are needed.

BILL: This is a ___*formal office*___ party, isn't it? What if I wear my _____ tie?
        1. (office / formal)   **2. (silk / new)**

NANCY: That's fine, but don't wear that _____ shirt with it. People will think
        3. (purple / denim / ugly)

you don't have any _____ clothes.
                    4. (suitable / dress-up)

BILL: So what? Why should I pretend I like to dress up when I don't?

NANCY: Because there are going to be a lot of _____ businesspeople
                                                5. (interesting / important)

there, and I want to make a _____ impression. It's my job,
                            6. (memorable / good)

remember? I don't want people to think I have a(n) _____
                                                    7. (unstylish / sloppy)

dresser for a husband, which of course you're not. Humor me just this once, OK, sweetie?

Hmm . . . I wonder if I should wear my _____ earrings or the
                                        8. (round / sapphire / blue)

_____ ones.
9. (green / oval / emerald)

(Later, at the party.)

NANCY: Hi, Paul. This is Bill, my husband.

PAUL: Welcome. Bill, I'm glad to meet you. You two are our first guests to arrive. Help yourselves

to snacks. There are some _____ sandwiches. You know, Nancy, I'm
                            10. (tomato-and-cheese / excellent)

sorry I didn't make it clear this isn't a _____ party. You two look
                                        11. (dress-up / fancy)

great, but I hope you won't feel out of place.

BILL: Thanks. We'll be fine. By the way, Paul, I really like that _____ shirt
                                                                12. (beautiful / denim / purple)

you're wearing. Where did you get it?

EXERCISE 3: Compound Modifiers

(Grammar Note 6)

*Complete the sentences with compound modifiers. Add the indefinite article **a / an** in all but Item 8.*

Pam and Allen Murray took their son Joshua to a reading specialist because Joshua could

not read aloud in class. Dr. Tanaka, the specialist, asked Joshua a number of questions about his

problems with reading. Joshua said that he got frustrated in his reading class, that even though it

was only _____ *a 50-minute* _____ period, it seemed to him like a year. During this
1. (lasting 50 minutes)

particular semester, the teacher was giving the students oral reading assignments every day. At first

the teacher had called on Joshua to read aloud, and Joshua would panic every time, even if it was

only _____ assignment. Now she was no longer calling on him.
2. (one paragraph in length)

Dr. Tanaka asked Joshua if he had any problems with silent reading. Joshua said he didn't, adding

that he loved to read to himself and could finish _____ book in a
3. (300 pages in length)

day or two. Pam, Joshua's mother, noted that his reading comprehension was excellent.

Dr. Tanaka asked Pam and Allen how long this problem had been going on. Allen said it had

begun when Joshua was in the first grade. Since Joshua was now 12, the situation had been

_____ ordeal. Dr. Tanaka wondered how the problem had started.
4. (lasting six years)

Pam replied that she felt it was definitely _____ problem, for Joshua
5. (related to stress)

had lisped when he started school. Joshua added that he had felt bad when the other children would

laugh at him when he pronounced his "s" sounds as "th" sounds. The problem simply got worse until

Joshua was no longer able to read orally at all.

Dr. Tanaka agreed that teasing might have caused Joshua's problem but suggested another

possibility—that Joshua's inability to read aloud could be _____
6. (related to eyesight)

problem. He asked if it would be all right to test Joshua's vision. When the Murrays agreed,

Dr. Tanaka asked Joshua to read two eye charts, which he was able to read perfectly. He

then asked Joshua to read a short passage that he held at a distance. The passage went

like this: "Night was falling in Dodge City. The gunfighter walked down the street wearing

_____ hat."
7. (holding 10 gallons)

Joshua read the passage with no difficulty at all, and Dr. Tanaka said he felt he now

understood Joshua's problem well: He had _____ anxiety.
8. (induced by performance)

(continued on next page)

He told the Murrays he had distracted Joshua by referring to his vision. He then said he had

_____ program that would have Joshua reading aloud proficiently
9. (lasting two months)

if he was willing to try it. Joshua was more than willing, so the Murrays made arrangements to start

the program soon.

EXERCISE 4: Creative Sentences   *(Grammar Notes 2–4, 6)*

*Write a sentence for each phrase, changing the phrase so that the modifier appears before
the head noun. Use correct punctuation.*

1. a flight that takes 10 hours

   Last month I was on a 10-hour flight from Bogotá to Buenos Aires.

2. a cat that has long hair

   _____

3. a jacket that is old and comfortable

   _____

4. an experience that amuses and interests you

   _____

5. a child who is 11 years old

   _____

6. a movie that wins an award

   _____

7. a table that has three legs

   _____

8. people who look unusual

   _____

9. a skirt that is made of cotton, is short, and is blue

   _____

10. a bowl originating in China and made of jade

_____

11. a building that has 60 stories

_____

12. a bag that weighs 90 pounds

_____

EXERCISE 5: Editing

Read the entry from medical student Jennifer Yu's computer journal. There are eight mistakes in the use of modifiers. The first mistake is already corrected. Find and correct seven more.

FRIDAY: It's midnight, the end of a long day. My first week of ~~school medical~~ _medical school_ is over,

and I'm exhausted but happy! I'm so glad I decided to go to the university. It was

definitely a good decision. I'm not completely sure yet, but I think I want to go into

psychiatry child because I love working with children—especially nine- and

ten-years-old kids.

Yesterday our psychiatry class visited a large new hospital where many middle-class

troubled children go for treatment. I expected to see a lot of boys and girls behaving

badly, but most of them were pretty quiet and relaxed. They just looked like they

needed some warm, personal attention.

Today in our surgery class we had a bright, hardworking teacher, a Brazilian young

doctor who was substituting for our usual professor. We got a helpful foreign viewpoint

on things.

The only thing I don't like about medical school is the cafeteria disgusting food. I'm

going to have to start getting some hot tasty Chinese food from my local favorite place.

Well, it's time for me to get some sleep. I hope this computer new program works

correctly.

EXERCISE 6: Listening

A | *Joshua Murray is working on his reading program with Dr. Tanaka. Read the statements. Then listen to their conversation. Check (✓)* **True** *or* **False**.

		True	False
1.	The first session will last only 30 minutes.	✓	☐
2.	Joshua likes his own voice.	☐	☐
3.	A rapid growth period occurs during adolescence.	☐	☐
4.	Joshua is 13 years old.	☐	☐
5.	Joshua is afraid of reading aloud.	☐	☐
6.	The phrase that Joshua will say to distract himself will not be difficult to remember.	☐	☐
7.	The people in the story have three dogs.	☐	☐
8.	Large, warm, and furry dogs can keep you warm on a cold night.	☐	☐

B | *Complete selected sentences from the conversation. Include indefinite articles that you hear before the modifiers. Place commas between adjectives when the speaker pauses, and be sure to hyphenate compound modifiers.*

1. Our first meeting is only going to be _____*a 30-minute session*_____ .

2. I feel like _____ .

3. And I feel like I have _____ .

4. You're just going through _____ .

5. Now, the key to getting you over this _____

is to distract you from thinking about how well you're doing.

6. Let's think of _____

that you can keep in the back of your mind.

7. "It was _____ ."

8. "It promised to be one of those _____ ."

9. It's a night that's so cold that you need _____

to sleep with to keep you warm.

EXERCISE 7: Pronunciation

🎧 **A** | *Read and listen to the Pronunciation Note.*

Pronunciation Note

When the modifiers of a noun are in the same category, we normally pause between them. In writing, we place a comma between the modifiers.

EXAMPLES: It was an **icy, dark, stormy** evening.
(All three modifiers are in the same category, so speakers pause between them.)

I'm going to wear my **round blue sapphire** earrings.
(The three modifiers are in different categories, so speakers do not pause between them.)

Note: If you can logically insert the word **and** between modifiers, the modifiers are in the same category and will be separated by commas in writing.

It was an icy **and** dark **and** stormy evening.

🎧 **B** | *Listen to the sentences. Place commas between modifiers in the same category.*

1. The film is a serious, profound, heartwarming treatment of an important issue.

2. We have some delicious cheese-and-pepperoni sandwiches.

3. That ugly grotesque decrepit building should be torn down.

4. The trip we took was an expensive silly miserable waste of time.

5. She's going to wear her new red silk dress.

6. We bought a beautiful new hybrid car.

7. My intelligent gracious 25-year-old daughter just got married.

8. Our little old fox terrier is a delight to have in the family.

C | *PAIRS: Practice the sentences. Take turns, making sure to pause between modifiers in the same category.*

EXERCISE 8: Story Discussion

A | *Read a famous Arabic story.*

> ### Death Speaks
>
> Long ago, a wealthy nobleman lived in Baghdad. One day, he sent a servant to the marketplace to buy food. Before long, the servant returned, terribly frightened. "Master," he said, "when I was in the marketplace just now I had a terrifying experience. I was about to pay for things when a woman bumped me, and I turned to see that it was Death. She waved her hands and put a spell on me. Master, may I please borrow your horse? It is not my time to die, so I will ride to Samarra to avoid my fate. Please let me have the horse; I must ride quickly." The nobleman gave the servant his horse, and the servant rode away as fast as he could.
>
> Curious, the nobleman went to the marketplace and soon encountered me in the crowd. "Why did you wave your arms at my servant and cast a spell on him?" he asked me.
>
> "I did not cast a spell on him," I answered. "When I saw him I waved my hands because I couldn't believe my eyes. You see, I was very surprised to see him in Baghdad since I am to meet him tonight in Samarra."

B | *PAIRS: Circle the letter of the correct answer. Then discuss your answers.*

1. In the story, Death is _____.
   - **a.** a personification
   - **b.** a normal human character

2. In the story, Death is _____.
   - **a.** male
   - **b.** female

3. In the last two paragraphs of the story, "I" and "me" refer to _____.
   - **a.** the merchant
   - **b.** Death

4. The servant expects to _____.
   - **a.** escape from Death
   - **b.** be captured by Death

5. The story suggests that _____.
   - **a.** it's possible to escape fate
   - **b.** it's not possible to escape fate

C | *Report your answers to the class. The class decides what the story shows about expectations.*

EXERCISE 9: Picture Discussion

A | *GROUPS:* Look at the picture of the sinking of the *Titanic in April 1912. Describe what you see, using as many modifiers as possible. Share your sentences with other groups.*

   EXAMPLE: The ship was sinking into the dark, icy ocean waters.

B | *Discuss what the picture suggests about expectations with the other groups.*

   EXAMPLE: The builders of the *Titanic* didn't expect it to sink.

EXERCISE 10: Writing

A | *Write three or four paragraphs about a situation that did not turn out as you expected it would. Did the situation have anything to do with the expectation syndrome? Pay special attention to the modification of nouns.*

> **EXAMPLE:** A year ago our school basketball team was having a great year. In the regular season, we had a 19-1 record: 19 wins and one loss, and that one loss was in our first game. It seemed like we couldn't lose. When we got to the playoffs, however, things didn't turn out as we expected they would. In our first playoff game . . .

B | *Check your work. Use the Editing Checklist.*

Editing Checklist

Did you use . . . ?
- ☐ adjectives correctly
- ☐ noun modifiers correctly
- ☐ modifiers in the correct order

Check your answers on page UR-2.
Do you need to review anything?

A | *Put the modifiers in the correct order.*

1. a (humid / summer / sweltering) _____ day

2. a (late / chilly / winter) _____ day

3. my (silk / pink / new) _____ tie

4. the (European / young / handsome) _____ actor

5. our (brick / new / beautiful) _____ house

6. the (little / dirty / old) _____ cabin

B | *Rewrite the phrases so that the modifiers come before the noun.*

1. a son who is eleven years old _____

2. a novel that has 900 pages _____

3. a bandit who had short hair _____

4. six periods of 55 minutes each _____

5. a proposal initiated by voters _____

6. people who look strange _____

7. a statue from China made of ivory _____

8. a cat that is gray and has short hair _____

C | *Circle the letter of the one underlined word or phrase in each sentence that is not correct.*

1. <u>The two first films</u> in <u>the film festival</u> were <u>the most popular ones</u> in   **A B C D**
        A   B   C
<u>the current series</u>.
        D

2. <u>A new skier</u> has <u>a hard time</u> with <u>steep dangerous slopes</u> on <u>cold days</u>.   **A B C D**
        A   B   C   D

3. My <u>film-buff friends</u> praised the <u>Academy Award-winning</u> *Avatar* for   **A B C D**
            A   B
its <u>awesome special effects</u> and <u>strange looking creatures</u>.
            C   D

4. There's <u>a medical condition</u> called "<u>focal dystonia</u>," an   **A B C D**
                A   B
<u>abnormal, muscle function</u> caused by <u>extreme concentration</u>.
            C   D

5. <u>One of</u> my <u>best bargains</u> was <u>a silk blue shirt</u> from <u>a street market</u>.   **A B C D**
        A   B   C   D

PART III

From Grammar to Writing

AGREEMENT

A key aspect of clear and effective writing is **agreement** of verbs with their subjects and pronouns with their antecedents. Singular and plural nouns must combine with singular and plural verbs, respectively. Singular and plural pronouns must similarly link with singular and plural antecedents, and they must also agree in gender.

EXAMPLES OF SUBJECT-VERB AGREEMENT:
Koalas live in Australia.
(The plural noun *koalas* must have a plural verb *live*.)

The **list** of students **was** posted on the bulletin board.
(The list was posted, not the students; *list* must have the singular verb *was*.)

There **are** 20 **students** in my English class.
(The plural subject *students* must have a plural verb *are*.)

EXAMPLES OF PRONOUN-ANTECEDENT AGREEMENT:
All the **students** brought **their** books to class on the first day.
(*Their* agrees in number with *students*.)

Jack ate **his** lunch quickly.
(*His* agrees in number and gender with *Jack*.)

Martha stopped by to see **her** mother after class.
(*Her* agrees in number and gender with *Martha*.)

Be Careful! In formal English, the pronouns *everyone / everybody, anyone / anybody, no one / nobody, someone / somebody* are considered grammatically singular. In conversation, however, they are often used in a plural sense.

EXAMPLES: **Everyone** brought **his / her / his or her** own lunch. (formal)
Everyone brought **their** own lunch. (conversational, informal)

In most writing it is best to use the forms *his, her,* or *his or her* with these pronouns.

1 | *In sentences 1–5, underline the subject and circle the correct verb to go with it.*

1. A list of available jobs <u>was / were</u> posted on the bulletin board.

2. One of my best friends <u>has / have</u> nine credit cards.

3. Mathematics <u>is / are</u> often considered a difficult subject.

4. Bipolar disorder and schizophrenia <u>is / are</u> two serious mental disorders.

5. The director and star of the film <u>was / were</u> Ben Affleck.

In sentences 6–10, circle the correct pronoun and underline its antecedent. Draw a line between the two. Use formal English.

6. All the students brought his / their books to class on the first day.

7. Each student must bring his or her / their own lunch to the picnic.

8. Frank drives his / her own car to school.

9. If any students come late, tell him / them where the picnic is.

10. Everybody may leave whenever he or she / they wishes.

2 | *Read the letter to the editor. In the blanks write the correct pronoun or correct form of the verb in parentheses. Use forms correct for formal English.*

Editor, The Times:

Many parts of our once-beautiful city _____ (be) starting to look like mini garbage dumps. You will recall that legislation requiring recycling within the city limits _____ (be) passed last year, and the mayor and other local politicians _____ (encourage) us to recycle, but in my apartment complex there _____ (be) no bins for recycling. The result is that people take no responsibility for _____ own actions, and everyone tosses _____ trash and recyclables—glass, plastic bottles, cans, etc.—right in with the food that is being thrown away. The manager of the complex and the owner of the building _____ (have) not bought any new containers for items that _____ (be) supposed to be recycled. So what else can residents do but mix _____ trash together? The owner _____ (be) responsible for breaking the law here. Not us! Meanwhile, trash cans in the downtown area _____ (be) overflowing with garbage, and vacant lots all around the city _____ (be) littered with soda cans, broken glass, and paper. The owner and publisher of your newspaper, Stanford Black, _____ (have) always been a supporter of a clean environment. I urge your paper to take leadership in solving this problem.

1. Think about a significant environmental or societal issue that concerns you. State the problem as you see it. Why do you feel as you do?
2. Describe your issue to a partner. Listen to your partner's issue.
3. Ask and answer questions about your concerns. For example: What are the main reasons why you feel as you do? What examples can you give that support your experience? What do you think should be done about the problem?

4 | *Write a draft of a three-paragraph composition about your issue. Follow the model. Remember to include information that your partner asked about.*

The problem and reasons why I feel as I do:

_____

_____

_____

_____

Possible reasons people have the opposite point of view:

_____

_____

_____

_____

What I think should be done about the issue:

_____

_____

_____

_____

1. The writer used subjects, verbs, and pronouns correctly.   **Yes** ☐   **No** ☐

2. What I liked in the composition:

   _____

   _____

   _____

3. Questions I'd like the writer to answer about the issue:

   Who _____?

   What _____?

   When _____?

   Where _____?

   Why _____?

   How _____?

   (Your own question) _____?

6 | *Work with your partner. Discuss each other's chart from Exercise 5. Then rewrite your own composition and make any necessary changes.*

IV

NOUN CLAUSES

Noun Clauses: Subjects, Objects, and Complements

HUMOR

STEP 1 GRAMMAR IN CONTEXT

Before You Read

PAIRS: Discuss the questions.

1. What kinds of things make you laugh?
2. What benefits do humor and laughter provide us?

Read

Read the story about brothers competing for their mother's love.

THE THREE BROTHERS

There once was a lady who had three sons. In many ways the relationship between the woman and her boys was exemplary. The sons were good citizens, well-off financially, and admirable persons overall. **What wasn't so admirable** was their rivalry, for a spirit of one-upmanship had always characterized their relationship. Each brother constantly tried to figure out **how he could outdo the other two. What the sons wanted** was a secure place in their mother's affections. They didn't understand **that their mother loved each boy for his own uniqueness. That the boys were intensely competitive** had always bothered the lady, but she didn't know what to do about it.

Time passed, and as the mother aged, she began to lose her sight. Before long, she was almost blind. The boys realized **that their mother's final days were approaching,** and, competitive to the end, each searched for a way to supplant the others. Each promised to buy her **whatever she wanted.** Their mother said **there was nothing she needed,** but the boys didn't believe her.

Moe, son number one, bought his mother a mansion. At first he wondered **whether he could afford it,** but money was no object **where his mother was concerned.** He was sure **that the mansion would be her favorite gift.**

Joe, son number two, felt **that he had to outdo Moe,** so he bought his mother a luxury car complete with a chauffeur on call 24 hours a day. Joe thought **that he would certainly win his mother's approval with this gift.**

Curly, son number three, was in a dilemma, wondering **what he could do to top his brothers.** While

The formula for the area of a circle is πr^2.

downtown one day, he happened to see a beautiful parrot in a pet store window. The store owner told him **that this specially trained parrot had memorized the entire** *Encyclopedia Britannica*. One could ask the parrot **whatever one wanted to know**, and the parrot would answer accurately. Curly was ecstatic and bought the parrot, convinced **this would make him number one in his mother's eyes.**

Soon the mother invited the boys over to her mansion. "Boys," she said, "I want to thank you all for your wonderful gifts. I don't know **if you believed me**, though, when I said **I didn't need anything**. Moe, this is a gorgeous house, but it's much too big for me. I live in only two rooms and don't have the energy or inclination to take care of the place. Please sell it.

"And Joe, that car you bought me is beautiful and luxurious, but I don't drive anymore. Plus, **the fact that the chauffeur doesn't speak English** is a problem. Please sell it."

Then she turned to Curly, saying, "But Curly, yours was the best gift of all. I just can't thank you enough."

Curly was pleased **that he was now number one in his mother's affections.** "That's great, Mom. Have you learned a lot from him?"

Puzzled, his mother said, "I don't know **what you mean**, son. All I know is **that the chicken you gave me was delicious.**"

After You Read

A | **Vocabulary:** *Circle the letter of the best meaning for the* **blue** *words and phrases from the reading.*

1. The relationship between the woman and her boys was **exemplary**.

   a. predictable   **b.** admirable   **c.** formal   **d.** troubled

2. A spirit of **one-upmanship** had always characterized their relationship.

   a. gaining an   **b.** becoming   **c.** getting angry   **d.** achieving
   advantage   wealthier   satisfaction

3. Each brother was constantly trying to figure out how he could **outdo** the others.

   a. anger   **b.** do better than   **c.** tease   **d.** amuse

4. The mother loved each boy for his own **uniqueness**.

   a. strangeness   **b.** unselfishness   **c.** individual   **d.** energy
                                                     qualities

5. Each boy searched for a way to **supplant** the others.

   a. take the place of **b.** stimulate   **c.** anger   **d.** learn from

6. The car was accompanied by a chauffeur **on call** 24 hours a day.

   a. in charge   **b.** on duty   **c.** present   **d.** available

7. Curly, son number three, was **in a dilemma**.

   a. facing others'   **b.** facing a difficult **c.** facing danger **d.** facing financial
   anger   choice   problems

8. Curly was **ecstatic** and bought the parrot.

   a. satisfied   **b.** amused   **c.** delighted   **d.** pleased with
                                                                        himself

9. I don't have the energy or **inclination** to take care of the place.

   a. ability   **b.** desire   **c.** time   **d.** permission

B | **Comprehension:** *Circle* **T (True)** *or* **F (False)**. *Correct the false statements.*

1. A spirit of cooperation characterized the brothers' relationship.	**T**	**F**
2. Each son desired to be first in his mother's affections.	**T**	**F**
3. The boys' mother encouraged the spirit of competition between them.	**T**	**F**
4. The boys' mother told them she needed a lot of things.	**T**	**F**
5. All three brothers bought their mother things to earn her love.	**T**	**F**
6. The mother was pleased by the gifts of all three brothers.	**T**	**F**
7. The parrot knew a great deal.	**T**	**F**
8. The mother was aware of what the parrot could do.	**T**	**F**

NOUN CLAUSES: SUBJECTS, OBJECTS, AND COMPLEMENTS

Noun Clauses Beginning with *That*

Subject	Object
That she loves them is obvious.	You can see **(that) she loves them**.
That they give gifts is unfortunate.	She knows **(that) they give gifts**.

Complement	
SUBJECT COMPLEMENT	The problem was **(that) the car was so expensive**.
ADJECTIVE COMPLEMENT	It is important **(that) people develop a sense of humor**.

Noun Clauses with Question Words

Subject	Object
What I should give her is obvious.	I wonder **what I should give her**.
Why he did that wasn't evident.	Can you explain **why he did that**?

Complement	
SUBJECT COMPLEMENT	The mystery is **how he could afford the car**.
ADJECTIVE COMPLEMENT	It's amusing **what she did with the bird**.

Noun Clauses with *Whether* or *If*

Subject	Object	
Whether she'll like it is hard to tell.	I wonder **whether / if she'll like it**.	
Whether it's useful or not matters to me.	I care about	**whether / if it's useful (or not)**.
		whether (or not) it's useful.

Complement	
SUBJECT COMPLEMENT	The issue is **whether she needs such costly gifts**.
ADJECTIVE COMPLEMENT	He's uncertain **whether she'll like it**.

GRAMMAR NOTES

1 | Noun clauses are dependent clauses that perform the same functions as regular nouns:
a. subjects

- **What I like** is a good joke.
- **What makes me laugh** is slapstick comedy.

b. objects

- I don't understand **why you find that funny**.
- You can see **that I am easily amused**.
- We're impressed by **what she's done**.

c. subject complements

- The question is **whether people will laugh**.

d. adjective complements

- It's clear **that laughter involves an emotion**.

Noun clauses begin with *that*, question words, words formed from *-ever* (*whatever, whoever, whomever, whichever*), or *whether* or *if*.

- We realize **that she was joking**.
- I don't understand **what it means**.
- **Whatever you decide** is fine with me.
- He doesn't know **if / whether it's true or not**.

---

2 | We use the word ***that*** to introduce certain noun clauses. In such cases, *that* is a grammatical word that simply introduces a clause. It has no concrete meaning.

- **That she was a funny person** was apparent.

That can be omitted when it introduces an object noun clause or a complement noun clause, especially in speaking.

- I believe **(that) humor is healthy**.
- I told Sue **(that) she was a funny person**.
- It's odd **(that) you laugh so little**.

When *that* introduces a subject noun clause, it is **never omitted**.

- **That Joe has a good sense of humor** is obvious.
  Not: Joe has a good sense of humor is obvious.

Subject noun clauses beginning with *that* are formal.

BE CAREFUL! Do not confuse *that* and *what*. The word *that* simply introduces a noun clause. The word *what* refers to something definite. It serves as the object in the noun clause. It cannot be omitted.

- I know **(that) she is coming**.

- I don't know **what she is bringing**.
                       O   S   V

---

3 | ***The fact that*** is sometimes used in place of *that* in subject noun clauses.

- **That you can laugh** is good.
- **The fact that you can laugh** is good.

The fact that **must** be used in place of *that* in noun clauses that are objects of prepositions.

- I'm impressed by **the fact that Bob is here**.
  Not: I'm impressed by that Bob is here.

It often functions as the subject of a sentence, with the noun clause coming at the end. Like the word *that*, *it*, when used with a noun clause, is a grammatical word with no concrete meaning.

- **It**'s funny **(that) you should say that**.

4	A **question** that is **changed to a noun clause** is called an **embedded question**. We use statement word order in embedded questions, not question word order.	• I don't even know **if she's from around here**. • I don't know **who she is**. NOT: I don't know ~~who is she~~.
	USAGE NOTE: An embedded question is more polite than a direct question.	• What time is it? *(direct)* • Do you know **what time it is**? *(more polite)*
	An embedded question can occur within a statement or within another question. An embedded question within a statement is followed by a period. An embedded question within another question is followed by a question mark.	• I'm not sure **what *incongruous* means**. • Do you know **how far it is to the nearest town**?
5	*Wh-* **question words** introduce **embedded** *wh-* **questions**.	• Do you know **when she arrived**? • I'm not sure **how many children she has**.
	The subject of an embedded *wh-* question takes a singular verb.	• I'm not certain **who is going** with us.
	BE CAREFUL! Do not use *do, does,* or *did* in embedded questions.	• I have no idea **what she meant**. NOT: I have no idea ~~what did she mean~~.
6	We use *if* and *whether (or not)* to introduce **embedded *yes / no* questions**.	• Do you know **if she came to work today**? • Who knows **whether she's here**? • I have no idea **whether she came or not**.
	Note that *if* and *whether (or not)* are similar in meaning and can often be used interchangeably.	• We're not sure **if / whether (or not)** Bob is in town.
	BE CAREFUL! Do not use *if* to introduce a subject noun clause.	• **Whether (or not) she understood** is questionable. NOT: ~~If she understood is questionable~~.
	BE CAREFUL! Do not omit *if* or *whether (or not)* in embedded *yes / no* questions.	• It is difficult to say **if / whether (or not)** his plan will work. NOT: It is difficult to say ~~his plan will work~~.
7	*Whether . . . or not* can replace *whether* in all noun clauses.	• We don't know **whether** she got the job. OR • We don't know **whether** she got the job **or not**.
	If . . . or not can replace *whether* in all but subject noun clauses.	• No one has told me **whether / if** she received the letter **or not**. • **Whether** she received it isn't known. NOT: ~~If she received it or not isn't known~~.

REFERENCE NOTE
For work on **noun clauses used to report speech**, see Unit 11.

EXERCISE 1: Discover the Grammar

A | *Read the sentences. Underline each noun clause and identify it as **S** (used as a subject), **O** (used as an object), or **C** (used as a complement).*

_____ **1.** Moe was sure that the mansion would be her favorite gift.

_____ **2.** What wasn't so admirable was their rivalry.

_____ **3.** All I know is that the chicken you gave me was delicious.

_____ **4.** Their mother said there was nothing she needed.

B | *Look at the sentences. Underline the embedded question in each. For each embedded question, write the direct question it was derived from.*

1. Each brother constantly tried to figure out <u>how he could outdo the other two.</u>

    How can I outdo the other two?

2. Curly was wondering what he could do to top his brothers.

_____

3. At first he wondered if he could afford it.

_____

4. I don't know if you believed me.

_____

5. I don't know what you mean.

_____

EXERCISE 2: Embedded Questions   *(Grammar Notes 4–7)*

Based on the exchanges in the chart, complete the story with embedded **yes / no** *and* **wh***-questions. Put the verbs in the simple past or the past perfect.*

1. A: Excuse me. How far is the nearest town?   **B:** I don't know.
2. A: Well, what's the name of the nearest town?   **B:** I'm not sure.
3. A: Can I borrow your cell phone?   **B:** What's a cell phone?

4. **A:** Well, are there any towing companies nearby? **B:** I don't know that either.
5. **A:** Do you know the people in that house there? **B:** No, I don't.
6. **A:** How long have you lived around here? **B:** That's private information.
7. **A:** What's your name? **B:** I'm not going to tell you.
8. **A:** Do you know anything at all? **B:** Yes, I do. I'm smarter than you are. At least I know where I am, and you don't.

My wife and I had an irritating experience a year ago when we were traveling in the Midwest. Our car broke down, and I saw a farmer working in a field. I was sure he could help me, so I went up to him. I asked him ____*how far the nearest town was*____. He

1.

said he didn't know. Then I asked him _____. He

2.

said he wasn't sure. I asked him _____. He asked

3.

me what a cell phone was. Then I asked him _____.

4.

He said he didn't know that either. I asked him _____

5.

the people in a nearby house. He said he didn't.

I asked him _____ in the area. He said that was

6.

private information. Then I asked him _____. He

7.

said he wasn't going to tell me. I asked him _____.

8.

He said he did and that he was smarter than I was. He said he at least knew where he was, and I didn't.

EXERCISE 3: Embedded Questions

(Grammar Notes 4–5)

A | *Write negative answers to the direct questions. Use an embedded question inside a phrase, such as* **I don't know, I'm not entirely sure, I have no idea, I don't have a clue,** *and so on.*

> **EXAMPLE:**　What happens to our diaphragm when we laugh?
> I have no idea what happens to our diaphragm when we laugh.

1. What is a pun?

   _____

2. What does *hyperbole* mean?

   _____

3. What is the humor of the unexpected happening?

   _____

4. How does repetition work in humor?

   _____

5. What is the humor of the incongruous situation?

   _____

6. How does sarcasm differ from other humor?

   _____

7. What are endorphins?

   _____

A Thumbnail Sketch of Humor

Pun

A pun is a kind of humor that depends on similarities in sound or meaning between two words. Example: A woman saw a bear a week before her baby was born. Frightened, she asked the doctor, "Will seeing that *bear* affect my baby?" The doctor said, "Yes. Your baby will have *bare* feet."

Hyperbole

Hyperbole, much used in humor, is exaggeration. Example: A: Why are you so tired? B: I got stuck in a traffic jam on the freeway. They've been working on that stupid freeway since about 1905!

Humor of the unexpected happening

A great deal of humor depends on what is called the humor of the unexpected happening. Example: In a movie, a woman in a restaurant opens her purse, and a bird flies out of it.

Repetition

Many humorous stories are structured on the basis of repetition of an element, most often three times. Example: A man can't find his car in a parking lot and tries to hitchhike. It is pouring rain. The first driver who drives along honks his horn and doesn't stop. The second car that comes by splashes water from a mud puddle all over him. Then another man comes out and unlocks the door of his parked car, next to the first man. Furious, the first man goes up to him, shakes him, and says, "I wouldn't accept a ride from you if you paid me."

Incongruous situation

The humor of the incongruous situation depends on normal things happening in unusual places. Example: No one thinks twice about seeing a dog in someone's yard, but if a dog enters an elevator in a downtown building, people will laugh.

Sarcasm

Sarcasm is a kind of irony. It can be mild and gentle, but it is more often biting and hurtful. Example: A: What do you think of Jones as a political candidate? B: Oh, he's sharp, all right. He's got a mind as good as any in the 12th century.

Physiological aspects of laughter

When we laugh, our diaphragm moves quickly up and down. Endorphins, hormones that are created in the brain when we laugh or exercise, are instrumental in lessening pain and contributing to a sense of well-being.

EXERCISE 4: Noun Clauses

(Grammar Notes 1–3)

PAIRS: *Examine the bumper stickers and discuss the meaning of each one. On a separate piece of paper, write one or two sentences explaining the meaning of each, making sure to use a noun clause. Use phrases like those from the box.*

the fact that	what this is about	what this means
what the humor depends on	what this is referring to	what's funny about this

EXAMPLE:

Is there life before coffee?

What this is referring to is the fact that many people cannot start the day without coffee. They act like they're dead.

1.

HONK
if you're illiterate

2.

IF YOU DON'T LIKE THE WAY I DRIVE,
STAY OFF THE SIDEWALK!

3.

MISSING: HUSBAND AND DOG.
ATTENTION: $100 Reward for Dog.

4.

CHANGE IS INEVITABLE—
EXCEPT FOR VENDING MACHINES.

5.

I'm in no hurry.
I'm on my way to work.

6.

Everyone is entitled to my opinion.

7.

FORGET ABOUT WORLD PEACE.
VISUALIZE USING YOUR TURN SIGNAL.

8.

ESCHEW OBFUSCATION.

166 UNIT 10

EXERCISE 5: Editing

Read the following statements about the proper way to tell a joke. There are eight mistakes in the use of noun clauses. The first mistake is already corrected. Find and correct seven more.

Eight Pieces of Advice About Telling a Joke

1. Make sure ~~is~~ the joke you're telling ^{is} funny.

2. The best jokes are broad enough so that everyone can enjoy them. Be certain that no one will be embarrassed by that you tell.

3. Ask yourself is the joke you want to tell vulgar. If it is, don't tell it.

4. Before you begin, be certain you remember what are the key details. Run through them in your mind before you start speaking.

5. Make sure what you have everybody's attention when you're ready to start.

6. Be certain whether you remember what the punch line of the joke is. Nothing is worse than listening to a joke when the teller can't remember the punch line.

7. The fact can you remember a joke doesn't guarantee success. You have to make the experience a performance. Be animated and dramatic.

8. If to laugh at your own jokes is always a question. Many comedians are criticized because they laugh at their own jokes. Don't laugh at what you're saying. Let others do the laughing.

EXERCISE 6: Listening

A | *Listen to the conversation. Where did the incident in Jean's story take place?*

_____

B | *Read the questions. Listen to the conversation again. Write answers to the questions, using a noun clause in each case.*

1. What bothers Greg about jokes?

   What bothers Greg about jokes is that they're too programmed.

2. According to Greg, what is the expectation when someone tells a joke?

   _____

3. According to Greg, what does everyone think if you don't laugh?

   _____

4. What is Greg's basic problem about jokes?

   _____

5. What does he feel like in this situation?

   _____

6. What was the problem that some girls were causing?

   _____

7. What did the principal decide?

   _____

8. According to Jean, what did the principal want to show the girls?

   _____

EXERCISE 7: Pronunciation

A | *Read and listen to the Pronunciation Note.*

> **Pronunciation Note**
>
> Remember that in *wh-* questions, your voice goes up near the end of the sentence and then falls at the end. In *yes / no* questions, your voice gradually rises and is still rising at the end of the sentence. In embedded questions, your voice rises at the end whether or not the embedded question is a *wh-* question or a *yes / no* question.
>
> **EXAMPLES:** Where did he go?
>
> Do you know where he went?
>
> Did he go?
>
> Do you know if he went?

B | *Listen to the questions. Draw downward slanting or upward slanting arrows, depending on whether the voice drops at the end or continues to rise.*

1. Did she come?

2. When did she come?

3. How did they get here?

4. Did they get here?

5. Did he leave?

6. Why did he leave?

7. What does *ecstatic* mean?

8. Does *ecstatic* mean *happy*?

C | *PAIRS: Listen to the embedded questions. Then practice the questions, paying close attention to your intonation. Take turns.*

1. Do you know if she came?
2. Do you know when she came?
3. Do you know how they got here?
4. Do you know if they got here?
5. Do you know if he left?
6. Do you know why he left?
7. Do you know what *ecstatic* means?
8. Do you know if *ecstatic* means *happy*?

A | *Read this article about airline humor.*

They *Do* Have a Sense of Humor

by David Field, *USA Today*

Airline crews may not seem like a humorous group as they walk through the airport terminal with that look of determination and dedication on their faces. But behind the serious behavior, they are a funny lot. Here are some classic airline jokes selected from the collective memory of aviation writers.

Flight Attendant Remarks

Before the no-smoking announcement: "This is a nonsmoking flight. If you must smoke, please ring your attendant call bell and one of us will escort you out to the wing."

After the no-smoking announcement: "Any passenger caught smoking in the lavatories will be asked to leave the plane immediately."

First-Time Fliers

Then there was the woman who, when asked if she wanted a window seat, responded, "No, not by the window. I've just had my hair done."

One passenger wanted to know how a plane could get from Chicago to Detroit, cities separated by a time zone, in just 15 minutes.

Although the flight time was 75 minutes, the time zone made their airline's scheduled departure seem like the flight took only 15 minutes. He was finally satisfied with the explanation that it was a *very* fast airplane.

Pilot Humor

When controllers are uncertain what a pilot plans or wants to do, they usually say, "Please state your intentions."

Few pilots are daring enough to respond literally. But one was once overheard: "I intend to retire to a small farm in Georgia and raise peaches."

Pet Stories

Two airline cargo handlers were removing a pet carrier from a plane's cargo hold and discovered the cat inside was dead.

Fearful of the saddened owner's anger, the two went to the nearest cat pound and found an animal of the same breed, size, and color, and proudly delivered it to its destination.

As the animal leaped out of the cage, the owner gasped in shock, turned to the cargo handlers, and exclaimed, "This is not my cat! My cat was dead when I shipped him! He was stuffed!"

Plane Humor

Pilots and maintenance crews usually communicate in writing. A pilot typically writes up an item to be repaired such as a cockpit gauge or switch.

An overnight maintenance crew responds in writing that the work was done or wasn't needed or couldn't be done.

A pilot once left a note complaining, "Dead bugs are on the cockpit windshield." When the pilot came back in the morning, maintenance had replied: "Sorry, live bugs not available."

B | PAIRS: *Tell your partner which jokes you find funny and which ones you don't. If you do find a particular joke humorous, explain what makes you laugh or smile about it. Explain to your partner what makes each joke a joke.*

EXAMPLE:　**A:** What I think is funny is the pilot's answer about retiring to Georgia to raise peaches.
　　　　　　B: Why?

EXERCISE 9: Class Discussion

A | *Prepare to present a joke or amusing story in class. Practice before you present it. Be prepared to explain what you find funny about it.*

B | *Present the joke or amusing story in class.*

C | *CLASS: Discuss whether or not you find the joke or story funny. Explain why or why not.*

EXERCISE 10: Writing

A | *Choose one of the activities for a writing assignment. Use noun clauses where appropriate.*

1. Write three to five paragraphs about a situation that you witnessed or participated in that you found humorous. Describe the situation fully, using a number of supporting details. Explain why the situation was funny for you.

2. If you know an extended joke (like the one in the opening reading of this unit), write it.

EXAMPLE:　One of the funniest situations I've ever been involved in happened in our office last year. It was April Fools' Day, and everyone in the office thought that we needed to play a practical joke on the office manager. She's always playing jokes on us, so we had to get back at her. Here's what we did . . .

B | *Check your work. Use the Editing Checklist.*

Editing Checklist
Did you use . . . ? ☐ subject noun clauses correctly ☐ object noun clauses correctly ☐ complement noun clauses correctly

A | Circle the correct noun clause to complete each sentence.

1. I'm not sure <u>what the punch line of the joke was / what was the punch line of the joke</u>.

2. I don't know <u>why does he always tell that joke / why he always tells that joke</u>.

3. I'm not sure <u>what time does the meeting start / what time the meeting starts</u>.

4. I don't remember <u>what *hyperbole* means / what means *hyperbole*</u>.

5. I don't know <u>whether Samira liked the party / Samira liked the party</u>.

6. I have no idea <u>that Mary does for a living / what Mary does for a living</u>.

7. I'm not sure <u>how long she's been a writer / how long has she been a writer</u>.

8. We're not sure <u>if or not / whether or not</u> Danilo will be able to play.

B | Correct the mistakes in the underlined phrases.

1. Do you have any idea <u>what did Mary mean</u>? _____

2. We're not sure <u>if or not Bob</u> is coming. _____

3. <u>However you want</u> to do is fine with me. _____

4. <u>Alison loves Kahlil</u> is obvious. _____

5. I wonder <u>that we should give Russell</u>. _____

6. We're pleased by <u>that Ben helped us</u>. _____

7. Alice told Jim <u>what she was</u> delighted. _____

C | Circle the letter of the choice that correctly completes each sentence. Note: Ø means no addition needed.

1. A person who is telling a joke needs to remember _____ the key details are. **A B C D**
   (A) the fact that   (B) that   (C) why   (D) what

2. I'm impressed by _____ Bill showed up to help. **A B C D**
   (A) that   (B) the fact that   (C) what   (D) Ø

3. Most people don't think _____ airline pilots have a sense of humor. **A B C D**
   (A) Ø   (B) what   (C) the fact that   (D) whether

4. _____ she understood the joke is questionable. **A B C D**
   (A) If   (B) Whatever   (C) Whether or not   (D) Ø

Direct and Indirect Speech
COMMUNICATION AND MISUNDERSTANDING

Before You Read

PAIRS: Discuss the questions.

1. In your experience, what are the most difficult kinds of misunderstandings to deal with? Give examples.
2. How can misunderstandings best be avoided?

Read

Read the interview with an expert on communication.

Understanding Misunderstandings

AN: Hello, everyone. I'm Ann Ness. Please welcome today's guest: communication expert Ellen Sands.

ES: Thanks for having me. You know, Ann, I think we're seeing a lot more verbal conflict these days than in the past. There seems to be a lot more rancor and a lot less civility. Today I want to talk about ways to avoid verbal conflict, or at least minimize it.

AN: Sounds good, Ellen. Let's roll.

ES: All right. First: People need to listen actively to each other. People hear things, but often they don't really listen. A couple of weeks ago I was at a restaurant in Los Angeles, sitting near a Japanese couple being served by an American waitress. The service was slow, and the couple seemed distressed. When the waitress brought the check, the man said, **"The bill seems very high. Did you include the service in it? How much is the service?"** The waitress said, **"You have to pay the tax."** The man said, **"The service was very slow. We have never waited so long to be served. We will pay the bill, but we won't pay for service."** Then they left angrily. The waitress just glared at them and didn't say anything. It wasn't a good situation, mainly because the waitress didn't listen actively.

(*continued on next page*)

Understanding Misunderstandings

AN: Let me see if I understand. When the waitress brought the check, the man said **the bill seemed very high**. He asked **how much the service was**. The waitress said **they had to pay the tax**. The man said **the service had been very slow** and **they had never waited so long to be served**. He said **they would pay the bill** but **they wouldn't pay for service**. Now what did the waitress do wrong?

ES: She didn't listen carefully. The man asked **if she had included the service in the bill**. Unfortunately, she never answered his question. That was the key thing he wanted to know.

AN: Did she do anything else wrong?

ES: She didn't address his concern about the slow service. She could have said, **"Yes, I'm really sorry about the service. We're short-handed today."**

AN: Very interesting. Now what's another way to avoid verbal conflict?

ES: One really good strategy is to state things positively instead of negatively. Recently I was sitting in as a consultant at a school board meeting. Right at the start the chair said, **"We're on a very tight schedule. Make your reports brief; no one will be allowed to take more than three minutes. And no one will be allowed to interrupt the person who's speaking. No one will ask any questions."** It wasn't a good meeting. You could have cut the silence with a knife.

AN: How could the chair have done better?

ES: He told them **to make their reports brief**, but he could have asked them **to try to limit their reports to three minutes**. He said **no one would be allowed to interrupt the person who was speaking**. He also said **no one would ask any questions**. He used a self-righteous tone and treated the attendees like schoolchildren. He could have asked them **to save questions until everyone had finished**. The bottom line is this: You don't have to sugarcoat your statements, but people will respond much better if you put a positive spin on things.

AN: All right. Thanks, Ellen. We'll be back shortly, after this commercial break.

After You Read

A | Vocabulary: *Match the blue words and phrases on the left with their meanings on the right.*

_____ 1. There seems to be a lot more **rancor** and a lot less civility.

_____ 2. There seems to be a lot more rancor and a lot less **civility**.

_____ 3. I want to talk about ways to **minimize** verbal conflict.

_____ 4. The couple seemed **distressed**.

_____ 5. The waitress just **glared** at them and didn't say anything.

_____ 6. We're **short-handed** today.

_____ 7. How could the **chair** have done better?

_____ 8. The **bottom line** is this: put a positive spin on things.

_____ 9. You don't have to **sugarcoat** your statements.

_____ 10. People will respond much better if you put a positive **spin** on things.

a. person in charge of a meeting

b. key point

c. courteous behavior

d. interpretation

e. bad or bitter feelings

f. looked angrily

g. make something appear to be nice

h. reduce to the smallest possible amount

i. without enough help

j. upset

B | Comprehension: *Refer to the reading and complete each statement with a single word.*

1. Ellen Sands is a(n) _____ expert.

2. Sands believes there is _____ rancor in communication today than in the past.

3. She also believes there is _____ civility today than previously.

4. Sands says that a key aspect of good communication is _____ listening.

5. In her first example, Sands talks of a couple from _____.

6. The couple thought the service was too _____.

7. The waitress never answered the man's question about whether the _____ was included in the bill.

8. In her second example, Sands talks of the need to state things in a(n) _____ manner.

9. The chair in her second example treated the attendees like _____.

.

STEP 2 GRAMMAR PRESENTATION

DIRECT AND INDIRECT SPEECH

		Statements: Direct Speech	
Subject	**Reporting Verb**	**Direct Statement**	
He	said,	"The food **is** delicious."	
		"The bill **includes** service."	
		"The service **was** slow."	

			Statements: Indirect Speech	
Subject	**Reporting Verb**	**Noun / Pronoun**	**Indirect Statement**	
He	said	Ø*	(that)	the food **was** delicious.
	told	Miriam / her		the bill **included** service.
				the service **had been** slow.

*Ø: not used.

		Yes / No Questions: Direct Speech	
Subject	**Reporting Verb**	**Direct Question**	
The chair	asked,	"**Have you finished** your report?"	
		"**Do you think we are going** to have time to finish?"	

			Yes / No Questions: Indirect Speech	
Subject	**Reporting Verb**	**Noun / Pronoun**	**Indirect Question**	
The chair	asked	(Marta)	**if**	**she had finished** her report.
		(her)	**whether (or not)**	**she thought they were** going to have time to finish.

		Wh- Questions: Direct Speech	
Subject	**Reporting Verb**	**Direct Question**	
The customer	asked,	"**What time does the manager arrive**?"	
		"**Who is the manager**?"	

			Wh- Questions: Indirect Speech	
Subject	**Reporting Verb**	**Noun / Pronoun**	**Indirect Question**	
The customer	asked	(the waitress)	**what time**	**the manager arrived.**
		(her)	**who**	**the manager was.**

.

.

.

.

.

.

.

.

Verb Changes in Indirect Speech

Direct Speech				Indirect Speech			
		Verb				**Verb**	
He said,	"I	report	the news."	He said	(that) he	reported	the news.
		am reporting				was reporting	
		reported				had reported	
		have reported					
		had reported					
		will report				would report	
		can report				could report	
		should report				should report	

Other Changes in Indirect Speech

	Direct Speech	Indirect Speech
PRONOUNS	"Andy, are **you** listening?" Mary asked.	Mary asked Andy if **he** was listening.
POSSESSIVES	The boss said, "Sue, bring **your** camera."	The boss told Sue to bring **her** camera.
THIS	"Can I have **this** film?" Sam asked.	Sam asked if he could have **that** film.
HERE	Mrs. Brown asked, "Will you be **here**?"	Mrs. Brown asked if I would be **there**.
AGO	"We came a year **ago**," Jim said.	Jim said (that) they had come a year **previously / before**.
NOW	Bob asked, "Are you leaving **now**?"	Bob asked if I was leaving **then**.
TODAY	"I need to work **today**," Jack said.	Jack said (that) he needed to work **that day**.
YESTERDAY	The reporter asked, "Did you call **yesterday**?"	The reporter asked if I had called **the previous day / the day before**.
TOMORROW	"Are you arriving **tomorrow**?" Sarah asked.	Sarah asked if we were arriving **the next day**.

GRAMMAR NOTES

1

We can **report speech** in two ways: direct speech and indirect speech. **Direct speech** (also called **quoted speech**) is the exact words (or thoughts) of someone speaking (or thinking). It is enclosed in quotation marks and is often introduced by a reporting verb such as *asked, claimed, said, stated, told,* and *wondered*.

Indirect speech (also called **reported speech**) is someone's report of direct speech. It does not contain the exact words of a speaker and is not enclosed in quotation marks. Indirect speech reports what a speaker said in a **noun clause or phrase** introduced by a reporting verb.

If a statement is reported, the noun clause can be introduced by *that*. If a question is reported, the noun clause is introduced by *if, whether (or not),* or a *wh-* question word.

BE CAREFUL! Don't use quotation marks in indirect speech.

- She said, "**I want to talk about ways to avoid verbal conflict.**"
- The man asked, "**Does the bill include service?**"

NOUN CLAUSE

- She said **(that) she wanted to talk about ways to avoid verbal conflict**.

NOUN CLAUSE

- The man asked **if the bill included service**.

- John said **(that) he would be there**.
  Not: John said "he would be there."

2

The verbs **say** and **tell** are the most common **reporting verbs**. We usually use the simple past form of these verbs in both direct and indirect speech.

BE CAREFUL! *Say* and *tell* have similar meanings, but they are used differently. We *say something* but *tell someone something*.

USAGE NOTE: When the listener is mentioned, it is preferable to use *tell*.

BE CAREFUL! Don't use *tell* when the listener is not mentioned.

- Hal **said**, "Martha, we have to leave."
- Hal **told** Martha they had to leave.

- Andy **told Freda** (that) she shouldn't worry.
  Not: Andy said Freda that she shouldn't worry.

- The chair **told us** to pay attention.
- The chair **said** to pay attention.

- Ms. Sasser **said** (that) she was going to sit in on the meeting.
  Not: Ms. Sasser told (that) she was going to sit in on the meeting.

3	To **report indirect questions**, we normally use *ask* in its simple past form.	• Mrs. Mason **asked** Mary if she was going to resign.
	BE CAREFUL! Indirect questions end with a period, not a question mark. Do not use *do*, *does*, or *did* in an indirect question.	• Sue asked Helen **if she had talked with her boss**. Not: Sue asked Helen ~~did she talk~~ with her boss.
	Use *if* or **whether (or not)**, not *that*, to introduce an **indirect yes / no question**. *If* and *whether (or not)* are similar in meaning and are often used interchangeably. We often use *whether (or not)* to emphasize alternatives or different possibilities.	• Bob asked, "Do you think she'll take the job?" • Bob asked **if / whether (or not)** I thought she would take the job.
	Use statement word order, not question word order, to report *yes / no* questions.	• I asked if **we would** know the answer soon. Not: I asked ~~would we~~ know the answer soon.
4	Use **question words** to introduce **indirect wh- questions**.	• The man asked, "How much is the service?" • The man asked **how much the service was**. • "Which entrée do you prefer?" the waiter asked. • The waiter asked **which entrée I preferred**.
	Use statement word order to report indirect questions about the predicate.	• My daughter asked, "Why didn't he take our order?" • My daughter asked **why he hadn't taken our order**.
	Use question word order to report indirect questions about the subject.	• "Who is going to do the dishes?" Mom asked. • Mom asked **who was going to do the dishes**.
5	If the reporting verb is in the simple past, the **verb in the noun clause** often changes: • imperative ➔ infinitive	• The teacher said, "**Open** your books." • The teacher told us **to open** our books.
	• simple present ➔ simple past	• Bill said, "I **invest** in the stock market." • Bill said (that) he **invested** in the stock market.
	• present progressive ➔ past progressive	• Mary asked, "John, **are** you **studying** political science?" • Mary asked John if he **was studying** political science.
	• simple past ➔ past perfect	• "Priscilla **prepared** a delicious meal," Mark said. • Mark said (that) Priscilla **had prepared** a delicious meal.
	• present perfect ➔ past perfect	• "Sam, **have** you ever **eaten** at that restaurant?" Jack asked. • Jack asked Sam if he **had** ever **eaten** at that restaurant.

(continued on next page)

Direct and Indirect Speech   **179**

6	In spoken English, we sometimes do not change verbs in a noun clause, especially if what we are reporting happened a short time ago.	• Yesterday Amy said, "Jack **didn't come to** work." • Yesterday Amy said Jack **didn't come to work**. OR • Yesterday Amy said Jack **hadn't come** to work.
	Even in formal English, we often do not change verbs to past forms if general truths are reported.	• "**Does it snow** here in the winter?" Kenny asked. • Kenny asked if it **snows** here in the winter. OR • Kenny asked if it **snowed** here in the winter.
	When the reporting verb is in the simple present, present progressive, present perfect, or future, the verb in the noun clause does not change.	• Betty says, "I**'m going to** buy a new car." • Betty says she**'s going to** buy a new car.
7	Certain **modals** often change in indirect speech. *Can, may, must,* and *will* → *could, might, had to,* and *would,* respectively.	• "Sam, **can** you call me at 6:00 P.M.?" Ann asked. • Ann asked Sam if he **could** call her at 6:00 P.M. • "I **won't** be able to," replied Sam. • Sam replied that he **wouldn't** be able to.
	Could, might, ought to, should, and *would* do not change in indirect speech.	• I said, "Helen, I **might** attend the conference." • I told Helen (that) I **might** attend the conference. • "Sarah, you **should** be more careful," Dad said. • Dad told Sarah (that) she **should** be more careful.
8	In addition to verbs, certain **other words** change in indirect speech. To keep the speaker's original meaning, make these changes as well: • pronouns and possessive adjectives → other forms	• Jeremy said, "**My** boss just promoted **me**." • Jeremy said **his** boss had just promoted **him**.
	• *this* → *that* and *these* → *those*	• Don asked, "Have you read **this** book?" • Don asked if I had read **that** book.
	• *here* → *there*	• "Please be **here** for the meeting," Sally asked. • Sally asked me to be **there** for the meeting.
	• *now* → *then*	• Mack said, "Alan's just arriving **now**." • Mack said Alan was just arriving **then**.
	• *ago* → *before* or *previously*	• Julie said, "I got the job three years **ago**." • Julie said (that) she had gotten the job three years **previously / before**.
	• *yesterday* → *the day before / the previous day* *today* → *that day* *tomorrow* → *the next day / the day after*	• "I can see you **tomorrow**," said Kayoko. • Kayoko said (that) she could see me **the next day**.

REFERENCE NOTE

For a list of **reporting verbs for reported speech**, see Appendix 23 on page A-10.

EXERCISE 1: Discover the Grammar

A | *Look at these sentences from the opening reading. Match the sentences on the left with the description of the change to indirect speech on the right.*

___h___ **1.** He told them to make their reports brief.

_____ **2.** He said they wouldn't pay for service.

_____ **3.** The waitress said they had to pay the tax.

_____ **4.** He asked how much the service was.

_____ **5.** He said they had never waited so long to be served.

_____ **6.** He said the bill seemed very high.

_____ **7.** He said the service had been very slow.

_____ **8.** He asked if she had included the service in the bill.

a. present of *be* → past of *be*

b. simple present → simple past

c. present perfect → past perfect

d. simple past → past perfect

e. *will* → *would*

f. *have to* → *had to*

g. past of *be* → past perfect of *be*

h. imperative → infinitive

B | *Read each direct speech sentence. Is the change to indirect speech correct (**C**) or incorrect (**I**)?*

___C___ **1.** Direct: "We will pay the bill."

Indirect: He said we would pay the bill.

_____ **2.** Direct: "You have to pay the tax."

Indirect: She said they had to pay the tax.

_____ **3.** Direct: "We have never waited so long to be served."

Indirect: He said they'd never waited so long to be served.

_____ **4.** Direct: "Does the bill include service?"

Indirect: He asked does the bill include service.

_____ **5.** Direct: "How much is the service?"

Indirect: He asked how much was the service.

_____ **6.** Direct: "We're short of time."

Indirect: He said they had been short of time.

_____ **7.** Direct: "I'm really sorry about the service."

Indirect: She said she was really sorry about the service.

_____ **8.** Direct: "Make your reports brief."

Indirect: He said them to make their reports brief.

EXERCISE 2: Direct Speech to Indirect Speech

(Grammar Notes 5–7)

Both direct and indirect speech are used in headlines. Put the headlines into indirect speech.

1.
SPACESHIP ONE'S REPEAT TRIP EARNS $10 MILLION

2.
Scientist Linda Buck Has Unlocked the Secret of the Sense of Smell

3.
MT. ST. ANDREA VOLCANO MAY ERUPT AGAIN

4.
A NEW TAX CUT WILL BE PASSED SOON

5.
UNEMPLOYMENT IS INCREASING

6.
Mercury-Contaminated Fish Is Dangerous to Eat

7.
A FACE TRANSPLANT PROCEDURE HAS BEEN PERFECTED BY SPANISH SURGEONS

8.
Three Local Schools Will Close Next Month

1. *The headline said Spaceship One's repeat trip earned $10 million.*

2. _____

3. _____

4. _____

5. _____

6. _____

7. _____

8. _____

EXERCISE 3: Indirect Speech to Direct Speech

(Grammar Notes 3–4)

*A substitute teacher came to a class and was asked many questions by the students. Read the teacher's answers to the students' questions. Write the questions in direct speech. Six of the questions will be **wh-** questions and two will be **yes / no** questions.*

1. She told Mary that Leonardo da Vinci had painted the Mona Lisa.

   Mary asked, "Who painted the Mona Lisa?"

2. She told Sammi where the Rosetta Stone had been found.

   _____

3. She told Roberto how long World War II had lasted.

   _____

4. She told Mei-ling that Magellan had been from the country of Portugal.

   _____

5. She told William that a person born outside the United States couldn't become president.

   _____

6. She told Ewa in what century the modern Olympics had begun.

   _____

7. She told Amanda how many countries had joined the European Union.

   _____

8. She told Zelda that population growth was gradually increasing worldwide.

   _____

EXERCISE 4: Multiple Changes to Indirect Speech
(Grammar Notes 3–7)

Read the conversation. Then complete the account with indirect speech forms. The number in parentheses indicates how many words are needed in each case.

SALLY: Dad, can you help me with my homework?

DAD: Yes, I can. What do you need?

SALLY: I have to write a report for my communications class. It's on a quotation.

DAD: OK. What's the quotation?

SALLY: It's by William Mizner, and it says, "A good listener is not only popular everywhere, but after a while he gets to know something."

DAD: What do you think it means?

SALLY: Well, maybe it's that people will like you if you're a good listener.

DAD: Good. That's part of it. Do you think it means anything else?

SALLY: Well, maybe that you can learn something if you listen.

DAD: Very good! You understand it really well.

My daughter Sally asked me _____*if I could help her with her*_____ homework. I told her
                                                1. (7)

_____ and asked her _____.
       2. (2)   **3. (3)**

She said _____ a report on a quotation for
                  4. (4)

_____ communications class. I asked her
       5. (1)

_____. She said _____ by William
       6. (4)   **7. (2)**

Mizner and went like this: "A good listener is not only popular everywhere, but after a while he

gets to know something." I asked her _____. She said she thought
                                    8. (5)

maybe _____ that people _____
           9. (2)   **10. (2)**

you if you were a good listener. I told her that _____ part of it
                                           11. (1)

and asked _____ anything else. She said she thought maybe
             12. (5)

it meant you _____ something if you listened. I told her
              13. (2)

_____ it really well.
     14. (2)

EXERCISE 5: Editing

Read the letter. It has eight mistakes in the use of direct and indirect speech. The first mistake is already corrected. Find and correct seven more.

November 20

Dear Emily,

   I just wanted to fill you in on Tim's school adventures. About two months ago

Melanie said she ~~feels~~ *felt* we should switch Tim to the public school. He'd been in a

private school for several months, as you know. I asked her why did she think

that, and she said, "He's miserable where he is, and the quality of education is

poor. He says he doesn't really have any friends." I couldn't help but agree. She

said she thought we can move him to the local high school, which has a good

academic reputation. I told that I agreed but that we should ask Tim. The next

morning we asked Tim if he wanted to stay at the private school. I was surprised

at how strong his response was. He said me that he hated the school and didn't

want to go there any longer. So we changed him. He's been at the new school for

a month now, and he's doing well. Whenever I ask him does he have his homework

done, he says, "Dad, I've already finished it." He's made several new friends.

Every now and then he asks us why didn't we let him change sooner. He says

people are treating him as an individual now. I'm just glad we moved him when

we did.

   Not much else is new. Oh, yes—I do need to ask are you coming for the

holidays. Write soon and let us know. Or call.

Love,

Charles

EXERCISE 6: Listening

A | *Listen to the next part of Ellen Sands's presentation. What are the two methods of minimizing verbal conflict that Sands has already mentioned?*

_____

_____

B | *Read the questions. Listen again. Then answer each question in a complete sentence.*

1. What is a third method of reducing verbal conflict?

   A third method is speaking about yourself instead of about the other person.

2. Does this method involve returning anger for anger?

   _____

3. Two sisters came to Sands for help with what kind of dispute?

   _____

4. What were they arguing about?

   _____

5. What did Rosa say about Alicia?

   _____

6. What did Alicia say in response to Rosa?

   _____

7. What is the first thing Alicia could have said?

   _____

8. What is the second thing Alicia could have said?

   _____

EXERCISE 7: Pronunciation

A | *Read and listen to the Pronunciation Note.*

> **Pronunciation Note**
>
> In English, consonant blending often occurs when a /t/ sound or a /d/ sound is followed by a /y/ sound. The combination /t/ + /y/ → /tʃ/ , and the combination /d/ + /y/→ /dʒ/. The letters following /t/ or /d/ that indicate this blending are most commonly **u** and **y** and sometimes **i** and **e**.
>
> **EXAMPLES:** The couple was from **Portugal**. /pɔrtʃəgəl/
> **Did you** finish your homework? /dɪdʒu/

B | *Listen to and repeat the sentences. Underline the word in which consonant blending occurs. Then write the letter that represents the /y/ sound.*

1. It wasn't a good <u>situation</u>.   <u>u</u>

2. We're on a very tight schedule.   _____

3. The quality of education is poor at that school.   _____

4. The chair used a self-righteous tone.   _____

5. Unfortunately, she never answered him.   _____

6. Tim will graduate in 2014.   _____

7. No one will ask any questions.   _____

8. The modern Olympics began in the 19th century.   _____

9. Spanish surgeons recently perfected a face transplant procedure.   _____

10. He says people are treating him as an individual.   _____

C | *PAIRS: Practice the sentences. Take turns, making sure that the words with consonant blending are pronounced correctly.*

EXERCISE 8: Group Reporting

GROUPS: Form two large groups, with each group sitting in a circle. Each group appoints a director. The director writes down a sentence about a general truth and whispers it to another student, who then whispers what was heard to the next student. The last student to hear the sentence writes it on the board. The director says whether the sentence is accurate. If it is not, the director locates where the message changed. Make the sentence long enough to be challenging but short enough to be easily remembered.

> **EXAMPLE:** **A:** Water freezes at 0 degrees Celsius.
> **B:** She said (that) water freezes at 0 degrees Celsius.

EXERCISE 9: Picture Discussion

A | *GROUPS: Discuss what happened to cause the accident. Invent conversations for the police officers, the drivers, and the bystander. Report them in indirect speech.*

> EXAMPLE: The woman said that the driver of the other car had been speeding but that she hadn't been.

B | *CLASS: Discuss who is most likely to give the most objective report of what happened and why.*

> EXAMPLE: Neither driver is likely to give an objective report. The bystander is likely to give a disinterested report because . . .

EXERCISE 10: Writing

A | *Write a few paragraphs about a recent news story that interested you. The news story should contain examples of direct speech. Then write a summary of the article, changing direct speech forms to indirect speech.*

EXAMPLE: The headline said, "He gave her his heart, then got a new one." Here's what the story was about:

A few hours before his wedding, Steven Dulka went to a hospital in Detroit, Michigan, to get a new heart. Dulka, who is 51 years old, was scheduled to marry Deidre Jacobsen. Unfortunately, Dulka had a heart inflammation and needed a transplant. About two hours before the wedding was set to start, Dulka got a call from a hospital administrator telling him that a heart had become available. Dulka told the administrator that he was getting married at 2:00 P.M. that day . . .

B | *Check your work. Use the Editing Checklist.*

Editing Checklist

Did you . . . ?
- ☐ use direct speech correctly
- ☐ use indirect speech correctly
- ☐ make verb changes in indirect speech correctly
- ☐ make other changes in indirect speech correctly

UNIT 11 Review

Check your answers on page UR-2.
Do you need to review anything?

A | Circle the correct word or phrase to complete each sentence.

1. Min-Ji told Ho-Jin <u>it's / it was</u> time to get up.

2. Mom told Mary she hoped she <u>had finished / have finished</u> her homework.

3. Rob asked Marisol <u>are you / if she was</u> ready to leave.

4. Dad told Tadao <u>to be sure / be sure</u> to feed the pets.

5. Juan told Maria <u>don't / not to</u> forget to turn off the TV.

6. John asked Dad <u>would he / if he would</u> pick him up.

7. Sally said that <u>"she would come by" / she would come by</u>.

8. She assured us she <u>could / can</u> be there by 8:00.

B | Correct the mistakes in the underlined words or phrases.

1. Marta asked José <u>would he</u> be late for dinner.   _____

2. José <u>said</u> Marta he wouldn't be late.   _____

3. Emiko told her father <u>"I don't feel well."</u>   _____

4. Emiko's father told her she <u>need</u> to take her medicine.   _____

5. Ali asked him <u>had he ever</u> seen snow.   _____

6. He said, "I <u>had seen</u> snow many times."   _____

7. The teacher told the students <u>don't</u> write in ink.   _____

8. The students said, <u>We didn't.</u>   _____

C | Circle the letter of the one incorrect word, expression, or punctuation mark in each sentence.

1. Ben <u>asked</u> Amanda <u>how long</u> <u>she had</u> lived <u>there?</u>
      A   B   C   D   A B C D

2. Amanda <u>said</u> Bill <u>she</u> <u>had lived</u> <u>there</u> for six months.
          A   B   C   D   A B C D

3. Jim <u>asked, "Dad,</u> what <u>does mean</u> <u>insipid</u>?"
      A B   C   D   A B C D

4. Frank <u>told,</u> <u>"Sami,</u> I <u>won't</u> be able to give you a ride <u>today."</u>
       A B   C   D   A B C D

5. Alice <u>asked</u> <u>her mother</u> <u>could she spend</u> the night at her friend's <u>house.</u>
       A   B   C   D   A B C D

PART IV

From Grammar to Writing
DIRECT AND INDIRECT SPEECH

A strong piece of writing will sometimes contain a balance between statements in indirect speech and in direct speech. It is important for establishing good control of your writing properly to incorporate direct speech within indirect speech, and vice versa.

Direct speech (also called quoted speech) states the exact words of a speaker. **Indirect speech** (also called reported speech) reports the utterances of a speaker but does not repeat all of the speaker's exact words.

In direct speech, quotation marks enclose the quotation. The reporting verb, such as *said* or *asked*, is followed by a comma if it introduces the quotation. Quotation marks come **after** a final period, question mark, or exclamation point.

EXAMPLES:
    Direct: Mary said, "John, we need to talk about our problems."
  Indirect: Mary told John they needed to talk about their problems.
    Direct: John asked, "Mary, are you mad at me?"
  Indirect: John asked Mary if she was mad at him.

If the quotation is divided by the reporting verb, each part of the quotation is enclosed in quotation marks. The part of the quotation after the reporting statement does not begin with a capital letter unless the remainder of the quotation is a new sentence.

EXAMPLES:
    Direct: "Asha," Daud said, "what time shall I pick you up?"
  Indirect: Daud asked Asha what time he should pick her up.

1 | *Punctuate the sentences in direct speech. Add capital letters if necessary.*

1. Dad, I want to quit school and go to work, Jim murmured.

2. Jim, how would you evaluate your education his father queried

3. I absolutely hate going to school Jim responded (exclamation)

4. Jim, Frank said, you're crazy if you think it's going to be easy to get a job

5. Frank said Jim, don't be a fool (exclamation)

6. Jim's parents asked, Frank, when are you going to start taking your future seriously

The other night my friend Linh and I had a fun conversation about our recent mishaps. Linh and I are both rather clumsy guys, which can lead us to some hilarious experiences. Linh told me about the time he'd been invited to a Thanksgiving dinner he'd just as soon forget.

So what happened I asked.

Well, Linh said, we were all seated around an enormous table. I guess there were about 12 people there. Several of them were high-society types.

What were you doing with a bunch of high-society people I asked.

Good question, Linh answered. Actually, I was visiting my cousin, and I was her guest.

So what did you do wrong I asked.

I was telling a joke and gesturing energetically with my hands, Linh said. I was sitting just in front of the door to the kitchen. Just as the maid was bringing in the turkey on a big platter, I made a big gesture and knocked the turkey off the platter. It fell on the floor.

Oh, no I said. Then what?

Well, Linh said, the hostess just started laughing. She said she was glad she wasn't the only person who had ever done something like that. Then she told the maid to take the turkey back into the kitchen and wash it off. The maid did and eventually brought it back, as good as new.

How did you feel about the whole thing I asked.

Mortified at first Linh answered. But it all turned out OK because of the hostess. It's great when people make you feel you're not the only person who can make a stupid mistake.

3 | *Before you write . . .*

1. Talk with a partner about a short, humorous incident that happened to each of you.
2. Ask and answer questions about the incidents. Why do you find the situation funny? What about it interests you?

4 | *Write a draft of a one- or two-paragraph composition about your own humorous situation in direct speech, paying particular attention to correct use of commas and quotation marks. Use* **asked, said, told,** *and any other appropriate verbs. Then rewrite your composition in indirect speech. Follow the model. Remember to include information that your partner asked about.*

The events of my humorous situation:

_____

_____

_____

What I find interesting about it:

_____

_____

_____

What I learned from the situation:

_____

_____

_____

5 | *Exchange compositions with a different partner. Complete the chart.*

1. The writer used subjects, verbs, and pronouns correctly. **Yes** ☐ **No** ☐

2. What I liked in the composition:

   _____

   _____

   _____

3. Questions I'd like the writer to answer about the composition:

   Who _____?

   What _____?

   When _____?

   Where _____?

   Why _____?

   How _____?

   (Your own question) _____?

6 | *Work with your partner. Discuss each other's chart from Exercise 5. Then rewrite your own composition and make any necessary changes.*

1 Irregular Verbs

Base Form	Simple Past	Past Participle	Base Form	Simple Past	Past Participle
arise	arose	arisen	forgo	forwent	forgone
awake	awoke	awoken	forsake	forsook	forsaken
be	was/were	been	freeze	froze	frozen
bear	bore	born/borne	get	got	gotten/got
beat	beat	beaten/beat	give	gave	given
become	became	become	go	went	gone
begin	began	begun	grind	ground	ground
bend	bent	bent	grow	grew	grown
bet	bet	bet	hang	hung*/hanged**	hung*/hanged**
bite	bit	bitten	have	had	had
bleed	bled	bled	hear	heard	heard
blow	blew	blown	hide	hid	hidden
break	broke	broken	hit	hit	hit
bring	brought	brought	hold	held	held
broadcast	broadcast/broadcasted	broadcast/broadcasted	hurt	hurt	hurt
build	built	built	keep	kept	kept
burn	burned/burnt	burned/burnt	kneel	knelt/kneeled	knelt/kneeled
burst	burst	burst	knit	knit/knitted	knit/knitted
buy	bought	bought	know	knew	known
cast	cast	cast	lay	laid	laid
catch	caught	caught	lead	led	led
choose	chose	chosen	leap	leaped/leapt	leaped/leapt
cling	clung	clung	learn	learned/learnt	learned/learnt
come	came	come	leave	left	left
cost	cost	cost	lend	lent	lent
creep	crept	crept	let	let	let
cut	cut	cut	lie (down)	lay	lain
deal	dealt	dealt	light	lit/lighted	lit/lighted
dig	dug	dug	lose	lost	lost
dive	dived/dove	dived	make	made	made
do	did	done	mean	meant	meant
draw	drew	drawn	meet	met	met
dream	dreamed/dreamt	dreamed/dreamt	pay	paid	paid
drink	drank	drunk	plead	pleaded/pled	pleaded/pled
drive	drove	driven	prove	proved	proved/proven
eat	ate	eaten	put	put	put
fall	fell	fallen	quit	quit	quit
feed	fed	fed	read	read	read
feel	felt	felt	rid	rid	rid
fight	fought	fought	ride	rode	ridden
find	found	found	ring	rang	rung
fit	fitted/fit	fitted/fit	rise	rose	risen
flee	fled	fled	run	ran	run
fling	flung	flung	saw	sawed	sawed/sawn
fly	flew	flown	say	said	said
forbid	forbade/forbid	forbidden			
forget	forgot	forgotten			
forgive	forgave	forgiven			

* hung = hung an object
** hanged = executed by hanging

(continued on next page)

BASE FORM	SIMPLE PAST	PAST PARTICIPLE	BASE FORM	SIMPLE PAST	PAST PARTICIPLE
see	saw	seen	stand	stood	stood
seek	sought	sought	steal	stole	stolen
sell	sold	sold	stick	stuck	stuck
send	sent	sent	sting	stung	stung
set	set	set	stink	stank/stunk	stunk
sew	sewed	sewn/sewed	strike	struck	struck/stricken
shake	shook	shaken	swear	swore	sworn
shave	shaved	shaved/shaven	sweep	swept	swept
shear	sheared	sheared/shorn	swim	swam	swum
shine	shone*/shined**	shone*/shined**	swing	swung	swung
shoot	shot	shot	take	took	taken
show	showed	shown	teach	taught	taught
shrink	shrank/shrunk	shrunk/shrunken	tear	tore	torn
shut	shut	shut	tell	told	told
sing	sang	sung	think	thought	thought
sink	sank/sunk	sunk	throw	threw	thrown
sit	sat	sat	understand	understood	understood
slay	slew/slayed	slain/slayed	upset	upset	upset
sleep	slept	slept	wake	woke	woken
slide	slid	slid	wear	wore	worn
sneak	sneaked/snuck	sneaked/snuck	weave	wove/weaved	woven/weaved
speak	spoke	spoken	weep	wept	wept
speed	sped/speeded	sped/speeded	win	won	won
spend	spent	spent	wind	wound	wound
spill	spilled/spilt	spilled/spilt	withdraw	withdrew	withdrawn
spin	spun	spun	wring	wrung	wrung
spit	spat/spit	spat	write	wrote	written
split	split	split			
spread	spread	spread			
spring	sprang	sprung			

* shone = intransitive: *The sun shone brightly.*
** shined = transitive: *He shined his shoes.*

2 Non-Action Verbs

EXAMPLES: She **seems** happy in her new job.
I **have** a terrible headache.
The food **smells** good.
Mary **owes** me money.

APPEARANCES	EMOTIONS	MENTAL STATES		SENSES AND PERCEPTION	POSSESSION	WANTS AND PREFERENCES
appear	abhor	agree	hesitate	ache	belong	desire
be	admire	amaze	hope	feel	have	need
concern	adore	amuse	imagine	hear	own	prefer
indicate	appreciate	annoy	imply	hurt	pertain	want
look	care	assume	impress	notice	possess	wish
mean (= signify)	desire	astonish	infer	observe		
parallel	detest	believe	know	perceive		**OTHER**
represent	dislike	bore	mean	see		cost
resemble	doubt	care	mind	sense		include
seem	empathize	consider	presume	smart		lack
signify (= mean)	envy	deem	realize	smell		matter
	fear	deny	recognize	sound		owe
	hate	disagree	recollect	taste		refuse
	hope	disbelieve	remember			suffice
	like	entertain (= amuse)	revere			weigh
	love	estimate	see (= understand)			
	regret	expect	suit			
	respect	fancy	suppose			
	sympathize	favor	suspect			
	trust	feel (= believe)	think (= believe)			
		figure (= assume)	tire			
		find (= believe)	understand			
		guess	wonder			

3 Non-Action Verbs Sometimes Used in the Progressive

EXAMPLES: The students **are being** silly today.
We**'re having** dinner right now. Can I call you back?
Mary **is smelling** the roses.
The cook **is tasting** the soup.

ache	bore	expect	hear	include	perceive	sense
admire	consider	favor	hesitate	indicate	presume	smell
agree	deny	feel	hope	lack	realize	sympathize
amuse	disagree	figure	hurt	look	refuse	taste
annoy	doubt	find	imagine	notice	represent	think
assume	empathize	guess	imply	observe	see	wonder
be	entertain	have	impress			

4 Irregular Noun Plurals

SINGULAR FORM	PLURAL FORM	SINGULAR FORM	PLURAL FORM	SINGULAR FORM	PLURAL FORM
alumna	alumnae	elf	elves	paramecium	paramecia
alumnus	alumni	fish	fish/fishes*	people***	peoples
amoeba	amoebas/amoebae	foot	feet	person	people
analysis	analyses	genus	genera	phenomenon	phenomena
antenna	antennae/antennas	goose	geese	—	police
appendix	appendixes/appendices	half	halves	policeman	policemen
axis	axes	index	indexes/indices	policewoman	policewomen
basis	bases	knife	knives	protozoan	protozoa/protozoans
businessman	businessmen	leaf	leaves	radius	radii
businesswoman	businesswomen	life	lives	series	series
cactus	cacti/cactuses	loaf	loaves	sheaf	sheaves
calf	calves	louse	lice	sheep	sheep
—	cattle	man	men	shelf	shelves
child	children	millennium	millennia/millenniums	species	species
crisis	crises	money	moneys/monies**	thesis	theses
criterion	criteria	moose	moose	tooth	teeth
datum	data	mouse	mice	vertebra	vertebrae/vertebras
deer	deer	octopus	octopuses/octopi	wife	wives
dwarf	dwarfs/dwarves	ox	oxen	woman	women

   * fishes = different species of fish
  ** monies/moneys = separate amounts or sources of money
*** a people = an ethnic group

5 Non-Count Nouns

ABSTRACTIONS
advice
anarchy
behavior
chance
decay
democracy
energy
entertainment
evil
freedom
fun
good
happiness
hate
hatred
honesty
inertia

integrity
love
luck
momentum
oppression
peace
pollution
responsibility
slavery
socialism
spontaneity
stupidity
time
totalitarianism
truth
violence

ACTIVITIES
badminton
baseball
basketball
biking
billiards
bowling
boxing
canoeing
cards
conversation
cycling
dancing
football
golf
hiking

hockey
judo
karate
reading
sailing
singing
skating
soccer
surfing
taekwon do
talking
tennis
volleyball
wrestling

DISEASES
AIDS
appendicitis
bronchitis
cancer
chickenpox
cholera
diabetes
diphtheria
flu (influenza)
heart disease
malaria
measles
mumps
pneumonia
polio
smallpox
strep throat
tuberculosis (TB)

FOODS
barley
beef
bread
broccoli
cake
candy
chicken
corn
fish
meat
oats
pie
rice
wheat

GASES
carbon dioxide
helium
hydrogen
neon
nitrogen
oxygen

LIQUIDS
coffee
gasoline
juice
milk
oil
soda
tea
water

NATURAL PHENOMENA
air
cold
electricity
fog
hail
heat
ice
lightning
mist
rain
sleet
slush
smog
smoke
snow
steam
thunder
warmth
wind

OCCUPATIONS
banking
computer
 technology
construction
dentistry
engineering
farming
fishing
law
manufacturing
medicine
nursing
retail
sales
teaching
writing
work

PARTICLES
dust
gravel
pepper
salt
sand
spice
sugar

SOLID ELEMENTS
aluminum
calcium
carbon
copper
gold
iron
lead
magnesium
platinum
plutonium
radium
silver
sodium
tin
titanium
uranium

SUBJECTS
accounting
art
astronomy
biology
business
chemistry
civics
computer science
economics
geography
history
linguistics
literature
mathematics
music
physics
psychology
science
sociology
speech
writing

OTHER
clothing
equipment
film
furniture
news

6 Ways of Making Non-Count Nouns Countable

ABSTRACTIONS
a piece of advice
a matter of choice
a unit of energy
a type/form of entertainment
a piece/bit of luck

ACTIVITIES
a game of badminton/baseball/basketball/
   cards/football/golf/soccer/tennis, etc.
a badminton game/a baseball game, etc.

FOODS
a grain of barley
a cut/piece/slice of beef
a loaf of bread
a piece of cake
a piece/wedge of pie
a grain of rice
a portion/serving of . . .

LIQUIDS
a cup of coffee, tea, cocoa
a gallon/liter of gasoline
a can of oil
a glass of milk, water, juice
a can/glass of soda

NATURAL PHENOMENA
a bolt/current of electricity
a bolt/flash of lightning
a drop of rain
a clap of thunder

PARTICLES
a speck of dust
a grain of pepper, salt, sand, sugar

SUBJECTS
a branch of accounting/art/
astronomy/biology/chemistry/
economics/geography/linguistics/
literature/mathematics/music/
physics/psychology/sociology, etc.

OTHER
an article of clothing
a piece of equipment
a piece/article of furniture
a piece of news/a news item/an item
   of news
a period of time

7 Nouns Often Used with the Definite Article

the air
the atmosphere
the authorities
the Bhagavad Gita
the Bible
the cosmos
the Creator

the earth
the economy
the Empire State
   Building
the environment
the European Union
the flu

the gross national
   product (GNP)
the Internet
the Koran
the measles
the Milky Way
   (galaxy)

the moon
the movies
the mumps
the ocean
the police
the *Queen Mary*

the radio
the sky
the solar system
the stock market
the stratosphere
the sun

the Taj Mahal
the *Titanic*
the United Nations
the universe
the Vatican
the world

8 Countries Whose Names Contain the Definite Article

the Bahamas
the Cayman Islands
the Central African Republic
the Channel Islands
the Comoros
the Czech Republic

the Dominican Republic
the Falkland Islands
the Gambia
the Isle of Man
the Ivory Coast
the Leeward Islands

the Maldives (the Maldive Islands)
the Marshall Islands
the Netherlands
the Netherlands Antilles
the Philippines
the Solomon Islands

the Turks and Caicos Islands
the United Arab Emirates
the United Kingdom (of Great
   Britain and Northern Ireland)
the United States (of America)
the Virgin Islands

9   Selected Geographical Features Whose Names Contain the Definite Article

GULFS, OCEANS, SEAS, AND STRAITS

the Adriatic Sea	the Indian Ocean
the Aegean Sea	the Mediterranean (Sea)
the Arabian Sea	the North Sea
the Arctic Ocean	the Pacific (Ocean)
the Atlantic (Ocean)	the Persian Gulf
the Baltic (Sea)	the Philippine Sea
the Black Sea	the Red Sea
the Caribbean (Sea)	the Sea of Japan
the Caspian (Sea)	the South China Sea
the Coral Sea	the Strait of Gibraltar
the Gulf of Aden	the Strait of Magellan
the Gulf of Mexico	the Yellow Sea
the Gulf of Oman	

MOUNTAIN RANGES

the Alps	the Himalayas
the Andes	the Pyrenees
the Appalachians	the Rockies (the Rocky
the Atlas Mountains	Mountains)
the Caucasus	the Urals

RIVERS

(all of the following can contain the word *River*)

the Amazon	the Nile
the Colorado	the Ob
the Columbia	the Ohio
the Danube	the Orinoco
the Don	the Po
the Euphrates	the Rhine
the Ganges	the Rhone
the Huang	the Rio Grande
the Hudson	the St. Lawrence
the Indus	the Seine
the Jordan	the Tagus
the Lena	the Thames
the Mackenzie	the Tiber
the Mekong	the Tigris
the Mississippi	the Volga
the Missouri	the Yangtze
the Niger	

OTHER FEATURES

the Arctic Circle
the Antarctic Circle
the equator
the Far East
the Gobi (Desert)
the Kalahari (Desert)
the Middle East
the Near East
the North Pole
the Occident
the Orient
the Panama Canal
the Sahara (Desert)
the South Pole
the Suez Canal
the Tropic of Cancer
the Tropic of Capricorn

10   Verbs Used in the Passive Followed by a *That* Clause

EXAMPLE: It **is alleged that** he committed the crime.

allege	believe	fear	hold	predict	theorize
assume	claim	feel	postulate	say	think

11   Stative Passive Verbs + Prepositions

EXAMPLE: The island of Hispaniola **is divided into** two separate nations.

be bordered by	be divided into/by	be known as	be measured by
be composed of	be filled with	be listed in/as	be placed near/in
be comprised of	be found in/on, etc.	be located in/on, etc.	be positioned near/in
be connected to/with/by	be intended	be made (out) of	be related to
be covered by/with	be joined to	be made up of	be surrounded by

12   Verbs Followed by the Gerund

EXAMPLE: Jane **enjoys playing** tennis and **gardening**.

abhor	confess	endure	give up (= stop)	postpone	resume
acknowledge	consider	enjoy	imagine	practice	risk
admit	defend	escape	keep (= continue)	prevent	shirk
advise	delay	evade	keep on	put off	shun
allow	deny	explain	mention	recall	suggest
anticipate	detest	fancy	mind (= object to)	recollect	support
appreciate	discontinue	fear	miss	recommend	tolerate
avoid	discuss	feel like	necessitate	report	understand
be worth	dislike	feign	omit	resent	urge
can't help	dispute	finish	permit	resist	warrant
celebrate	dread	forgive	picture		

EXAMPLE: The Baxters **decided to sell** their house.

agree	care	determine	hurry	plan	say	venture
appear	chance	elect	incline	prepare	seek	volunteer
arrange	choose	endeavor	learn	pretend	seem	wait
ask	claim	expect	manage	profess	shudder	want
attempt	come	fail	mean (=	promise	strive	wish
beg	consent	get	intend)	prove	struggle	would like
can/cannot	dare	grow (up)	need	refuse	swear	yearn
afford	decide	guarantee	neglect	remain	tend	
can/cannot	demand	hesitate	offer	request	threaten	
wait	deserve	hope	pay	resolve	turn out	

14   Verbs Followed by the Gerund or Infinitive without a Significant Change in Meaning

EXAMPLES: Martha **hates to go** to bed early.
              Martha **hates going** to bed early.

begin	can't stand	hate	love	propose
can't bear	continue	like	prefer	start

15   Verbs Followed by the Gerund or the Infinitive with a Significant Change in Meaning

forget
   I've almost **forgotten meeting** him. (= At present, I can hardly remember.)
   I almost **forgot to meet** him. (= I almost didn't remember to meet him.)

go on
   Jack **went on writing** novels. (= Jack continued to write novels.)
   Carrie **went on to write** novels. (= Carrie ended some other activity and began to write novels.)

quit
   Ella **quit working** at Sloan's. (= She isn't working there anymore.)
   Frank **quit to work** at Sloan's. (= He quit another job in order to work at Sloan's.)

regret
   I **regret telling** you I'm taking the job. (= I'm sorry that I said I would take it.)
   I **regret to tell** you I'm taking the job. (= I'm telling you now that I'm taking the job, and I'm sorry I'm taking it.)

remember
   Velma **remembered writing** to Bill. (= Velma remembered the previous activity of writing to Bill.)
   Melissa **remembered to write** to Bill. (= Melissa didn't forget to write to Bill. She wrote to him.)

stop
   Hank **stopped eating**. (= He stopped the activity of eating.)
   Bruce **stopped to eat**. (= He stopped doing something else in order to eat.)

try
   Martin **tried skiing**. (= Martin sampled the activity of skiing.)
   Helen **tried to ski**. (= Helen attempted to ski but didn't succeed.)

16 Adjective + Preposition Combinations

These phrases are followed by nouns, pronouns, or gerunds.

EXAMPLES: I'm not **familiar with** that writer.
I'm **amazed at** her.
We're **excited about** going.

accustomed to	capable of	famous for	incapable of	poor at	suited to
afraid of	careful of	fascinated with/by	intent on	ready for	surprised at/about/
amazed at/by	concerned with/	fed up with	interested in	responsible for	by
angry at/with	about	fond of	intrigued by/at	sad about	terrible at
ashamed of	content with	furious with/at	mad at (=angry at/	safe from	tired from
astonished at/by	curious about	glad about	with)	satisfied with	tired of
aware of	different from	good at	nervous about	shocked at/by	used to
awful at	excellent at	good with	obsessed with/about	sick of	weary of
bad at	excited about	guilty of	opposed to	slow at	worried about
bored with/by	familiar with	happy about	pleased about/with	sorry for/about	

17 Verbs Followed by Noun / Pronoun + Infinitive

EXAMPLE: I **asked Sally to lend** me her car.

advise	choose*	forbid	invite	pay*	remind	tell	warn
allow	convince	force	need*	permit	require	urge	would like*
ask*	encourage	get*	order	persuade	teach	want*	
cause	expect*	hire					

*These verbs can also be followed by the infinitive without an object.

EXAMPLES: I **want** Jerry **to go.**
I **want to go.**

18 Adjectives Followed by the Infinitive

EXAMPLE: I was **glad to hear** about that.

advisable*	careful	disappointed	essential*	happy	lucky	proud	sorry
afraid	crucial*	distressed	excited	hard	mandatory*	ready	surprised
alarmed	curious	disturbed	fascinated	hesitant	necessary*	relieved	touched
amazed	delighted	eager	fortunate	important*	nice	reluctant	unlikely
angry	depressed	easy	frightened	impossible	obligatory*	right	unnecessary*
anxious	desirable*	ecstatic	furious	interested	pleased	sad	upset
ashamed	determined*	embarrassed	glad	intrigued	possible	scared	willing
astonished	difficult	encouraged	good	likely	prepared	shocked	wrong

* These adjectives can also be followed with a noun clause containing a subjunctive verb form.

EXAMPLES: It's **essential to communicate.**
It's **essential that she communicate with her parents.**

19 Sentence Adverbs

EXAMPLES: **Clearly**, this is the best course of action.
This is **clearly** the best course of action.
This is the best course of action, **clearly**.

actually	certainly	evidently	happily	mainly	perhaps	significantly	thankfully
amazingly	clearly	fortunately	honestly	maybe	possibly	surely	understandably
apparently	definitely	frankly	hopefully	mercifully	probably	surprisingly	unfortunately
basically	essentially	generally	importantly	overall			

20 Words That Begin Dependent Clauses

SUBORDINATING CONJUNCTIONS (TO INTRODUCE ADVERB CLAUSES)

after	no matter if
although	no matter whether
anywhere	now that
as	on account of the fact that
as if	once
as long as	only if
as many as	plus the fact that
as much as	provided (that)
as soon as	providing (that)
as though	since
because	so that
because of the fact that	so . . . that (= in order to)
before	such . . . that
despite the fact that	though
due to the fact that	till
even if	unless
even though	until
even when	when
everywhere	whenever
if	where
if only	whereas
inasmuch as	wherever
in case	whether (or not)
in spite of the fact that	while

RELATIVE PRONOUNS (TO INTRODUCE ADJECTIVE CLAUSES)

- that
- when
- where
- which
- who
- whom
- whose

OTHERS (TO INTRODUCE NOUN CLAUSES)

- how
- how far
- how long
- how many
- how much
- however (= the way in which)
- if
- that
- the fact that
- what
- what color
- whatever
- what time
- when
- where
- whether (or not)
- whichever (one)
- whoever
- whomever
- why

21 Transitions: Sentence Connectors

TO SHOW ADDITION
- additionally
- along with this/that
- also
- alternatively
- as a matter of fact
- besides
- furthermore
- in addition
- indeed
- in fact
- in other words
- in the same way
- likewise
- moreover
- plus

TO SHOW A CONTRAST
- actually
- anyhow
- anyway
- as a matter of fact
- at any rate
- despite this/that
- even so
- however
- in any case
- in contrast
- in either case
- in fact
- in spite of this/that
- instead (of this/that)
- nevertheless
- nonetheless
- on the contrary
- on the other hand
- rather
- still
- though

TO SHOW AN EFFECT / RESULT
- accordingly
- as a result
- because of this/that
- consequently
- for this/that reason
- hence
- in consequence
- on account of this/that
- otherwise
- then
- therefore
- this/that being so
- thus
- to this end

TO SHOW TIME AND SEQUENCE
- after this/that
- afterwards
- an hour later (several hours later, etc.)
- at last
- at this moment
- before this/that
- from now on
- henceforth
- hitherto
- in the meantime
- just then
- meanwhile
- next
- on another occasion
- previously
- then
- under the circumstances
- until then
- up to now

22 Transitions: Blocks of Text

all in all	in short	second(ly)	to conclude
another reason/point, etc.	in sum	the most important reason/factor, etc.	to resume
finally	in summary	third(ly) (fourth[ly], etc.)	to return to the point
first(ly)	last(ly)		to summarize
in conclusion	most importantly		

23 Reporting Verbs

EXAMPLE: "This is the best course of action," Jack **added**.

add	claim	maintain	point out	respond	tell
allege	comment	murmur	query	say	wonder
allow	confess	note	report	shout	yell
ask	exclaim	observe			

24 Verbs and Expressions Followed by the Subjunctive (Base Form)

EXAMPLES: We **demand (that)** he **do** it.
It is **essential (that)** he **do** it.
The professor **suggested (that)** we **buy** his book.

AFTER SINGLE VERBS
ask*
demand
insist
move (= formally propose something in a meeting)
order*
prefer*
propose
recommend
request*
require*
suggest
urge*

AFTER IT + ADJECTIVE + NOUN CLAUSE
it is advisable that
it is crucial that
it is desirable that
it is essential that
it is important that
it is mandatory that
it is necessary that
it is obligatory that
it is reasonable that
it is required that
it is unnecessary that
it is unreasonable that

* These verbs also take the form verb + object pronoun + infinitive.

EXAMPLES: We **asked that** she **be** present.
We **asked her to be** present.

These are the pronunciation symbols used in this text. Listen to the pronunciation of the key words.

VOWELS				CONSONANTS			
Symbol	Key Word	Symbol	Key Word	Symbol	Key Word	Symbol	Key Word
i	beat, feed	ə	banana, among	p	pack, happy	ʃ	ship, machine, station, special, discussion
ɪ	bit, did	ɚ	shirt, murder	b	back, rubber		
eɪ	date, paid	aɪ	bite, cry, buy, eye	t	tie	ʒ	measure, vision
ɛ	bet, bed	aʊ	about, how	d	die	h	hot, who
æ	bat, bad	ɔɪ	voice, boy	k	came, key, quick	m	men
ɑ	box, odd, father	ɪr	beer	g	game, guest	n	sun, know, pneumonia
ɔ	bought, dog	ɛr	bare	tʃ	church, nature, watch	ŋ	sung, ringing
oʊ	boat, road	ɑr	bar	dʒ	judge, general, major	w	wet, white
ʊ	book, good	ɔr	door	f	fan, photograph	l	light, long
u	boot, food, student	ʊr	tour	v	van	r	right, wrong
ʌ	but, mud, mother			θ	thing, breath	y	yes, use, music
				ð	then, breathe	t̬	butter, bottle
				s	sip, city, psychology		
				z	zip, please, goes		

GLOSSARY OF GRAMMAR TERMS

action verb   A verb that describes an action.
- James **telecommutes** three days a week.

active sentence   A sentence in which the subject acts upon the object.
- **William Shakespeare** wrote **Hamlet**.

adjective   A part of speech modifying a noun or pronoun.
- The **blue** sofa is **beautiful**, but it's also **expensive**.

adjective clause   A clause that identifies or gives additional information about a noun.
- The man **who directed the film** won an Oscar.

adjective phrase   A phrase that identifies or gives additional information about a noun.
- In that movie, the actress **playing the heroine** is Penélope Cruz.

adverb   A part of speech modifying a verb, an adjective, another adverb, or an entire sentence.
- Ben drives his **incredibly** valuable car **very carefully**.

adverb clause   A dependent clause that indicates how, when, where, why, or under what conditions things happen; or which establishes a contrast. An adverb clause begins with a subordinating conjunction and modifies an independent clause.
- We're going to leave for the airport **as soon as Jack gets home**.

adverb / adverbial phrase   A phrase that indicates how, when, where, why, or under what conditions things happen. An adverb phrase modifies an independent clause.
- We learned a great deal of Spanish **while traveling in Mexico**.

An adverbial phrase performs the same functions as an adverb phrase but does not contain a subordinating conjunction.
- **Having had the professor for a previous class**, I knew what to expect.

auxiliary (helping) verb   A verb that occurs with and "helps" a main verb.
- **Did** Mary contact you? No. She **should have** called at least.

base form   The form of a verb listed in a dictionary. It has no endings (-s, -ed, etc.).
- It is mandatory that Sally **be** there and **participate** in the discussion.

causative   A verb construction showing that someone arranges for or causes something to happen. **Get** and **have** are the two most common causative verbs.
- We **got** Martha to help us when we **had** the house remodeled.

clause   A group of words with a subject and a verb that shows time. An **independent clause** can stand by itself. A **dependent clause** needs to be attached to an independent clause to be understood fully.

INDEPENDENT	DEPENDENT

- We'll go out for dinner when Mom gets back from the bank.

comma splice   An error resulting from joining two independent clauses with only a comma.
- I understand the point he made, however, I don't agree with it. (comma splice)
- I understand the point he made; however, I don't agree with it. (correction)

common noun   A noun that does not name a particular thing or individual.
- We bought a **turkey**, cranberry **sauce**, mashed **potatoes**, and **rolls** for the special **dinner**.

complement   A noun or adjective (phrase) that describes or explains a subject or direct object.
- Hal is **a man with unusual tastes**. He painted his house **orange**.

compound modifier   A modifier of a noun that is composed of more than one word. A compound modifier is usually hyphenated when it precedes a noun.
- My **five-year-old** daughter can already read.

conditional sentence   A sentence containing a dependent clause showing a condition and an independent clause showing a result. The condition may or may not be fulfilled.

CONDITION	RESULT

- If I had enough time, I would visit Morocco.

coordinating conjunction A word connecting independent clauses or items in a series. The seven coordinating conjunctions are **and**, **but**, **for**, **nor**, **or**, **so**, and **yet**.

- *Mom had forgotten to buy groceries, **so** we had a supper of cold pizza, salad, **and** water.*

count noun A noun that can be counted in its basic sense. Count nouns have plural forms.

- *The **students** in my **class** all have at least one **sibling**.*

definite article The article **the**; it indicates that the person or thing being talked about is unique or is known or identified to the speaker and listener.

- *China is **the** most populous nation in **the** world.*

definite past The simple past form; it shows an action, state, or event at a particular time or period in the past.

- *I **lived** in Spain in the '90s and **visited** there again last year.*

dependent clause A dependent clause is a group of words that cannot stand alone as a sentence: It requires a main (independent) clause for its meaning.

MAIN CLAUSE   DEPENDENT CLAUSE

- *They saw the bandit, who was wearing a bandanna.*

direct object A noun or pronoun that receives the action of a verb.

- *Martin discovered an autographed **copy** of the novel.*

direct (quoted) speech The exact words (or thoughts) of a speaker, which are enclosed in quotation marks.

- *"**Barry**," Phyllis said, "**I want you to tell me the truth.**"*

embedded question A question that is inside another sentence.

- *He didn't know **what he should buy for his mother.***

focus adverb An adverb that focuses attention on a word or phrase. Focus adverbs come before the word or phrase they focus on.

- ***Even** I don't support that idea. It's too radical.*

fragment A group of words that is not a complete sentence. It is often considered an error.

- *Because he doesn't know what to do about the situation. (fragment)*
- *He's asking for our help because he doesn't know what to do about the situation. (correction)*

future in the past A verb construction showing a state, action, or event now past but future from some point of time in the past.

- *We **were going to help** Tim move but couldn't. Sam said he **would help** instead.*

generic Referred to in general; including all the members of the class to which something belongs.

- ***The computer** has become essential in today's world.*
- ***Whales** are endangered.*
- ***An orangutan** is a primate living in Borneo and Sumatra.*

gerund A verbal noun made by adding **-ing** to a verb.

- *Dad loves **cooking**, and we love **eating** what he cooks.*

identifying (essential) clauses and phrases Clauses and phrases that distinguish one person or thing from others. They are not enclosed in commas.

- *The student **who is sitting at the end of the second row** is my niece.*
- *The film **starring Johnny Depp** is the one I want to see.*

if clause The clause in a conditional sentence that states the condition.

- ***If it rains**, they will cancel the picnic.*

implied condition A condition that is suggested or implied but not stated fully. Implied conditional sentences use expressions such as *if so*, *if not*, *otherwise*, *with*, and *without*.

- *You may be able to get the item for half price. **If so**, please buy one for me as well. (= if you are able to get the item for half price)*

indefinite article The articles **a** and **an**; they occur with count nouns and indicate that what is referred to is not a particular or identified person or thing.

- *In the last year I have bought **an** old **house** and **a** new **car**.*

indefinite past The present perfect; it shows a past action, event, or state not occurring at any particular or identified time.

- *We **have seen** that movie several times.*

indirect object A noun or pronoun that shows the person or thing that receives something as a result of the action of the verb.

- *Martin gave **Priscilla** an autographed copy of his new novel. He also gave **her** a DVD.*

indirect (reported) speech   A report of the words of a speaker. Indirect speech does not include all of a speaker's exact words and is not enclosed in quotation marks.

- *Phyllis told Barry **that she wanted him to tell her the truth**.*

infinitive   ***To*** + the base form of a verb.

- *Frank Jones is said **to be** the author of that article.*

inverted condition   The condition of a conditional sentence, stated without the word *if*. Inverted conditions occur with the verbs *had*, *were*, and *should*, which come first in the sentence and are followed by the subject.

- ***Had I** known that would happen, I never would have agreed.*

main (independent) clause   A clause that can stand alone as a sentence.

MAIN CLAUSE   DEPENDENT CLAUSE

- *They saw the bandit, who was wearing a bandanna.*

mixed conditional   A conditional sentence that shows the hypothetical present result of a past unreal situation or the hypothetical past result of a present unreal situation.

- *If I had taken that job, I would be living in Bucharest now.*
- *Sam would have arrived by now if he were planning to come.*

modal (auxiliary)   A type of helping verb. ***Can, could, had better, may, might, must, ought to, shall, should, will***, and ***would*** are modals. They each have one form and no endings.

- *You certainly **can** do that; the question is whether you **should** do it.*

modal-like expression   An expression with a meaning similar to that of a modal. Modal-like expressions have endings and show time.

- *Russell **has to** find a new job.*

non-action (stative) verb   A verb that in its basic sense does not show action.

- *It **seems** to me that Joe **has** a problem.*

non-count noun   A noun that in its basic sense cannot be counted.

- ***Smoke** from the **fire** filled the **air**.*

nonidentifying (nonessential) clauses and phrases   Clauses and phrases that add extra information but do not distinguish one person or thing from others. They are enclosed in commas.

- *Henry, **who is a member of the hockey team,** is also a star basketball player.*

noun clause   A dependent clause that performs the same function as a noun. Noun clauses function as subjects, objects, objects of prepositions, and complements.

- ***What I want to do** is spend a week relaxing on the beach.*

noun modifier   A noun that modifies another noun.

- *What did you buy, **milk** chocolate or **chocolate** milk?*

parallelism (parallel structure)   The placing of items in a series in the same grammatical form.

- *Marie loves **hiking**, **riding** horses, and **collecting** artifacts.*

participial adjective   An adjective formed from present and past participial forms of verbs.

- *The **bored** students were not paying attention to the **boring** speaker.*

passive causative   A verb structure formed with ***have*** or ***get*** + **object** + **past participle**. It is used to talk about services that you arrange for someone to do for you.

- *I usually **have my dresses made** by Chantal.*

passive sentence   A sentence that shows the subject being acted upon by the object.

- ***Hamlet** was written by **William Shakespeare**.*

perfect forms   Verb constructions formed with the auxiliary verbs ***had***, ***has***, and ***have*** and a past participle. They include the **past perfect**, **present perfect**, and **future perfect**.

- *I **had** never **been** to Brazil before 1990. Since then **I've been** there eight times. By this time next year, **I'll have been** there ten times.*

phrase   A group of related words without a subject or a verb showing time.

- ***Relaxing in the hammock,** I pondered my future.*

proper noun   The name of a particular individual or thing. Proper nouns are capitalized.

- ***Stella** and I both think that **Rio de Janeiro** and **Paris** are the world's two most beautiful cities.*

quantifier   A word or phrase showing the amount or number of something.

- *Ken earned **a lot of** money selling books. I bought **a few of** them myself.*

relative pronoun   A pronoun used to form adjective clauses. ***That**, **when**, **where**, **which**, **who**, **whom**,* and ***whose*** are relative pronouns.

- *The fairy tale **that** always scared me when I was a child was "Rumpelstiltskin."*

reporting verb   A verb such as ***said**, **told**,* or ***asked***, which introduces both direct and indirect speech. It can also come after the quotation in direct speech.

- *The mayor **said**, "I've read the report." OR "I've read the report," the mayor **said**.*

result clause   The clause in a conditional sentence that indicates what happens if the condition occurs.

- *If it rains, **they'll cancel the picnic**.*

run-on sentence   An error resulting from the joining of two independent clauses with no punctuation.

- *I think therefore, I am.* (run-on sentence)
- *I think; therefore, I am.* (correction)

sentence adverb   An adverb that modifies an entire sentence. It can occur at the beginning, in the middle, or at the end of a sentence.

- ***Fortunately,** Sarah was not hurt badly in the accident.*

stative passive   A passive form used to describe situations or states.

- *North and South America **are connected by** the Isthmus of Panama.*

subjunctive   A verb form using the base form of a verb and normally following a verb or expression showing advice, necessity, or urgency. The verb *be* has the special subjunctive form *were*, which is used for all persons.

- *We always **insist** that our daughter **do** her homework before watching TV.*
- *If I **were** you, I would pay off my mortgage as soon as possible.*

subordinating conjunction   A connecting word used to begin an adverb clause.

- *We were relieved **when** Jack finally called at 1 A.M.*

tag question   A statement + tag. The **tag** is a short question that follows the statement. Tag questions are used to check information or comment on a situation.

- *She's an actor, **isn't she?***

topic sentence   A general sentence that indicates the content of a paragraph.

- *There are several things to keep in mind when you visit a Japanese home.*

transition   A word or phrase showing a connection between sentences or between larger blocks of text.

- *Climate change is a serious problem. **However,** it is not as serious as the problem of poverty.*

unreal conditional sentence   A sentence that talks about untrue, imagined, or impossible conditions and their results.

- *If I were you, I would study a lot harder.*

zero article   The absence of a definite or indefinite article. The zero article occurs before unidentified plurals or non-count nouns.

- ***Whales** are endangered.*
- ***Water** is necessary for survival.*

UNIT REVIEW ANSWER KEY

Note: In this answer key, where the contracted verb form is given, it is the preferred form, though the full form is also acceptable. Where the full verb form is given, it is the preferred form, though the contracted form is also acceptable.

UNIT 1

A 1. are doing
2. loves
3. takes
4. 'm getting
5. seem
6. attends
7. is playing
8. like

B 1. have lived
2. has directed
3. has been working
4. have owned
5. have been remodeling
6. has been running

C 1. B 2. C 3. D 4. B 5. A 6. D

UNIT 2

A 1. got
2. have done
3. have been
4. have visited
5. was
6. went
7. wanted
8. have never known

B 1. met
2. attended
3. had invited
4. was
5. had known
6. proposed

C 1. D 2. B 3. A 4. D 5. C 6. D

UNIT 3

A 1. have to
2. 'll be
3. 'll call
4. lets
5. 'll stop by
6. get

B 1. taking
2. leaves OR is leaving
3. get
4. 'll have been flying OR will have flown
5. 'll be
6. 're spending OR 'll spend OR 're going to spend
7. 'll send
8. 're

C 1. C 2. B 3. C 4. A 5. C 6. D

UNIT 4

A 1. weren't supposed to
2. didn't have to
3. shouldn't have
4. could
5. 'd better not
6. must have
7. 's got to
8. aren't allowed to
9. could have
10. Hadn't we better

B 1. must OR have got to
2. should
3. can't OR must not
4. must (simply) OR has to (simply)
5. should you

C 1. A 2. A 3. C 4. B 5. C

UNIT 5

A 1. must
2. might
3. might
4. couldn't
5. should
6. ought not to
7. had to
8. 's got to be
9. must have been
10. must

B *Possible answers*
1. Jeremy may have had to work late.
2. Mari must have missed her flight.
3. They can't have heard the news.
4. We should know the answer soon.
5. You could have gotten a scholarship.

C 1. C 2. C 3. C 4. A 5. B

UNIT 6

A 1. C 3. NC 5. NC 7. NC
2. NC 4. C 6. C

B 1. **a.** any **b.** a drop of
2. **a.** some **b.** some pieces of
3. **a.** any **b.** a grain of
4. **a.** some **b.** a game of

C 1. C 2. D 3. C 4. B 5. A

UNIT 7

A 1. G 3. D 5. G 7. N
2. N 4. G 6. D 8. N

B 1. The 3. the 5. The 7. —
2. a 4. an 6. —

C 1. B 2. C 3. A 4. B 5. D

UNIT 8

A 1. Most
2. amount of
3. any
4. a lot of
5. a couple of
6. The number of
7. many
8. little
9. plenty of
10. no

B *Possible answers*
1. many
2. much
3. a lot of
4. a few
5. a lot of
6. Every

C 1. B 2. C 3. D 4. A

UNIT 9

A 1. sweltering humid summer
2. chilly late winter
3. new pink silk
4. handsome young European
5. beautiful new brick
6. dirty little old

B 1. an eleven-year-old son
2. a 900-page novel
3. a short-haired bandit
4. six 55-minute periods
5. a voter-initiated proposal
6. strange-looking people
7. Chinese ivory statue
8. a gray short-haired cat

C 1. A   2. C   3. D   4. C   5. C

UNIT 10

A 1. what the punch line of the joke was
2. why he always tells that joke
3. what time the meeting starts
4. what *hyperbole* means
5. whether Samira liked the party
6. what Mary does for a living
7. how long she's been a writer
8. whether or not

B 1. what Mary meant
2. whether or not Bob
3. Whatever you want
4. That Alison loves Kahlil
5. what we should give Russell
6. the fact that Ben helped us
7. that she was

C 1. D   2. B   3. A   4. C

UNIT 11

A 1. it was   5. not to
2. had finished   6. if he would
3. if she was   7. she would come by
4. to be sure   8. could

B 1. if he would   5. if he had ever
2. told   6. have seen
3. she didn't feel well 7. not to
   OR, "I don't . . ." 8. "We didn't."
4. needed

C 1. D   2. A   3. C   4. A   5. C

UNIT 12

A 1. who   3. whom   5. which   7. sees
2. where   4. whose   6. when   8. who

B 1. who lives next door
2. The book that Sara bought OR The book Sara bought
3. whose dog is barking
4. whom we met
5. where I was born
6. when we spoke
7. ,who is a student,
8. whose parents work here

C 1. A   2. A   3. D   4. D

UNIT 13

A 1. which   5. whom
2. whose   6. interested
3. whom   7. which was
4. which   8. starring

B 1. which   3. whom   5. whom   7. who
2. which   4. which   6. who   8. which

C 1. C   2. C   3. C   4. D

UNIT 14

A 1. is being constructed   5. been
2. had his car serviced   6. being
3. were caught   7. been
4. died   8. the job done by noon

B 1. is reported
2. is being reported
3. has been reported
4. was reported
5. was being reported
6. had been reported
7. will be reported
8. will have been reported

C 1. B   2. A   3. B   4. D

UNIT 15

A 1. is bordered by   5. by
2. as   6. is located in
3. is claimed   7. is thought to
4. is believed to be 8. are alleged

B 1. by   5. are believed
2. is said   6. is claimed
3. is surrounded   7. of
4. are alleged   8. is regarded

C 1. C   2. B   3. A   4. D

UNIT 16

A
1. not smoking
2. shopping
3. Emiko's
4. Not giving
5. to having
6. seeing
7. being awakened
8. not having been invited

B
1. finishing
2. Having missed
3. coming
4. driving
5. being told
6. seeing
7. having taken
8. mentioning

C 1. B   2. A   3. C   4. D

UNIT 17

A
1. to do
2. to accept
3. to give up
4. smoking
5. to lock
6. locked
7. to confront
8. to be criticized

B
1. strong enough
2. warned you
3. to postpone
4. be typed
5. to have had
6. not to get
7. to have forgotten
8. to finish

C 1. D   2. B   3. A   4. C

UNIT 18

A
1. just don't
2. had we
3. he even thinks
4. only members
5. don't just
6. even he can
7. does Eva
8. comes the train

B
1. are kangaroos
2. ,clearly
3. but he should
4. does our team lose
5. Just members
6. is the money
7. Actually,
8. goes the plane

C 1. C   2. D   3. D   4. A

UNIT 19

A
1. unless
2. Even though
3. in case
4. As
5. Once
6. now that
7. wherever
8. as soon as

B
1. whenever
2. As soon as
3. Even if
4. Because
5. Only if
6. Although
7. Whereas
8. unless

C 1. B   2. A   3. A   4. D

UNIT 20

A
1. Not knowing
2. Caught cheating
3. Having gotten the tickets
4. before leaving
5. On realizing
6. Relaxing
7. Having visited
8. being given

B
1. Having heard
2. while doing
3. Having eaten
4. finishing
5. Having been
6. being taken
7. Fearing
8. Given

C 1. A   2. C   3. D   4. B

UNIT 21

A
1. however
2. though
3. Because
4. consequently
5. besides
6. and
7. or
8. otherwise

B *Possible answers*
1. so
2. besides
3. or
4. consequently
5. Although
6. After
7. Besides
8. consequently

C 1. B   2. C   3. D   4. B

UNIT 22

A
1. rains
2. doesn't
3. rained
4. wouldn't
5. weren't
6. hadn't rained
7. 'd
8. were going to

B
1. wishes
2. wouldn't
3. hadn't
4. have had to
5. wouldn't
6. made
7. wouldn't
8. had listened

C 1. B   2. A   3. C   4. D

UNIT 23

A
1. Without
2. If not
3. If so
4. otherwise
5. With
6. if not
7. without
8. with

B *Possible answers*
1. otherwise
2. If I hadn't
3. call
4. Should that happen
5. But for
6. understand
7. if so
8. likes

C 1. A   2. B   3. C   4. B

UNIT 7

9. Game

Answers				
The type of tree that used to grow on Easter Island What is the (Chilean) wine palm?	The ship that sank in the Atlantic in 1912 on its first voyage What is the *Titanic*?	The place in a city or town where one keeps one's money What is a / the bank?	The home country of the first European to see Easter Island What is Holland / the Netherlands?	The name of the people who settled Easter Island Who are the Polynesians?
The animals that have been reintroduced in national parks What are wolves?	The circular object that was not used in moving the Easter Island statues What is the wheel?	The outer covering of a tree What is bark?	The body of water in which Easter Island is located What is the Pacific (Ocean)?	The people in a particular circumstance who have a great deal of money Who are the rich / wealthy?
The material from which the Easter Island statues are made What is stone?	A form of precipitation that is necessary for crops to grow What is rain?	A form of energy that involves the use of radioactive material What is nuclear power?	The device invented by Easter Islanders to move their statues What is the / a canoe rail?	A liquid substance used to produce gasoline What is petroleum / oil?
The place in a city or town where one can mail letters What is a / the post office?	A type of natural phenomenon that devastated the country of Haiti in 2010 What is an earthquake?	The part of the human body that is the seat of intelligence What is the brain?	The nation over which Hurricane Katrina formed What is the Bahamas?	The electronic device invented in 1944 by Farnsworth and Zorinsky What is the computer?
A type of animal killed by wolves in Yellowstone National Park What is the / an elk?	A woodwind instrument that uses a reed and was invented about 1700 What is a / the clarinet?	The people in a particular circumstance who are badly off economically Who are the poor?	A polluting material in the ocean that birds and fish mistake for food What is plastic?	In the Arctic and subarctic region, the part of the soil that doesn't thaw in the summer What is (the) permafrost?

8. Game

Team A

1. **A:** Which country has fewer people, Canada or Mexico?
   B: Canada has fewer people.

2. **A:** Which country has more land area, Canada or the United States?
   B: Canada has more land area.

3. **A:** Which country produces less oil, Venezuela or Mexico?
   B: Venezuela produces less oil.

4. **A:** Which country has no snowfall, Somalia or Tanzania?
   B: Somalia has no snowfall.

5. **A:** Which country has fewer rivers, Libya or Nigeria?
   B: Libya has fewer rivers.

6. **A:** Which country has a smaller number of people, Monaco or Cyprus?
   B: Monaco has a smaller number of people.

7. **A:** Which country produces a large amount of gold, Nigeria or South Africa?
   B: South Africa produces a large amount of gold.

8. **A:** Which city has less rainfall, Aswan, Egypt, or Athens, Greece?
   B: Aswan, Egypt, has less rainfall.

Team B

1. **A:** Which country has fewer people, Great Britain or Spain?
   B: Spain has fewer people.

2. **A:** Which country has more land area, Australia or Brazil?
   B: Brazil has more land area.

3. **A:** Which country produces less oil, the United States or Saudi Arabia?
   B: The United States produces less oil.

4. **A:** Which country has no military, Colombia or Costa Rica?
   B: Costa Rica has no military.

5. **A:** Which country has fewer rivers, Yemen or Turkey?
   B: Yemen has fewer rivers.

6. **A:** Which country has a smaller number of people, San Marino or Kuwait?
   B: San Marino has a smaller number of people.

7. **A:** Which country uses a larger amount of nuclear energy, the Netherlands or France?
   B: France uses a larger amount of nuclear energy.

8. **A:** Which city has less rainfall, Antofagasta, Chile, or Nairobi, Kenya?
   B: Antofagasta, Chile, has less rainfall.

8. Game

Team A

1. **A:** Which island is composed of the nations of Haiti and the Dominican Republic?
   B: Hispaniola is composed of the nations of Haiti and the Dominican Republic.

2. **A:** Which Central American country is bordered by Panama and Nicaragua?
   B: Costa Rica is bordered by Panama and Nicaragua.

3. **A:** Which people are considered by some to be the descendants of Atlanteans?
   B: The Basque people are considered by some to be the descendants of Atlanteans.

4. **A:** Which legendary creature is thought to live in the Himalayas?
   B: The yeti is thought to live in the Himalayas.

5. **A:** Which individual is claimed to have been the assassin of U.S. President John F. Kennedy?
   B: Lee Harvey Oswald is claimed to have been the assassin of U.S. President John F. Kennedy.

6. **A:** Which individuals are regarded as great humanitarians?
   B: Albert Schweitzer and Mother Teresa are regarded as great humanitarians.

Team B

1. **A:** Which Caribbean nation is composed of many islands?
   B: The Bahamas is composed of many islands.

2. **A:** Which Caribbean nation is located about 90 miles south of Florida?
   B: Cuba is located about 90 miles south of Florida.

3. **A:** Which forest creature is said to live in the Pacific Northwest?
   B: Bigfoot is said to live in the Pacific Northwest.

4. **A:** Which lost continent is thought to have been located in the Atlantic Ocean?
   B: Atlantis is thought to have been located in the Atlantic Ocean.

5. **A:** Which planet was thought to be the center of the universe before Copernicus?
   B: Earth was thought to be the center of the universe before Copernicus.

6. **A:** Which presidents are regarded by many as the greatest American presidents?
   B: George Washington and Abraham Lincoln are regarded by many as the greatest American presidents.

9. Conditional Game

Team A

1. **A:** Where would you be if you were in the capital of Honduras?
   B: You would be in Tegucigalpa if you were in the capital of Honduras.

2. **A:** How old would you have to be if you were the president of the United States?
   B: You would have to be at least 35 years old if you were the president of the United States.

3. **A:** Where would you be traveling if the monetary unit were the won?
   B: You would be traveling in North or South Korea if the monetary unit were the won.

4. **A:** Where would you be if you were visiting Angkor Wat?
   B: You would be in Cambodia if you were visiting Angkor Wat.

5. **A:** Who would you have been if you had been the emperor of France in 1804?
   B: You would have been Napoleon if you had been the emperor of France in 1804.

6. **A:** Who would you have been if you had been the first prime minister of India?
   B: You would have been Jawaharlal Nehru if you had been the first prime minister of India.

7. **A:** What country would you have been from if you were Marco Polo?
   B: You would have been from Italy if you had been Marco Polo.

8. **A:** What mountain would you have climbed if you had been with Edmund Hillary and Tenzing Norgay?
   B: You would have climbed Mt. Everest if you had been with Edmund Hillary and Tenzing Norgay.

Team B

1. **A:** How old would you be if you were an octogenarian?
   B: You would be between 80 and 89 if you were an octogenarian.

2. **A:** Where would you be traveling if you were in Machu Picchu?
   B: You would be traveling in Peru if you were in Machu Picchu.

3. **A:** What would you be if you were the largest mammal?
   B: You would be a blue whale if you were the largest mammal.

4. **A:** What country would you be in if you were standing and looking at Angel Falls?
   B: You would be in Venezuela if you were standing and looking at Angel Falls.

5. **A:** Who would you have been if you had been the inventor of the telephone?
   B: You would have been Alexander Graham Bell if you had been the inventor of the telephone.

6. **A:** What kind of creature would you have been if you had been a stegosaurus?
   B: You would have been a dinosaur if you had been a stegosaurus.

7. **A:** What would your occupation have been if you had been Genghis Khan?
   B: You would have been an emperor if you had been Genghis Khan.

8. **A:** Who would you have been if you had been Siddartha Gautama?
   B: You would have been the founder of Buddhism if you had been Siddartha Gautama.

CREDITS

INDEX

This index is for the full and split editions. All entries are in the full book. Entries for Volume A of the split edition are in black. Entries for Volume B are in red.

Punctuation. *See also* Commas; Periods
of adjective clauses, 215–216, 229
of adjective phrases, 229
of adverb clauses, 326
of adverb phrases, 344
of connectors, 360, 362
of direct/indirect speech, 178–179, 191
exclamation points, 191
question marks, 191
quotation marks, 178, 191
semicolons, 362, 414

Quantifiers
in adjective clauses, 214–215
with count nouns, 122–125
forms of, 122
with non-count nouns, 122–125
uses of, 123–125
Question marks, in direct/indirect speech, 179, 191
Question words
to introduce embedded questions, 161
to introduce indirect questions, 179
noun clauses beginning with, 159, 161
Questions
changed to noun clauses, 161
in direct/indirect speech, 176–179
embedded, 161
speculation in, 73–74
wh- questions
in direct/indirect speech, 176, 178–179
noun clauses, 159, 161
yes/no questions
in direct/indirect speech, 176, 179
if to introduce embedded, 161
whether to introduce embedded, 161
Quotation marks, in direct/indirect speech, 178, 191
Quoted speech. *See* Direct speech

Real conditionals, 381–383
Reason, adverb clauses of, 326, 343, 345

Regret, conditionals for, 384
Relative clauses. *See* Adjective clauses
Relative pronouns
in adjective clauses, 199–202, 215
omitting, 201–202, 215
Reported speech. *See* Indirect speech
Reporting verbs
changing form of, 179
in direct/indirect speech, 176, 178–180
Result clauses, in conditional sentences, 381–384, 399–400
Run-on sentences, correcting, 414

Sadness, conditionals for expressing, 384
Say, *tell* vs., 178
Semicolons
to correct comma splices, 414
to correct run-on sentences, 414
with transitions, 362
Sentence adverbs, 312
Sentence fragments, avoiding, in writing, 45
Sentences. *See* also Conditionals
adverbs to modify, 312
complete, 45
complex, 327
run-on, avoiding, 414
topic, 85
transitions in connecting, 361–363
word order in, 176, 179, 382
Shall, to ask for advice, 55
Should (not)
for advisability, obligation, and necessity, 53–55, 239
in passive sentences, 239
for speculation about the future, 72, 74
with subjunctive in unreal conditions, 400
Should (not) have, for advisability in the past, 55
Simple action verbs
forms of, 4
uses of, 5

Simple future
forms of, 35
in passive voice, 237–239
Simple gerunds
forms of, 273
uses of, 275
Simple infinitives
forms of, 289
uses of, 291
Simple modals, uses of, 54
Simple non-action verbs
forms of, 4
uses of, 6
Simple past
in adverb clauses, 345
changing to past perfect in indirect speech, 179
changing simple present to, in indirect speech, 179
as definite past, 17–18
forms of, 17
with *if only* statements, 384
in passive voice, 237
uses of, 18
Simple present
action and non-action verbs in, 4
changing to simple past in indirect speech, 179
forms of, 4, 35
in passive voice, 237
in present real conditional, 383
uses of, 5–6, 36
Since
in adverb clauses of reason, 328
in adverb clauses of time, 327, 344
deleted in adverbial phrases, 345
with present perfect progressive, 5
So, as coordinating conjunction, 360–362
Some
in affirmative statements, 124
with count nouns, 122, 124
with non-count nouns, 94–95, 122, 124
in questions, 124
Speculation, modals for
future, 72, 74
past, 72–73
present, 72–73
Speech. *See* Direct speech; Indirect speech
Statements, in direct/indirect speech, 176, 178–179